ENDORSEMENTS FOR
A FRAGILE THREAD OF HOPE

"Congratulations to Andi Buerger and Beulah's Place in fighting for the rights of innocent children and teens worldwide who have been victimized by traffickers and abusers. Her inspirational book tells of her first-hand journey as a survivor and of the lives she is rescuing every day. Our fight is a hard one—but critical. We are making a difference serving as the source of hope to those abused and vulnerable. Blessings, dear friend, from across the border, as we say, 'Together we can make a difference.'"

–Rosi Orozco, *human rights activist, Commission Unidos Vs Trata, (Safe House Tijuana Mexico)*

"A Fragile Thread of Hope is a memorable and inspiring read. Four heartrending stories of real at-risk teens and the woman who took them in, whose own aching abuse is also captured, makes this book a celebration of our fragile yet resilient humanity. These intertwined stories are important reminders that by noticing those around us, we can each make a difference, and that caring is the midwife of hope and possibility. Andi Buerger's book is a recipe for how we heal ourselves; and, while I can't imagine her sacrifice, I sense her reward and am grateful for this book."

–Gary W. Goldstein, *American film producer, author, speaker, consultant*

"A Fragile Thread of Hope could be classified as a titanium cable of faith, grit and pure power! As I read the amazing and terrifying saga of Andi's childhood, braided into the stories of four homeless teens, my eyes opened, my heart felt sick (then rejoiced!) and I came away humbled. For Andi to change from the victim and become the victor after so much trauma is awe-inspiring. I've never personally been subject to or been around the problem of homeless trafficked youth in our country. Everyone should read this story of strength, faith and courage! Let it open your eyes and your heart so that you become aware—so we all do our part in helping people overcome tragedy and triumph!"

–Kedo Olson, World renowned rodeo announcer and member of the International Hall of Fame of Rodeo Announcing

"I was eighteen, homeless and suicidal when I found the courage to call Andi Buerger's hotline at Beulah's Place. There I found shelter, unconditional love and a way out of the destructive cycles I couldn't seem to control. My story is included in *A Fragile Thread of Hope* and I hope it helps others. Five years have passed since then, and I've experienced some ups and downs, made lots more mistakes and been hurt many more times. That's how life goes, I guess. What I've discovered is that support and consistent love, the kind I've received from Ed and Andi Buerger, has helped me to believe in myself, to grow and learn, and, most importantly, to live in hope."

–Allison, former resident of Beulah's Place

"Beulah's Place completely changed my life. I'm Evelyn in *A Fragile Thread of Hope* and I was going down a rabbit hole with no end in sight. I don't know what would have happened to me, assuming I'd still even be alive, if I hadn't received help from Andi and Ed Buerger. I learned that I didn't have to do everything alone—sometimes you need a helping hand. They believed in me and helped me, and now I have college degrees in philosophy, criminology and sociology. I'm blessed with my son, Malachi, a great job, and, most importantly, I have found myself. For that I am forever grateful."

    –Evelyn, former resident of Beulah's Place

"Beulah's Place has not only proven to be a stepping stone to a better life, but has provided me with the support I lacked throughout my life. My name is Nevaeh in this story, and I'm sharing my story to let people know there *is* hope for a better life, no one deserves to be mistreated in any way, and you are worthy of being loved and supported."

    –Nevaeh, a former resident of Beulah's Place

"A few months after our son began his eighth-grade year of school, his girlfriend started gossiping about him with friends at a sleep-over birthday party. The girls decided to launch the worst cyberbullying attack our local police had ever seen, complete with death threats delivered in explicit detail. Our son and our family crumbled. He became angry, depressed, rebellious and impossible to control. A straight 'A' student that was loved for his sarcastic wit, caring heart, and great artistic abilities, became suicidal and took pills to end his suffering. That was just the beginning. He began staying with friends whose parents actively engaged him with drugs and alcohol, convincing him he couldn't return home. Eventually he ended up on the street, and that's when we found Andi Buerger. Her personal experiences, her love for us and our son was so desperately needed. I believe without her compassion and God's love we would've completely collapsed. Our family's experience and Andi's story has drawn us into the world of street kids who so desperately need to know love and what it means to hope again."

    –Keri S., mom and business owner

"You actually explained how I felt as a kid—how my childhood abuse affected my heart and soul. You expressed the actual abuse accurately without going into grave detail. It's not easy to write an emotion, but you did it so effectively that I was so caught up in the story, I couldn't put it down. Andi's story intertwined with those of the girls will help people relate to the pain, depth and severity of a lifetime of abuse with a hopefulness that we can survive and thrive with help and support."

    –D. Keefer

"Fantastic read! The horrific stuff that I just don't see in the community and I don't know it really exists. Wow! Thank you for sharing this with me and preparing to share it with the world."

    –James Tofolo, ND, PT

"Force of nature meets fountain of joy. That's the first impression everyone has of my sweet, ferocious friend, Andi Buerger. I'm so honored to share part of her story with you and so grateful for the opportunity our family has had to be partner in her passion project from its beginnings in 2008. There is no story so hopeless it can't be redeemed. Great job! I was riveted, and I already know the story!"

    –Lauri Deason

"What an incredible woman! What an incredible voice of hope and promise of a future she is for others enduring such atrocities! God can bring beauty out of ashes. HE IS OUR HOPE AND OUR FUTURE!"

    –Lana Reed

11/10/2020

Siena,

Thank you for your support! Be blessed always!

♡ Andi!

A Fragile Thread of Hope

ONE SURVIVOR'S QUEST TO RESCUE

ANDI BUERGER

WITH **KAY FARISH**

Certain names and identifying characteristics have been changed, and certain events have been reordered.

A Fragile Thread of Hope
© 2019 by Andi Buerger

Printed in the United States of America
First Printing, 2019

ISBN 978-1-7333605-0-0

Rights and Permissions:
Living Joyously Today LLC.
Post Office Box 5,
Redmond, OR, 97756, United States

DEDICATION

First and foremost, to the God of the big blue sky, who met a little red-haired girl sitting alone on the curb, and she has never been the same.

To the young women of Beulah's Place who bravely told their stories.

There really aren't words to express the deep and abiding gratitude for those God sent to share my life journey, to demonstrate genuine unconditional love, and to help me navigate the destiny designed for me. Somehow, I hope each and every person celebrated here knows that their presence and their love in my life has forever impacted my heart for all eternity.

My husband, Ed: You are the most amazing human I've ever known. If I didn't already know God, I would know Him because of your unconditional, unyielding love for me. You are the best life I've ever had. I love looking into your beautiful Jesus-rimmed eyes! You are the calm in my journey and a man after God's own heart. I am always and forever honored to be your friend, your love, and your wife.

Kay: Without you, this book simply would not be. Your passion to tell my story and that of other innocents who became victors made the pain, the tears, and the anxiety of writing my truth less terrifying. The mountains of notes, scribbles, interviews, and downloads from conversations became your inspired work. When we began, you skillfully and compassionately drew out the message from my trauma. Your inspired title and words will forever impact the "walking wounded" who read this book of hope and those we still need to rescue. Thank you for making my life matter in print.

Diane and **Michael:** My dearest friends before Ed. You showed me for the first time in my life what a real family is... and how each member has to work hard to make that family unit work. You walked with me through disasters and triumphs, all without judgment. Your prayers, gifts, support and experiential love in action showed me Jesus in action. You are my first family.

Dee Dee: Without you, Beulah's Place might not have begun. God put you in my life during a very trying season. As I reevaluated my life, you helped me put the first web page together to share the vision Ed and I had for the homeless at-risk teens in Redmond. You turned what seemed to be negative situations into positives for me and harnessed my passion to save others who were like me.

Scott Burns: From the day Ed and I were engaged, you have always shown up for way too many things to note here. Your friendship and immense talent got us from one website or video function to another to build up Beulah's Place. Your tremendous intellect with computers and audio visual "stuff" kept Ed and me operating as non-techie people! You have never said "no" when it came to volunteering or helping us to help more teens in some way. You, Tracy, Cameron and Caitlin are forever forged in the success of the stories here, and in my heart.

Dea and **Rich:** Without the love, Emmy-winning talent, branding strategy, and support from this dynamic duo, since the beginning of Beulah's Place (and even before as pillars of encouragement and reason for Ed and me), I really don't know where Beulah's

Place would be. Simply not enough space to thank these gifts from Heaven. Forever grateful!

Kevin Badami: Your servanthood to me and to Beulah's Place is beyond just a thank you. You never complain. You so underestimate your value and talent, but know that you have contributed greatly to the real successes in this book.

Pastor Mike and **Patty Ferry:** God brought both of you into our lives when Ed and I most needed spiritual guidance and the opportunity to grow individually, as a couple, and as a couple who minister to others. What we didn't expect was to receive such unspeakable love and devotion as "family," wisdom extraordinaire, and the coaching and encouragement to use our unique giftings boldly in the world. You were the first to regularly support Beulah's Place with monthly giving and always have our backs when it comes to the kids. You are forever life friends who make Ed and me better ambassadors of God's unconditional love.

Gary W. Goldstein: A chance meeting years ago morphed into an amazing friendship and the sort of smart coaching and strategies that helped propel Beulah's Place to greater heights. Gary, thanks for sharing your wisdom and knowledge, for seeing the possibility and value of Beulah's Place, and helping the human victories in this book become our reality.

Angels who left my life and left a piece of their heart in mine:
Elijah Buerger: Our son lost through miscarriage.
Janet Drew: My friend, confidant, and eventual sister through adoption.

Paul and **Betty Jo Beard:** My mom and dad. They adopted me as an adult so I could have a family to bring Ed home to; they loved me, were proud of me, and adored my husband—like good parents do.

Ted Eberhard: My first real friend in Oregon. Safe. Kind. Thought I could be anyone and do anything. Always a gentleman.

Lorri Sipe: Can't begin to cover who this "sister" was in my life. We brought great things to the other spiritually, emotionally, and as visionaries. Lorri was Ed's counterpart. She just *got me.* Believe. Lorri taught me well. This first book is proof.

CONTENTS

Chapter One

ANDI—HOMELESS THANKSGIVING

I didn't run away for good. I can't say why, really, except that I didn't know where I would go. I was trapped in a maze of an extraordinary normal. One in which abuse was a daily occurrence—the angry cursing and volatile outbreaks that ended in bruises I had to hide from the outside world were the everyday of my life. The woman who gave birth to me, the one person in my life who should've been safe, violated me sexually from the time I was an infant. Because of this, I conceived a plan for my suicide when I was only five years old. Anything was better than the constant hell in which my older brother, Joe Jr. and I, lived. The attempt was foiled the first time by the very mother I was trying to escape. The second time, a few days later, my attempt at death was interrupted by someone who gave me the single thread of hope that would carry me through until now.

Along the way, I learned to cope with the beatings and the verbal and sexual abuse. Over the years, I disassociated with the reality of my pain, though it took years to actually begin healing. Walking into wholeness is still a process and a choice for me. That is why, I'm sure, my husband, Ed, and I noticed the two young mothers who walked into the soup kitchen on Thanksgiving Day of 2008. We were there to help feed the many homeless that find themselves caught in the tumultuous winter climate of Central Oregon, where we live. The weather in Central Oregon is conducive to living outdoors much of the year, so it seems to be a good place for homeless and transient people to set up their lives. The line was long and the community center was bustling with volunteers in the kitchen preparing turkey and dressing and at the tables dishing out the feast. As we arrived, we could smell the pungent aromas of sage and thyme as the buttered herbs seeped into the skin of the turkey breast, crisping it for the knife that would soon break the shiny brown surface, allowing the juices inside to come pouring out. Fresh rolls were in the oven and there were two ladies in aprons standing over the stove creating gravy with flour and milk as they chirped merrily to each other. I watched as an older gentleman opened cans of congealed cranberry sauce that plopped in scarlet cylinders onto a waiting platter.

"What do you need us to do?" I asked, already lifting my sweater from my shoulders and looking for an apron.

"Here," said a woman close by, "spread these out on the tables." And she handed Ed and me a roll of paper tablecloths and tape.

"We're on it!" Ed said with that smile of his that gets me every time.

With me on one end and Ed on the other, we spread the paper lengthwise, cut it to fit, and taped the white expanse to the table edges. "Smells good in here, huh?" Ed asked.

"It does!" I replied. "It's making me hungry."

Within a few minutes of our finishing our chore, a local pastor came into the dining area where many of the guests had already gathered. "It's time for us to have Thanksgiving dinner!" he declared. "Wonder if you'd all bow your heads with me, and let's thank God for this great meal that's been prepared for us."

Dutifully, the congregation of people gathered bowed their heads. The prayer was short. The line was growing. Dinner was served. While I worked in the kitchen, Ed found himself dishing up dressing at the serving table. In order to be what they considered presentable, many of the men had found the community center restroom and made an effort to slick back their hair and maybe wash their hands. Their eyes, the ones that would meet ours, were warm with gratefulness. The smiles were genuine, and revealed the collateral damage of years on the streets—missing teeth, deep lines around their eyes and around their mouths from years of sun exposure, and lips cracked and chapped from the elements. Ed noticed their dirty ragged fingernails and the growing sunspots on their hands when they reached a chinet plate toward him to pile it high with stuffing. I wondered what memories the festivities and the kitchen aromas brought back to these men and women as they mingled at the tables eating heartily. Wondered where the family was that ate without them somewhere in Any Town, USA.

Toward the end of the evening when Ed and I were preparing to leave, a young woman wandered reticently across the threshold and into the community center. Her long curly brown hair was unkempt and dirty at the roots and her eyes darted around the room like a doe's checking to see if it's safe in a clearing. Around her neck was a sling fashioned from an old faded orange pashmina. As she moved closer to me and Ed, I could see the baby squirming in the makeshift pouch on her mother's chest. *Dear God.* She couldn't have been older than sixteen—seventeen. A child with a child. As she approached me, I smiled into a weary face, broken already by a callous world she couldn't possibly know I thought I might just understand. She smelled of the streets, and of cigarette smoke and marijuana. In her eyes was the glazed look of someone whose expectations of the world had been reduced to bare minimum. Survival for her and her child was the only thing keeping her alive and connected to the universe.

Sitting off to the side as we left was another young mother whose hair was cut short in uneven chunks as though she'd taken scissors to it in the dark. Tattoos were sprinkled over every visible surface of her body and I could see daylight through the large holes in her ears made by two large round plugs. A rhinestone sparkled from her left nostril and she held a wriggling one-year-old boy in her tiny arms. She was smiling and talking to an older gentleman who was admiring her baby, and I could see the streets and perhaps drugs they offered had already rotted several of her teeth. *What hell has she run away from?*

I felt protective of them as they packed up their babies to go back onto the streets of Redmond. To what kind of life were they headed out that night? It brought back the feelings of a familiar desperation—the need to run. Only it wasn't safe out there. The chairs they vacated would be quickly filled with other revelers and the never-ending line of hungry wayfarers holding out plates for turkey and dressing. And the girls will have wandered in and out of our lives, street phantoms, waifs holding waifs.

As we walked through the kitchen to grab our things, I asked Ed, "Did you see those young mothers?" My heart still breaking at the thought of them.

"I did," he said as he reached for my sweater and his coat from a rack near the back door of the kitchen where a dishwasher hummed and the odor of antibacterial floor cleaner mixed with smells of Thanksgiving still hanging in the air. "They couldn't have been older than sixteen, Andi," Ed mused. "It's hard to imagine why they are on the streets...especially with kids."

"Not hard for me," I mused. "I get why kids run away."

"Everyone's got a story," Ed replied as he helped me into my sweater then reached his arms into his own. "Theirs must be pretty bad."

We waved good-bye to the volunteers still cleaning the stove and began walking to our car. As we turned the corner toward the downtown street parking where our car had been for hours, we were surprised to see one of the young homeless mothers standing at the open trunk of her battered old Honda Civic. We heard the baby crying before we actually saw her, and I wondered if she'd been there when we first came to the community center and we simply hadn't noticed her. She was changing the child's diaper on top of what looked like a pile of their belongings thrown randomly into the trunk. A beaten-up stroller was lying on the ground beside the girl's feet as were a bag of disposable diapers and an old leather purse stuffed full, with the nipple of a baby bottle peeking over the top. The orange pashmina that had cradled the woman's baby hung slack in front of her like a hammock as she shushed her angry child.

"They're living out of the car," said Ed with a very real degree of horror. "She and that baby are living *out of a car*."

"There must be some way to help these girls," I said to Ed as I opened the passenger seat door of our car and eased in beside him. I could guess their history. Maybe even write some of it for them. That's how familiar my heart was with the pain etched on their faces. Homeless. Needy. Nowhere to go. How does a sixteen-year-old find herself in a small town in Oregon with nothing but an old car and a baby clutching at her shirt? Who doesn't have a mother? What father let her out of his sight? What backstory led to such abject loneliness? Their stories couldn't be that far from my own, I thought. The possibilities of why the girls would be on the streets were not as endless as one might imagine. Many homeless teens are running *from* something before they find themselves trying to cope with life on their own. I know how desperately I needed to be rescued from my parents when I was growing up—the feelings of hopelessness and despair.

On the way home that night I couldn't shake the need to do something. I couldn't help but put myself in their shoes. A nagging ache long buried, but still alive, crept into me, urged me to rescue them simply because no one rescued me. I could atone for the misery that put them on the streets. Victimhood is a vast wilderness where there is no respite. Ed and I could give them a place to land in safety. "What if we established some kind of haven for these young women, Ed?"

"That's a big undertaking," he said. "I'm not even sure what that would look like."

"Well…we'd have to start with their needs, maybe." My mind was racing forward, seeing girls graduating from high school, getting good jobs and building a future. "Teens need education, transportation, a job and a place to live." A plan was beginning to take shape in my mind. "I bet we could do something like that for them!"

"Something like what?" Ed asked, a smile sliding slowly across his face. He is used to my enthusiastic optimism.

"Like set up a place for homeless girls where they can live safely. Not forever, but long enough to help them get cars, jobs and eventually a better life." I couldn't wait!

That night Beulah's Place was born. Named after Ed's amazing mother, Beulah. It would be five years, however, before we took in our first central Oregon teen.

Chapter Two

ANDI—RESCUING ALLISON

The morning light was streaming through our guest room window, warming it from the chill of a cold Friday night in February of 2014, as I carried the sheets in from the hall closet and set them on a nearby chair. It had been a little while since anyone had slept there. I took a deep breath as I removed the fluffy beige comforter and emptied the matching shams of their down pillows. Tiny white feathers floated in the air, and I blew one higher just for the fun of it, then watched as it floated to the floor. The linens smelled fabric softener clean as I stretched the contoured bottom sheet tautly over the mattress cover then flipped the top sheet and sent it flying over the width and length of the bed. The tucking and fluffing felt right—setting things in order. The young woman I'd met the week before at a coffee shop now needed a place to stay that was safe and quiet. Free from the drama her life had become. Allison. She was surviving, that's all. I knew the drill; surviving, I mean.

I received two calls on the Monday before. The first was from Nevaeh, who'd seen an interview about Beulah's Place on television and called our hotline. She was deathly ill and living in a filthy apartment with a man of dubious character and his small child. Nevaeh's voice was weak and pleading. Not only did she need shelter, she needed medical attention, and soon.

The second call was from Allison, who was living in a three bedroom home with eight other people—Marge, her two children, her boyfriend and four other homeless or near homeless people Marge had met at her Narcotics Anonymous meetings. That's where she met Allison. Asked her home to dinner. Let her stay. That was May of 2013, nine months ago, and in that time things had evidently gone from bad to worse. Marge caught her boyfriend sleeping with her sixteen-year-old daughter. Food was in short supply. Allison was squeezed out. Trying to stay clean of the drug habit that brought her to this point in the first place. *Trying.* It was all a mess.

"Hello, is this Andi Buerger?" she asked. "From Beulah's Place?" Her voice was thin and tenuous. I could tell she was nervous.

"It is!" I chirped, wanting to calm her fears. "Who is this?"

"My name's Allison. Uh…I, uh, saw you on television and got this hotline number." The girl paused. I could hear her breathing. "I need a place to stay. I'm getting bounced out of where I am now." She waited. "Is that something you can help me with?"

"Probably," I answered. "Can you tell me a little more about you?"

"My psychiatrist told me to tell you I have suicidal ideation and dissociative disorder. Is that the kind of thing you need to know?"

Whoa! "Okay." I said. I took a breath.

Allison stumbled forward. "My dad molested me when I was younger. Mom is an alcoholic. I've abused drugs and alcohol, too, but I'm self-rehabilitating. I want to finish high school." It came out of her in a litany of super-charged issues pared down to short phrases. Facts of her life blurted out in the most minimal manner possible like she was summarizing only the high points of a very long movie that needed a much longer explanation.

It left me wanting to say, "Wait, *what?*" Instead I calmed my outrage at the awful abuse Allison hinted at and said, "I'm really sorry you've experienced those things, Allison." My mind was already figuring out how to get her out of her present situation. "Do you have a car? Could you meet me somewhere?"

"Yeah, I do. We don't have any food in our house, either," she said. "Could you help with that, too?"

"Tell you what," I replied, "meet me in the Albertson's parking lot and we'll get some food and talk. Would that work?"

"Yes." Allison sounded relieved. "Yes, thank you."

"Okay. I'll be there in an hour."

"I know what you look like from the television interview. I'll look for you." Then she hung up.

Our local television station, KTVZ 21, aired an interview they'd done with me and two of our rescued teens on January 22, 2014. We'd received several calls from troubled teens or their friends or relatives because they'd also seen the news blurb. Featured on the interview were Chelsea and a young man we'd helped. I explained our program and its origins, mentioning the fact that I'd also been trafficked growing up. Each of the teens told snippets of their stories and agreed to be filmed for the news show, putting faces to our outreach. It was compelling. Chelsea lived from man to man before she found Beulah's Place. And the young man had family problems that made it difficult for him to stay at home. Allison's call was a courageous gesture—reaching out in her desperation to a lady she saw on television, grasping at one last straw, hoping for redemption.

It was one of those rare rainy days in Redmond, Oregon. We usually get more sunny days a year than San Diego, although the winters can be brutally cold. The city was built in 1910 and is named after Frank T. Redmond. It is nestled on the eastern edge of the Cascade Mountain range in the high desert of central Oregon where the city is known for picturesque hiking trails and steep buttes. Juniper trees and pines randomly dot the grassy flatlands and rustic ranches. Most of the year, the climate and the environment attract a variety of homeless people who congregate here where I've lived since the mid-nineties when I took a corporate job with a local resort.

I dug deep in the hall closet to find my umbrella. I punched it open as I walked out the door of our house and headed to the car, seriously irritated at the sun for giving way to the rain. The wind had picked up in the afternoon, chilling the air and challenging my umbrella to stay put over my head. I raced to the car, unfolded the dripping umbrella and threw it to the floorboard of the passenger side; then I started the engine.

I never quite know what to expect when I first meet someone who's heard about Beulah's Place. I know what it's like to be abused. To never feel safe anywhere. To want love more than anything else in the world but to feel incapable of giving or receiving it. It's the common thread that runs through the story of all the young men and women who call us for help. Who need a safe place to stay while they get on their feet. It's heartbreaking, really. While the car warmed up and the windshield wipers sputtered and whined in their effort to clean the dirt off the rain-streaked window, I wondered about this new girl. *Suicidal ideation and dissociative disorder.* I put the car in gear and headed to the grocery store thinking how brave it was of Allison to share those things with a total stranger. I wondered at the amount of therapy she'd had in order to even understand her needs so profoundly…and clinically.

Allison was already waiting for me when I pulled into the Albertson's parking lot. I knew her without asking. Understood the hunch of her shoulders. Could tell her heart was pounding as she searched each face peering out from the windshield of every car that pulled into a parking space. I smiled broadly at her as I unhooked my seatbelt and opened the door of my car. She lowered her head for a moment, almost imperceptibly shuffled her right foot on the slick sidewalk where she stood, then watched me walk toward her.

"Hi, I'm Andi," I said. "Let's get out of this rain." I touched her shoulder to turn her toward the entrance as she half-smiled at me. She was shivering beneath the flimsy blouse that was way too thin to keep her warm. Her fingers were fumbling idly with the backpack slung across her chest. She was short, her hair tousled, her nails ragged, her eyes anxious. "You hungry?" I asked.

"Yes." Allison looked at me forlornly. "We only had a box of granola bars to feed everyone yesterday. We gave most of them to the kids. I had part of the last one this morning."

"Let's go to Walmart, then. They have a deli. We can hop in my car," I said as I steered her back to the parking lot with my hand gently on her back.

On the way, Allison told me more about her living situation. I assured her I'd find her a place soon. I wasn't sure where, though. I'd have to leave that up to God. "So, Allison, I want to hear about you. Can you tell me a little bit more about why you need a place to stay?"

"There are just too many of us there at the house. And…Marge thinks it's time for me to move on." Allison adjusted her glasses on her face and repositioned her body in the passenger seat.

"Marge is…?" I asked.

"The lady who took me in. It's her place…and I don't really get along with her daughter, anyway." Allison wasn't looking at me but glancing idly out of the window. I'm quite sure she was measuring her responses. Just how much would she be able to tell me before I wouldn't listen to her anymore? Before I'd be so disgusted I'd write her off as I'm sure others have. I recognized shame when I saw it. It had crawled up onto her face when she finally looked over at me a few minutes later. A hint of dimples made tiny craters in her cheeks as her lips arced in a half-smile. Resignation, I thought.

"What about your parents? Are they involved in your life?" I was guessing not.

Allison played with her short reddish-blonde hair, hanging straight and unwashed around her chin and met my gaze for the first time. Her lily pad green eyes were rimmed with a muddied sadness. "Not really." Once again she shifted in the seat uncomfortably, and knocked over a bottled water I had in the console, spilling its contents onto her lap and splashing beads of water onto the leather seat. I grabbed a tissue from my purse and cleaned up the mess. "I'm so sorry," Allison said with a nervous laugh while she brushed water from her jeans.

"It's all good," I said as I patted her knee. "I should've screwed the cap on tighter." I brushed my hand in the air as if the water bottle incident somehow resided there and I was getting rid of it. "Anyway, about your parents…can you tell me about them?"

"I've had some problems with drugs and alcohol. Mom couldn't take it anymore. And she married a man who doesn't like me." The tilt of her head, the slight shrug of her shoulders—Allison sighed, and her body slumped slightly forward, as if she'd run out of air.

"So you ran away?"

"Something like that."

I parked the car and turned to face Allison. "Would you like to tell me about it?" I asked, wanting a better understanding of why she found herself in such dire straits. "Why you ran away…why you were involved with drugs."

"Okay." Allison adjusted herself in the passenger side of the front seat, pushed her glasses up on her nose, and looked at me. "I hope you'll still help me when I'm done telling you all of this…I'm not proud of it." She looked down at her hands that were fidgeting in her lap and began a story that broke my heart.

When she finished, we sat for a few minutes in silence. I wasn't quite sure how to respond. Much of what she told me resonated with my own history of abuse. I wanted even more to protect her. Wished with all my heart I could undo the damage done to her young heart. Finally, I said, "Allison, I am so sorry…"

Tears sparkled in her eyes as she responded, "Well…I know some of it's my fault…" She wiped her nose with the back of her hand. "I don't seem to make the best decisions."

"Maybe we can help with that," I said as I patted her knee and handed her a tissue.

We both took a deep breath. "How about that lunch I promised?" I said with a smile.

"Yeah," she said. "I'm still hungry!"

We got out of the car and headed for the deli located at the front of the Walmart. "Pick out what you want to eat and I'll pay, then while you're eating, I'll shop for groceries," I said as we stepped up to order. Beside the counter was a windowed refrigerator that displayed a variety of drinks. "What would you like?" I asked as I pointed toward it.

"Oh, chocolate milk! I haven't had that since I was a kid!" Allison's eyes lit up like a child's on Christmas morning.

Once she was settled in at a deli table, I took a shopping cart and began filling it to the brim with boxed macaroni and cheese, spaghetti and sauce, cereals, milk and other essentials for Marge's house. I paid and we loaded my car with the groceries then drove back to Albertson's to transfer the bags to her car.

"You may not understand this," I said after we'd closed the trunk and stood looking at each other, "but I love you and want to help you."

Allison's eyes widened and her brow tightened slightly, smoothing out the tension that lined her face earlier. "I think I can...understand, that is. Thank you for all of this." She lowered her head. "Really...thanks."

I called Allison the next day and she was exuberant. "Oh, my gosh! Everyone is so grateful for the food!" I went by the house the following day with toiletries because I knew from Allison they were the last thing on any grocery list. I wanted her to be taken care of until we could find her a place. Marge was there when I dropped by. She was a woman in her late thirties or early forties. It was hard to tell because it was clear life had taken its toll on her. Stress had etched crow's feet at the edges of her dull gray eyes and created ashy colored half-moons that drooped lightly from beneath her lower eyelids where they rested upon her pale cheeks. The woman had the body of a former meth addict, slender and slightly concave. She greeted me with a weary smile when she opened the door to find me standing there with a large grocery bag in my arms.

"Hi," I said. "I'm Andi Buerger, and you must be Marge."

"Yes, yes. I'm her all right." I couldn't help but notice the woman's ruined teeth as they peeked at me from her mouth when she spoke, though she obviously tried to hide them by curling her upper lip over them when she was talking. She held the screen open for me to enter. "I guess you're here for Allison?"

"For her and for you," I replied. "I have some toiletries for your home. I was thinking you might need them with so many mouths to feed in one household." I set the package I was carrying down on the soiled forest green carpet that crept over the living room floor like a fungus.

"Thank you for the food you sent home with Allison," Marge said as she wiped her hands nervously on her soiled jeans. I noticed her nails were dirty, her hands calloused. "It was very nice of you." The woman seemed to avoid looking into the grocery bag, embarrassed possibly at seeming too anxious for its contents.

"It was my pleasure," I said as I looked around. "Allison said you have several people in recovery living here with you. It was good of you to take them in."

"Hey," she said, smiling sheepishly, "I know what that's like."

I could see into the kitchen where a teenage girl was sitting idly on a plastic chair at the formica table. I knew it must be the daughter Allison told me about. Behind her was a sliding glass door over which an old sheet was draped, sagging in the middle as if it were about to drop to the floor, tired. The place was dark, all the windows closed as if the household were filled with day sleepers. Aluminum foil substituted for dark shades in the bedroom I could see across the hall from the living room. The home smelled of body odor, fried eggs and cigarettes.

"We are working to place Allison in a stable situation," I told Marge. "If you can keep her until we can get her situated, I'll provide groceries." And I pointed to the bag I'd set on the floor.

"Sure." Marge said with an audible sigh. "No big deal." But I could tell from the weariness that hunched her shoulders and hollowed her cheeks that it was a big deal and I needed to do something quickly.

A few days later, one of the residents at Marge's brought in some meth. Allison panicked and called me. "Can I please come stay with you until you find me a place? I can't do this anymore." I could feel her desperation, and I couldn't leave her there in the chaos.

"Sure, Allison." *What else could I do?* I gave her my address and readied the guest room. There was so much I didn't know about this young woman's life. But the story she told me when I met her that first day was soul rending and hopeless. We could offer a room, a bed and a plan. I smoothed the bedspread back over the fresh sheets and patted the throw pillows into place, then breathed a prayer.

Chapter Three

ALLISON—SUICIDAL IDEATION
AND PURPLE HAIR

I didn't really know how much to tell Andi Buerger. My life so far has been more of a spectacle than I wanted to admit. She seemed like such a nice lady. I mean, what if I told her all this stuff about me? What if then she decided I was just too messed up to be picked for Beulah's Place? I was really jazzed after I watched the interview on Channel 21. There was this girl, Chelsea, who didn't even have a coat to wear. Andi found her one. And she looked so happy in the interview, saying she found peace. *That* would certainly be something new for me. I wanted Andi to like me like that…enough to take me in and take care of me. So, I told her most of it. Not everything. Not yet.

I was always wondering if I'd ever get it right. You know—life. I don't remember much of anything from my childhood. Dissociative disorder. That's what the psychiatrist I started seeing when I was twelve said. The few things I do remember from being a little kid make me think that's why I don't remember much else. Like the time my dad, who was a preacher, molested me then read me Bible stories and told me Jesus wants us to do those kinds of things. Memories like that are better left alone. I'm pretty sure that's why I buried them. Dad left us in Redmond, Oregon, when I was ten years old. Never came back. Moved to Texas to live with his mom and dad. Told us he was going to find a job and send for us. Well, that didn't happen. Turns out Dad moved to Afghanistan and met some Asian woman. Emailed Mom and said, "So long." Who does that? Breaks up a marriage by email?

Mom already drank too much, but when Dad left she became a full-blown alcoholic. Somehow she functioned at work, but there was nothing left when she came home to my older brother, Jeff, and me. I buried myself in my school work. I loved school, was a straight-A student and involved in a bunch of activities. I guess you could say it was my safe place. I could count on certain things to happen at school. My older brother just about quit life when Dad left. He stayed in his room playing video games, sleeping or watching television. It was like having Dad in the house still, because that's what he did for about a year before he left us. Mom hardly noticed Jeff, or me, for that matter. It's like she poured alcohol over her broken heart, first stinging it then numbing the pain. It made her sour. What do you do when your mom freaks out like that? Become her mom, I guess. That's what I did, anyway.

Somehow Dad figured out how bad things were and threatened to take us away from Mom, so she sobered up. But not before the wreckage of our lives was piled up pretty high. By the time I was fifteen, Jeff had moved out, our elderly dog was put down and Mom was never home. It just felt like everything that could fall apart did. I tried to figure it out. I'd always been the good kid. The one who made good grades. Who didn't want anyone to stress out. Did anyone notice that? Nope. Not even when I started cutting myself. I hid that pretty well at first. Only using a knife or razor on parts of my body no one could see. It helped. The pain, the blood, the epinephrine rush. Bleeding out of wounds I could see because I couldn't bleed out of the real ones.

Then Hal came along. Mom's new boyfriend, who is a whole lot older than she is. It was like I didn't exist after that. She'd load up the refrigerator with frozen dinners, say good-bye on Monday morning and not come back until the weekend. I was completely alone. With nothing to do. At least before, I took care of her and

Jeff. Now there wasn't even the dog to keep me company. And… some nights I was afraid. For good reason, too. One night someone tried to break in when I was in the house by myself. In a panic, I called Mom. Her cell phone rang and rang. *Pick up, Mom! C'mon!* Panicking, I called her over and over again, but her time with Hal was too important to answer the stupid phone. A friend from school finally came over with her dad and took me to their house for the rest of the night. The next morning, I finally got a hold of my mother.

"Why didn't you pick up last night, Mom?" I was so mad at her. "You know someone tried to break into the house?" I was screaming.

"Calm down," she was saying over my hollering. "I'll come home tonight."

I slammed the phone down and went to school. Didn't really trust she'd be home, though. So I was surprised when she walked in the door that evening. "Why is your hair purple?" That's what she had to say to me. Not, "Oh, my gosh, I'm so glad you are okay!" Arms around me, hugging me into herself. Nope. Not Mom. Just wanted to know why I'd dyed my hair. *Maybe so you'd notice me.* Oh, and then she saw my eyebrow piercing. "Why did you do that?"

"Can we talk about the fact that someone tried to break into the house last night, Mom?" *Sheesh! I always had to be the adult!*

"Well, I don't know what you want *me* to do about that now," she said as she tried to find a snack from the pantry.

"Will you listen to me?" I yelled. "You can't go to your boyfriend's house anymore and leave me all alone here!"

Mom blew up like a bomb detonated by a timer that had run out of seconds—suddenly and uncalled for! "What?" she screeched as she turned to face me, eyes locked onto mine. It didn't make sense, but I knew my telling her she couldn't go to his house was like I was telling a teenager she couldn't stay out past ten on week nights. She acted like a little kid! I swear! "I will go if I want to! You can't tell me what to do, Allison!" Something in her seemed to come unglued.

Mom needed this new guy the same way she'd needed alcohol. I could tell by the frenzied look in her eyes. Like she needed a drink… or two. He was her escape now, only she was escaping *me*.

"Well, if you have to sleep with him every night, make him come over here!" I hated her right then. And I couldn't think of a good enough way to get back at her. I stomped out of the house, making sure to slam the door on my way out, leaving the whole mess and Mom standing in the kitchen fuming like a volcano ordered not to blow. It made me glad to leave her there with her frustration and anger. She was holding an unopened granola bar she'd grabbed from the pantry in her left hand; her right one was balled up in a fist, ready to strike. My life didn't make any sense.

I used a pay phone at a drug store near our house and called this friend from middle school, Karen. I knew she got stoned back then, but I was never interested in it. Mom drilled it into us to never, ever do drugs. Getting sober was so hard for her. She didn't want us to go down that path. For that very reason, I said, "Hi, Karen, this is Allison…you know, from middle school…um…I was wondering…do you still smoke pot?"

Karen was pretty stunned. "Wait a minute. Is this the same Allison I knew a couple of years ago?"

"Yes." My heart was pounding with the thrill of this impulse. I pretty much do everything *right now*! As soon as it comes to my mind. "And I want to smoke pot tonight."

"You sure? I don't even really know you," Karen said.

"I'm cool with it," I replied. "I know I used to be all straight and everything, but not anymore." I wasn't sure what Karen wanted me to say that would make her know I wasn't going to narc on me or something. "I can pay for it."

There was silence on the other end of the phone. I could tell Karen was trying to figure out if I was legit. Then finally, "Not tonight, but let's get together tomorrow and I'll find us some." Then Karen paused. "You sure this is the same Allison?"

I just laughed. "Yeah, it's me. Tomorrow sounds good. I'll call you." I hung up and listened to the coins drop down into the pay phone. *Just once. That'll teach Mom to leave me by myself. I'll just do it once.*

The first time was in the garage of this guy Karen knew. He was pretty much a stoner. Since I was only going to smoke pot once, I did it all night long. Eight hours of smoking joints. Not only did I like the way it made me feel, I liked being with Karen and this guy. It beat being alone. My refrigerator was packed with the perfect stoner food—frozen dinners! For two weeks, every day, we'd drink, smoke pot and eat microwaved burritos. Karen knew some guys over twenty-one who'd buy us beer and hard cider or we'd steal it from the convenience store around the corner and come back to my house. But, really, when I looked at it, I was still alone. There was no one who cared what I was doing every night. I didn't see the point of it. Or of anything, for that matter. When the fog cleared, nothing had changed. Marijuana only created a haze that filtered out my real life. I couldn't stay high all the time, and when I came down it was always to a still house, a frozen dinner, a television and my bed. I felt like a lonely puppy left at the pound. Only nobody came looking for me.

The thought played on the edge of my mind for a few days. What it would be like not to *be*. How peaceful it might be to drift away to somewhere that wasn't here. Smoking pot was a trip to somewhere else where I wasn't necessarily me. Death was the ultimate escape. I was cutting myself more by then. My thighs, my shoulders, my abdomen. There were few places left on my body where I could draw the red line and cringe with the thrill of actual pain. It gave meaning to the stuff I couldn't handle that left me empty. And, I could control this pain. Nothing helped what was going on inside of me. Only death, I thought, would end that.

It was an impulse one night, though, which led me to the medicine cabinet. I opened the door, avoiding the mirror, and stared at all of our medications. Container after container of them lined the thin metal shelf. I reached to pick one out. A psychotropic drug Mom needed to control her mood swings. I read the label. *I wonder how many of these it would take to kill me.* Tranquilizers and my own prescriptions for depression and borderline dissociative disorder stood side by side, seemingly waiting for me to choose another from the lot. I flipped the child-proof cap off Mom's drugs and poured some into my hand. They were red. That seemed right. I swallowed them all dry. Then I chose some of my pills, throwing my head back and pouring them into my mouth in a steady stream. I washed them down with hard cider and waited. It didn't take long. Power surged through me like I'd been plugged into an electrical outlet, and I had a heightened awareness of light and sound as blood rushed to my face, pounding in my cheeks, making me dizzy and disoriented. I felt out of my body—my spirit soaring in full color as the rest of me shrank into some phantom, unreal and unnecessary to life. I knew I was losing myself. Eternity was close. Just on the other side of the bathroom door. Or up past the roof. A sleep away. The life I'd been given I was ending. A murder in our house. And I would be the one who did it. Mom would see that and be sorry she'd left me, never to see me alive again. It only dawned on me when it was almost too late, after the medicine bottles lay strewn over the countertop, their contents making my stomach churn and my head swirl, that no one might care enough to find me for days and days. That I might not like eternity that much. That instead of being omnipotent, I'd ceded my power to the belly of the medicine cabinet, and this might not end well. I needed to call my mom.

Already drowsy, I searched my room for my cell phone, frantically patting down the comforter on my bed to see where it landed when I'd thrown it there earlier in the evening. I wasn't wearing my glasses, so I fumbled in my search like a frantic blind person. Finally my hand came across the phone, which I grasped to my chest as though I'd found missing treasure. My eyes couldn't focus, but, by some miracle, I managed to punch in Mom's number on the first try. "Mom, come right now!" I know my voice was slurred. That's all I could think to say. I laid the phone down on my bed. She was still talking, but it wasn't making any sense to me. It's like my phone was making noises from another dimension...

She was over me then...and Hal, too. It seemed only seconds since I'd called. "Wake up! Wake up!" Mom was screaming. I was trying to understand why my body kept being slammed back against the pillow shams on my bed. "Hal, call 911!" *Why is Mom shaking me?* "Allison! You must wake up!" It was too loud and made me nauseated. I couldn't understand why my face was in her hands, her breath in my nostrils. Sudden fear woke me up, surging from some deep cavern where nightmares are created. *Those pills.* I didn't want to die. I changed my mind. "Mom."

"We are taking you to the emergency room, Allison." She stood me up. Propped me against her body and half-dragged me to the car where Hal was waiting to speed me to the hospital. I could hear sobbing and only vaguely thought of it as mine. A dam had broken somewhere down inside of me, spewing pain in wails fed by a cocktail of drugs intent on helping me end it once and for all. By the time the emergency room attendants heaved my sobbing body into a wheelchair and threw as much activated charcoal down my throat as I could swallow without choking, all I wanted to do was sleep. I awoke in a hospital in Portland three days later.

"Why am I here?" I asked, still in a groggy haze.

"You began hallucinating and resisting the emergency staff at the Redmond hospital. When they took you to ICU, your heart rate dropped. So, they put you into an induced coma and brought you here." It was my mom. Her hair was disheveled and she wasn't wearing any makeup.

"I just want to go home, Mom." I wasn't dead. It hadn't worked. I didn't understand what the big deal was at that point.

Before we had time to say too much to each other, a psychiatrist walked in to talk with Mom and me. The doctor knew I'd been smoking pot. They'd found it in my system. That's all Mom heard. He asked me a few questions about why I felt the need to overdose. Then he left, promising to return.

"You've been smoking pot?" The words flew out of Mom's mouth like bullets from a gun. *Really?* Her stomping around the room was so annoying. She was so mad she was almost snorting as she paced like a caged animal around my bed. I almost died from an overdose of her prescription drugs because I was just about the loneliest person on earth, and she was mad because I'd been smoking pot! *Yes, and cutting myself, and drinking every night, and piercing my ears, lips, eyebrows…whatever I could find to pierce! Why? Because no one gave a crap! Especially you, Mom!* I don't know why I still wanted to please her…but I kind of did.

I was put into the pediatric psychiatric ward at Providence Hospital in Portland for over a week. It was the Thanksgiving holiday from school and all I could think about was getting out of the hospital and going back to school. I decided to fake it with the staff so they'd discharge me. The first few days, though, I was resistant. I told them, "I'm just impulsive. This was no big deal. I'm alive, after all." But by the fourth day I began to be worried about myself. *Maybe something is wrong with me.* It scared me enough that I spent the rest of my time there trying to get better. I wanted to stay clean and sober. And I did. For a couple of months. Mom stayed home, I went to school and did well, as usual. But old patterns die hard, I guess. Mom decided I was well enough to fend for myself again. She missed her man. And I missed my drugs. I didn't seem to change much on the outside, put on a good show, mainly so I could smoke pot without anyone knowing. By March, though, the desperation that marijuana helped me keep more or less quiet, came back. I was barely sixteen and life was already more than I wanted to handle.

There was a bridge in town just high enough that if I jumped I was pretty sure it'd kill me. I thought about it for days. What it would be like to fly off the edge. The burst of freedom. The cold night air filling my lungs one last time. It had to be night. The darker the better. I'd look up at the stars. I'd curse my Mom for not caring. I'd take a few steps back then take a running leap into whatever is out there after this life. Down, down into blackness. Then it would all be over. The mistake I made was telling a friend. A good friend. Because she made sure Mom knew.

I was admitted into a psych facility in Eugene. Missing school again. Locked up with just the worst kids ever. Never mind the flying chairs and constant screaming, these kids were completely out of control in every possible way. I couldn't even think in that place. I knew the other patients just wanted attention. Maybe they were only used to getting it by lashing out. Me? I wasn't angry. Not like a little kid, anyway. Well, maybe a little. But I didn't act like *that*…

When they discharged me, I didn't even pretend I didn't smoke pot. I'd be straight for the weekdays so I could be at school, but on the weekends, it was pot and alcohol. I kept this up for about six months until my friends turned on me. They started making fun of my anxiety. Yes, I had anxiety issues. That shouldn't be surprising. There were some things I had hang-ups about. Like using public restrooms. I couldn't. The sound of someone urinating made me panic. I couldn't stand to hear it. Not even my own, sometimes. I'd clasp my hands over my ears to shut out the noise. My friends started making jokes about what my father probably did to me to make me so paranoid. Incessantly. Even when they knew I didn't think it was funny.

And then I'd have these memories pop up. Taking baths with my dad when I was four or five. I didn't need specifics because the feelings it brought up to see my little kid self in that tub assured me it was bad. The confusion. A need to cry out for help. An assurance no one would hear. The memory suffocated me, like I was under water where I couldn't breathe.

Meth was my answer for this. The bullying by the friends at school I thought I could trust turned my only safe place into hell. I ran from them. Wouldn't talk to them even though they pretty much stalked me. I refused to be the brunt of their jokes. Like a heat-seeking missile, I was drawn to Kathy, who I'd heard experimented with drugs. She had the look of a meth user: scrawny and agitated, her ashen face pimpled and her bleary eyes rimmed in red. We were together at her locker one afternoon after school when I casually asked her, "Do you know where I could get some meth?"

Shocked, she gingerly closed her locker door and almost whispered, "Why are you asking me that?"

"I dunno." I whispered back, my heart already beating in anticipation. "Don't get mad...I thought I'd like to try it. That's all." I looked around to see if anyone might have heard us talking.

"It'll make you want to live," she finally said after looking at me like she was trying to gauge whether or not I was telling the truth. The way she said that was like she was in love with the drug. She took my arm and drew me close to her as we walked slowly down the corridor toward our class. "It makes life beautiful. You should definitely try it!" Kathy's eyes glowed with this strange light that made me forget her hair was dry and stringy and her hand was boney as a skeleton's.

It wasn't that Kathy was such a good sales rep. I mean, it was obvious the effects meth had on her. But she said it would make me want to *live*. Like she read my mind. Winter break was coming up the next week, so we arranged to meet on Saturday. I went to her house then we walked to the grocery store to recycle bottles and cans for cash. "My grandma will give us money, too," Kathy said. "I can always trick her into stuff." I didn't know her grandma, so I didn't care as we walked toward the old lady's house that afternoon. I was on a mission to feel beautiful.

Kathy knocked on her grandmother's front door then went right in. "Grandma, you home?" she yelled as the screen door banged against the house. The lady appeared from the kitchen with a huge smile on her face. I expected an old person, but she was maybe fifty-five with a slim figure and short dirty blond hair. Dressed in jeans and a long tee shirt, she moved quickly toward Kathy with her arms already opened. I immediately felt guilty for what I knew her granddaughter was about to do. She had no clue. "Hi, Grandma!" She gave the woman a perfunctory hug.

"And who is this young lady?" asked Kathy's granny, looking over at me, smiling in such a welcome way that it suddenly made me want to cry. It pricked a yearning somewhere, but I couldn't identify it.

"This is my friend, Allison," Kathy replied, as she grabbed my arm and pulled me over to her. "We're going to the movies." She lied so well even I believed her—looked over at her like, *Really?*

"Nice to meet you," said Grandma as she reached for my hand and grabbed it between hers. I was thinking if I had a nice granny like that, I'd rather have a hug than the meth. But, I didn't have anyone. *Oh, well.*

"Could you give us some money for the show?" asked Kathy. "We're out of cash."

"Sure," said the woman as she reached for her purse from the dining room table where it sat slouched over like it had fallen asleep while sitting up. The house was small but very neat. It smelled of detergent and something on the stove… maybe soup. Grandma handed her granddaughter a twenty-dollar bill.

"Thanks!" said Kathy, and she didn't appear to feel the least bit guilty.

The dealer looked like this normal guy. He walked toward us with his shoulders hunched and his hands buried deep in the pockets of his dark blue parka. A lit cigarette hung from his mouth and the smoke from it circled his head as he peered at Kathy through his stringy black bangs. She signaled for me to wait for her as she walked with the dealer into an alleyway between two shops in the strip mall where we'd met him. She gave him all the money we had—ours and Grandma's. The next few hours were totally worth it. Meth made me feel…I don't even know how to describe it. Spiritual, maybe. Like my body didn't matter anymore. Love wrapped around me, warm and tingling like an adrenalin rush, but more powerful. Or I thought it was love. I *was* beauty, not just beautiful. I felt almost god-like…and so alive, like I was plugged into an amplifier. I never, ever wanted to come down. We stayed up all night in somebody's house…I don't even know whose. It didn't matter. Nothing did. The sun was rising when I left.

I floated home. Really. That's the way I felt. I slept. Read. Watched television. All like I was in a peaceful dream. The phone rang late in the day. "Hey, this is Kathy. You want to do it again?"

"Sure." My heart was racing. Who wouldn't want to feel invincible one more time?

"I know this guy who'll get it for us for ten dollars. Do you have ten dollars?"

I used meth every day for the next three weeks except for one night when the dealer took my last little bit of money and didn't show up with the drug. I was frantic. I didn't think I could live without a fix. By then I had to have it. Habit now, not choice. Thoughts of suicide and a call to my psychiatrist landed me back at the Eugene rehab facility.

"What have you been using?" my psychiatrist asked as he looked at me over the rims of his reading glasses. It's the normal question doctors ask when someone is brought to rehab.

"Pot and alcohol," I lied. I didn't want to be there any more than I did the last time they admitted me. And I certainly didn't want him to know I was using meth. In fact, all I could think about was getting out so I could use again. And…I desperately wanted a cigarette.

"When was the last time you abused?" The second normal psych question.

I didn't answer. A confusing fight was going on inside of me. The last shred of integrity I had was fighting with my almost desperate need to use. I felt my face flush. My hands sweat.

"Allison," repeated my doctor, "when was the last time you used?"

I felt the answer squeeze out of me, pushed up from this geyser building in my stomach. "This morning," I admitted. Vomited the words, really. And shame came up with them. *How had I gotten so bad so quickly?* It was like I was watching someone else sitting there crying like a baby, so dumb she'd been tricked into an addiction. I couldn't even look at my doctor. I couldn't look at myself. That's why the staff found me several days later lying on the bathroom floor with the string from my pajama bottoms looped around my neck. I was almost unconscious when I looked into the horrified face of a staffer and moaned as I heard her holler for someone to bring her some scissors. I came more fully awake hearing the sound of my own gasping for breath. Once again I'd failed.

The psychiatrist said my mental health problems were the root of my drug use. Maybe he's right. We never really got to the root of my mental health problems, though. The multiple reasons why I can't remember life before age twelve. Fleeting memories that not only bring conflicting visuals, but also create visceral panic. The little girl in those memories is lost to me. But the residual of her escape still hides down in me somewhere, peeking out once in a while to make me feel crazy.

They were going to tell Mom. About the meth. The drug and alcohol counselors agreed. The thought of that made me crazy! If she knew about the meth, there wouldn't be a shred of dignity left in me. I still don't know why I cared a flip about what she thought. Somewhere deep inside me was the idea that she left me alone because I wasn't valuable enough...didn't mean enough to her...for her to be with me. To take care of me. Or...deeper still…I didn't *deserve* her love. So I ran. Literally ran out of the room and across the street. Tried to climb a barbed wire fence. Resisted six staffers trying to get me down. Fought off the police. It wasn't the best way to handle the situation. Handcuffed and further shamed, the decision was made to send me back to Portland to a high security facility. They were able to stabilize me there—gave me different meds.

Back in the Eugene facility, I was clean and not suicidal anymore. Mom and Hal were getting married. Of course, her life went on without me. I can't say that didn't hurt, though. Mom's insurance ran out after six weeks in Eugene. I had to go home, but I wasn't ready to face the fact that everything would now be way different with Mom married. I was more aware of my triggers, too. Hal was definitely one of them. So, I made a plan. I'd go to a halfway house that sheltered homeless and trafficked teens. The Loft. Except they had no empty beds. Home was my only choice, short term. I knew I couldn't handle it for long. I just didn't know it would fall apart quite so fast.

It was all about what I was going to wear for her wedding. A wedding I hated the thought of anyway. Mom took me shopping a couple of times to find just the right dress. Her idea of the "right" dress and mine were completely opposite. My heart wasn't in it, anyway. It all made me want to implode. We returned without a dress one Saturday evening, arguing as we came through the back door. Hal was standing in the kitchen with a glass of cold water in his hands, the condensation from the ice slipping from the surface of the glass and spilling in droplets onto the man's protruding belly. I thought he looked disgusting in his overly tight red tee shirt, the long gray hairs that covered his body sprouting like grass from his forearms and his Lee jeans hanging low on his backside.

"I don't know why you can't just be happy with the dress I want you to wear," Mom was saying as she put a Macy's package on the kitchen counter. "After all, it's my wedding!"

Oh, man. The idea that she couldn't see why that hurt was beyond me then. It's beyond me now! I fit into her picture like I'd been cut out of some other photo and glued into place in this new picture she was trying to create. Not a *real* representation of our family. No. The one she made up. "Well, it's going to be *my* dress! I don't want to be in the stupid wedding, anyway!"

His hand went pounding down onto the countertop as Hal threw his glass into the sink and moved toward me, his eyes glaring with something worse than hate—condescension. He began yelling at the nothing I was to him. "You can drink and do drugs all you want, but you *can't* talk back to your mother that way!" All blustering and self-righteous, this man who'd stolen my mother from me in the first place. Who wasn't my father. Wasn't anything to me. I hated him even in my toes. I couldn't look at them. Either of them.

I flew out the back door, slamming it hard on my way out. There was no place to go once I left, though, except over the fence. I was halfway up when I felt Hal's hands on my legs. "Get down from there!" he yelled. "You get down from there right now and come apologize to your mom!"

"Leave me alone!" I screamed as I dug my hands into the sharp metal spikes on the fence. Hal kept pulling at the legs of my jeans, popping them open at my waist in the process. All I could think of was: *I have to get away from him!* But the more I resisted, the more aggressive he became, until I felt his hands on my bare flesh. He'd pulled my pants down around my thigh in his effort to get me down from the fence. There's a place in me his touch set off that is like coming in contact with an electric current. I literally felt electrocuted somehow. I couldn't scream loud enough. I couldn't fight him off violently enough. I was completely and utterly humiliated. And Mom just stood there.

"I'm going to call the police! You can't touch me that way!" I screamed as I jumped down from the fence. "I'm calling the police and they'll put you in jail!" I was embarrassed by my angry tears as I pulled up my pants, buttoned and zipped them closed.

"Go ahead. Call the police! They won't do anything to me!" Hal yelled back, the veins in his neck round and hard like a garden hose, his eyes ablaze with his own self-righteousness.

A few minutes later when the cop car pulled up and the policemen got out, Hal is the one who answered the question, "What happened here?"

Because the answer was that his girlfriend's crazy druggie daughter went ballistic, I was the one hauled into the police car and taken down to the station for observation. The official conclusion was that Hal had used "reasonable force" to get me down from the fence when I was hysterical. Reason wasn't anywhere to be found in that scenario. That was the irony.

Karen and her dad picked me up at jail and let me spend the night. The next day I checked in at The Loft. I felt like the universe had placed me in a coffin before I was dead—picked by some evil force to be completely alone, no matter how much I knocked on the sides of my pine box in order to be heard. I didn't like being the walking dead, so I made it known I was still alive. I met a guy at The Loft. Needy like me. We weren't supposed to, of course, so we slept together. And, of course, we got caught. I met some over-aged men in the neighborhood and slept with them. It was something to do to make me feel alive. Like I mattered for a minute. But, of course, I didn't. The Loft staff had to take me to the hospital three times for suicide attempts. Finally the director said, "We have to let you go, Allison. We aren't equipped to handle your needs and we don't think we can keep you safe anymore."

One good thing that happened at The Loft, though, was I got started in Narcotics Anonymous. I was such a mess. I felt so hopeless…and motherless. I'd stayed a couple of weeks with a friend when The Loft kicked me out, but that wasn't going well at all. The girl and I fought all the time. The N.A. group was full of people struggling with some of my same issues. Marge was one of them. In her late thirties or early forties, she was much further along in her rehabilitation than many of us. By this time I was ready to live out of the Olds Ninety-eight my mom bought me for my sixteenth birthday. But Marge asked enough questions to discover I was on my own, so she invited me to dinner at her place. It wasn't much, but it was home to her and her three children. She was a single mom working a huge paper route to put food on the table. I had to admire that.

"If you want to, you can stay with us," Marge offered as we cleared the dishes away from the modest meal she'd made—macaroni and cheese, maybe. Anyway, it was made with love. That's what I discovered about life with Marge. There is love out there.

"Really?" I couldn't believe it. "Yes!" I moved my things in. I moved my heart in. I wanted to be with Marge all the time. She let me ride with her on her paper route each night...way over a hundred miles round trip. And the entire time, we talked. She actually wanted to know about *me*. Listened to *me*. I've never laughed or talked so much in my life. At first, I kind of waited for the ball to drop. At some point I was expecting her to hit me or yell at me. To get enough of me and abandon me. But it didn't happen. Someone can care for me, Allison, without it involving hurting me. It was a new thought. And it was healing for a while. Until Marge couldn't say no to several other members of Narcotics Anonymous who were down on their luck.

I didn't tell Andi about the other woman, yet. The one who made me so crazy I got into drugs for a while again. Maybe I will someday. I think it might be too much. Too ugly. It's why Marge told me I had to leave. The other reason is that life is just one big disappointment even to those who try to help other people.

Chapter Four

ANDI—MOTHERS

Hearing Allison's story that day left my stomach in knots and my head pounding. It was a little too close to home. Ed and I established Beulah's Place in order to help teens and young adults who are homeless as a result of abuse or trafficking. Named it after Ed's absolutely fabulous mother whom he adored and whom I never had the privilege of meeting. My mother, on the other hand, created two children who desperately needed rescue: me and my brother, Joe Jr. Allison's experiences nudged awake the horror stories of my youth, dredging up so many memories obscured, for much of my young adult life, by my own dissociative disorder. It took years of therapy and intensive counseling to sort out the mess my parents made of my psyche. Driving home after telling Allison I'd find her a place to stay as soon as I could, I could hear once more my birth mother's voice screeching her pet names for me: "Stupid!" "Klutz!" "Pig!" "Idiot!" Allison's mother issues mirrored some of my own.

Mother is a word that connotes nurturing and comfort to most people—an endearing term of affection for the woman who loves her babies with all her heart. The one with a soft lap in which to curl up and fall asleep while she reads fairy tales at bedtime. The one who covers little tousled heads with hundreds of sweet kisses just because her child is so dear to her. Children read her eyes while she nurses them; read her lips when she whispers their names. Hers is the hand a child holds when he first crosses the street. Mommies are safe, with arms wide open for a child to careen into when life gets stormy or the path is piled with leaves that hide the way. When our heads are hung in shame, it's Mommy who lifts our chins and tells us to do better next time. Nightmares flee when she chases them from a bedroom filled with the darkness of midnight. She is the champion of her child, the protector and guide. It is why so many have "Mom" tattooed on their biceps. Mommy is the one who can always be counted upon to love her kids no matter what. The one to whom grown men and women still tell the secrets of their hearts. I can never call the woman who raised me, *Mom.* Her name was Leanne.

My first memory of Leanne was of her holding a butcher knife over my head and screaming at me when I was three years old. Joe Jr., who was six at the time, tiptoed with me toward the kitchen to see what our mother was doing there. We were on a reconnaissance mission to see how she blended oregano, basil and tomatoes to make the whole house smell like spaghetti sauce. The woman was short, trim… and ferocious, though that wasn't obvious as she stood at the stove stirring a pot, the steam from it curling up around her head. Beside her on the counter were small piles of fresh herbs and diced onion. I could see the bows of her apron tied around the back of her housedress, her legs, hanging like two baseball bats from beneath the hem, as she spread them apart for balance, her feet in white Keds, and the back of her head, her short dark hair cropped close around the nape of her neck like a man's. Curiously, even as young as I was, I remember feeling guilty looking at her there. Like I was breaking some silent rule that says babies can't look at mommies while they make dinner. Joe peeked around the corner first, putting his hand on the wall beside the doorframe as he leaned out to see what Leanne was doing. I found a place under his arm as I joined him in staring at the woman in the kitchen. I placed my hand on the wall a little lower than Joe's. She'd put down the spoon by then and was cutting up some meat to add to the sauce when she saw us there out of the corner of her eye. I don't know if we scared her, if we were supposed to be in our rooms doing other things or what exactly set her off. At three years old, all I remember was the visceral fear that overtook me next. Our mother rushed toward us waving a butcher knife in her hand, the blood from the meat she'd been chopping smudged onto its blade. Her face was crimson and her eyes wild as she screamed, "Get your hands off those walls, you filthy little brats!" The knife was a monster glinting in the light emanating from the dining room fixture as it swayed back and forth in her hands while she chased us through the living room and into the hallway. Her screaming made me scream as I ran with all my might behind Joe back to our bedrooms where I hid under my bed for the rest of the afternoon, fearing she'd come and kill me there.

Leanne hated her life. Despised her husband, Joe Sr. She felt she was made for better things. Her own mother died when she was three, so she was raised by her stepmother, who was always kind to us. Somewhere along the way, Leanne developed pretentious tastes and a haughty sense of entitlement. I guess that's why we were never allowed to sit on our couches though they were covered in plastic and remained pristine in the living rooms of all the homes we lived in while I was growing up. Or maybe it was because of Leanne's intense aversion to housework.

Joe Sr. was from Chicago. Left when he was sixteen years old and never turned back. He settled in California where he met and married Leanne in 1957. A Polish kid who always talked big and dreamed bigger, Joe was tall and relatively attractive and used it to his advantage to captivate our mother and any other woman who'd fall prey to his charms. Prone to depression, as most dry alcoholics are, Joe was in and out of sales jobs for their whole marriage. Leanne never missed an opportunity to tell him what a complete disappointment he was in every way…and she made her point very loudly. It's hard to live a lavish lifestyle when your husband is a loser, so Leanne got a teaching degree while we were young so there could be food on the table.

Joe Jr. came early in their marriage. A sickly kid, always small for his age, he was, nevertheless, the apple of Leanne's eye—her prize possession over whom she lauded every time an opportunity presented itself or even when it didn't. I was told on numerous occasions that Joe's IQ was 180. I have no idea if that is actually a fact. But he *was* smart. His early life was plagued by many stress illnesses that accompanied his very real asthma and exacerbated his constant agitation. Leanne seemed to actually pet him sometimes. When she wasn't beating him nearly to death.

Leanne made it clear to her husband that she never wanted another child after Joe's birth. The dreams of being a society matron were fast disappearing in the drudgery of life with a sickly kid and a lazy husband with a wandering eye. Leanne made such a big deal about never having another child that even her relatives knew it. When she became pregnant with me, it was common knowledge that I was completely unwanted and inconvenient. Liver problems and stress almost caused a premature birth in Leanne's eighth month of pregnancy, but I made it into the world in one piece. I had no idea that with the cutting of my umbilical cord I was placed in the arms of a woman who would torment and abuse me. From my first breath, I was just another mouth to feed. Never in my life did I feel wanted or loved. My father summed it up perfectly at a family gathering when I was eight years old: "Andrea was a mistake we couldn't give back! There was a no return policy with that one!" And the room fell into raucous laughter while I hung my head in shame.

Originally, I was to be named Maria. During my womb time, however, Leanne changed her mind. When she and Joe Sr. first married, they'd lived next to a kindly Christian woman who'd spent time with Leanne teaching her about God. Maybe even having a Bible study with her. It was a vague religious experience that certainly hadn't created a positive life change in Leanne. But she loved the woman enough to give me her name—Andrea: *strong heart.* At least that's what I've been told it means. From the Bible verse in 2 Thessalonians 3:3: The Lord is faithful and will keep you for Himself, protected from the evil one. Lord knows, I needed it!

Leanne would put Joe and me down for exceptionally long naps in the afternoons even after we were old enough to skip nap-time. It gave her the afternoon to do whatever she wanted, free of her kids. Bored and too energetic to sleep, I would devise things to do to keep myself distracted. One afternoon I decided I'd take my clothes off and put them on backwards. I'm sure I was also talking to myself as most kids do. Suddenly my bedroom door flew open and Leanne stepped into the room. I got very still. Already I was afraid of her quick temper and the meaty hands she used to pummel my face and chest when she was enraged. I was in some stage of undress when Leanne stomped over to my bed and threw back the covers, the suddenness of it making me gasp. "What are you doing under there?" she screamed. Instinctively my hands raced to cover my face. The insinuation in her voice was that I was up to something nasty; something nice little girls don't do. There was disgust in her face I couldn't read, yet. "You better be asleep when I come back to check on you!" Leanne demanded as she walked back toward the bedroom door. I hadn't noticed before, but there was a neighbor lady lurking in the doorway. When I dared to move my hands just the tiniest bit from my face, I could see that the lady was looking at me with a horrified expression. Even then I knew. Our neighbor wasn't appalled that a little girl was playing under the covers instead of taking a nap. It was the venomous way Leanne spit the words at me. The threat to hurt me implicit in her rage. And my little hands flying immediately to protect my face... and the terrified expression on it. She knew. This woman. Pity was dripping from her eyes, eyes that said to me, *This isn't normal.*

Normal is what happens to you in life, over and over again. Our normal was many degrees north of the line where most people live. Joe Jr. and I didn't know that, though. We were just kids trying to somehow make it through a day without being battered or cursed at or touched inappropriately. Leanne's adoration for her son became obsession as he grew older. But her abnormal perversities were visited on both of us very young. In her need to control every aspect of our lives, we were told when we should go to the bathroom—even if we didn't need to. If we didn't perform, Leanne would likely beat us for disobedience. I know now her need for ritualistic sadistic abuse fueled her urges with us kids, and we needed to be rescued. From very early I remember Leanne touching me in the bathroom. Under the guise of seeing if I'd peed. Her hands making me anxious, or even terrified. *Oh, Allison, I know why you can't stand the sound of your own pee.*

Normal for us was to be sitting in the living room watching television as Joe Sr. and I were one night. Normal was that no activity, no matter how mundane, was safe. Leanne, who'd been in her bedroom with the door closed, slammed out into the hallway and reeled toward the hall bath. Before she had a chance to actually enter the room, she noticed the toilet seat had been left up, again. And I could feel it before I even saw it. The explosion that sent her barreling into the living room screaming like she'd lost her mind. "You little shit!" And hovering over me with her face contorted and her large, stubby hands clenched for battle was the monster she so often became.

"How many times do I have to tell you to put that seat down!" She was pointing to the bathroom and shaking her arm, pumping it up and down like she was a well that needed priming.

"What?" Joe Sr. was irritated. "What are you talking about?" She'd interrupted his television show.

"I didn't go to the bathroom!" I defended myself at my own peril. I wanted to say, *There are two men in this house who leave the seat up. I'm not a man, so it wasn't my fault.* But I didn't dare. The last time she threatened to beat me was a few days earlier when she'd seen a drop of pee on the floor in front of the toilet. "If you don't clean that up right now, I'm going to rub your face in it then make you *lick* it up!" *Who, really, even thinks to say that to a child?*

She didn't hear my defense and wouldn't have listened to it anyway. The need to beat us was as intrinsic as breathing for her. A powerful fix, unsatisfied until we were left in a heap and she was completely exhausted. Before the words came out of my mouth, Leanne had already headed to her bedroom to pick out a belt. Brown or black? Her tools of torture hung in a neat row at the front of her closet. It seemed to me over the years that she delighted in the choice of instruments for our torture.

"Turn over! I'm going to beat the crap out of you!" she ordered as she rushed back into the living room with the folded belt dangling from her hand, the buckle looming hard and silver, jangling like a jailer's keys. Leanne caught me up by my tee shirt and threw me to my knees in front of the sofa. I was already crying. My head was pushed into the cushions and held there while this maniac of a mother battered me with the belt, careful not to hit me where the welts would show. And Joe Sr.? He sat there and listened for several minutes. Got tired of the noise. Made Leanne stop. Normal stuff, really.

***

Ed hadn't arrived yet when I pulled into the driveway of our comfortable three-bedroom home. The rain had finally stopped, leaving the air smelling clean and crisp. I took a deep breath and stepped out into the late afternoon sun, which was glowing like someone had finally turned the lights back on in a very dim room—so bright it made me squint. I shook off the dreariness of the weather and the darkness of my thoughts. I had work to do. Allison needed a place to stay and my man was going to need his dinner. The road that lay behind Ed and me was covered with debris, pocked with dips and teeming with detours. But we'd finally found each other.

I took a deep breath and opened the front door. "Strong Heart" finally had a home of her own, and it was good.

I made some tea and got right on the phone trying to locate a home for Allison. Beulah's Place is committed to finding a safe place for our young adults to live while they graduate high school, get a job, find transportation and stabilize their lives so they can live independently. We depend on families in our community to help in this process. I started going down the list of possible caregivers.

"Andi!" Ed called as he walked through the front door an hour later. "Where are you?" I heard the door slam and his work boots hit the tile in the entry way. "I'm home!"

"In here," I yelled back. "In the office."

Ed came in to kiss me on the forehead. "How'd it go?" he asked as he leaned over the desk and looked into my face. I'm always struck by how handsome my man is. His black curls have turned gray in the past fifteen years, but they still loop around his ears when his baseball hat is pulled over his head like it was as he put his ruddy face close to mine, electric blue eyes smiling. "What did you think of her?"

"She's heartbreaking." I smiled up at him. "Like they all are." I sighed and sat back in my chair.

"Do you think you can find her a place?" Ed asked as he stood and stretched his six feet, three inches to their full height, yawning as he raised his arms, his fingers almost touching the ceiling.

"I didn't have much luck this afternoon," I said. "But I know I will. We always do." It was our constant prayer: provision for these kids. What I knew from my own experience, though, is that God loves them more than we do. I simply needed to trust in that.

Ed helped me make dinner. He's a better cook than I am and doesn't have all the food issues I do, so we often cook together. I put gluten-free pasta on to boil while Ed cut up some veggies for a salad. "I wish I'd met Beulah," I mused.

"What made you think of my mom just now?" Ed asked.

"I've been thinking about my own…" I answered.

"Well, that's never a good thing," he said, smiling as he peeled carrots.

"This new girl…Allison…has such a marginal mom. An absentee parent that for some reason Allison still has a latent desire to please. No dad in the house." I turned from the stove and looked over at Ed. "But that's not all. Honestly, she could've been me, Ed. She's a cutter with dissociative disorder and a history of suicide attempts." There's still the memory of a desperate, lonely well down inside of me that can be tapped. Tears overtook me before I knew what was happening. "Talking with her made me remember what I'd rather forget," I said as I moved to the sink and put my arms around Ed, who is a foot taller than I.

"It's why you will help her, Babes," cooed Ed as he held me close. "It's why you even want to."

The steady beat of my husband's heart echoing in my ears eased me back into the moment. The pasta was boiling over and the sauce was bubbling. The ordinary goodness of our lives crashed in on the shadow of my bad memories, chasing them away for the moment. Leanne might have ruined my life then, but she has no power to ruin anything now.

"Back to your thought a minute ago," began Ed, "I wish Mom had met *you*." We carried our plates to the table and sat down. "She would've loved you! I tell you that all the time." A boyish grin transformed Ed into the kid his mom adored. It was there smeared across his face every time he spoke of her. Like she was still standing in the room with a plate of warm cookies in her hand and a satisfied smile on her face.

"And you loved her more than anything!" I laughed. He told me *that* all the time, too.

Ed was the youngest boy of Leroy and Beulah Buerger and grew up in El Cajon, California, with brothers, Jim and Daryl.

Ed's childhood experiences couldn't be more diametrically different from mine. I always get a vicarious thrill when Ed tells me about the cookies and pies his mom made. About his hard working, responsible, generous father. Their faith in Jesus permeated their home life. A genuine trust in God that transcended their circumstances. And, not unimportantly, Ed's childhood attention deficit disorder didn't affect the love his parents had for him one iota. My speech impediment was an embarrassment to my mother, who also believed me to be less intelligent because of it. So when Ed talks about family dinners, his Mom reading her Bible, the encouraging words he received when he didn't quite measure up... well, I want to put myself right there in that little home in El Cajon and soak it all up.

Chapter Five

ED—LIFE WITH BEULAH

My brothers and I were all born in December. Jim, the oldest, is twelve years my senior; Daryl, eight. I was the de facto baby of the brood, coddled and spoiled. My brothers were grown and out of the house by the time I was a pre-teen. Dad worked at North Island Civil Air Station on Coronado Island and Mom taught pre-school at Bancroft Baptist Daycare. We were "Father Knows Best" wholesome. A household with pies cooling on the stove and homemade cookies in the cookie jar. A Mom who smiled and patted our heads and a Dad who worked hard to put food on the table. I had Attention Deficit Disorder with Hyperactivity, restless leg syndrome and was a disruptive element in my school and I didn't even know it!

Mom encouraged my every triumph and minimized my failures. It made me always want to make her happy. I adored her from the moment I laid my infant eyes on her. A large, stocky woman with her graying hair cropped short, a generous figure and a ready smile, she reminded me of Aunt Bee from the television show "Mayberry." There wasn't a kid she didn't love, a stray she wouldn't take in or a time she wouldn't set another place at the table for whoever happened to be there for dinner. Her blue eyes danced when she laughed and her skin smelled like cupcakes. There was never anyone like my mom. Ever.

The Vietnam War broke out when I was young, and it took Jim away from us for a while. The morning of February 20, 1967, my dad and I took Jim to the airport before the sun was up. I remember when we got there it was filled with men in fatigues, their wives or moms holding onto them for dear life. Heartache was palpable. The brave among us were trying desperately not to cry. There hadn't been much conversation in our car on the way to the airport, although subtext hung in the atmosphere, waiting to be articulated. *What if I don't come back?* I know Jim was thinking that. I could see it in his eyes. *What if I never see my big brother again?* Fear of that made my stomach feel tight and my eyes water a little. *I'm proud of my boy.* Dad didn't say it in the car. The air was too close; the moment not quite right. But before Jim turned and walked away from us to head off to war, Dad gave him a bear hug, shook his hand, and said it. Said, "I'm proud of you." And Jim was gone.

Afterward, on the way home, Dad and I stopped at Tasty Burger for something to eat. Food in the stomach of a twelve-year-old goes a long way in easing sorrow…or just about anything. We didn't talk about Jim or the war. It was a Monday and I was out of school, excited about having the rest of the day off. Maybe I'd ride my bike or something. Dad and I weren't prepared for what happened when we got home.

We could see a tower of smoke in the distance as we pulled off the freeway, but thought nothing of it. February is the wrong time of year for forest fires in California. Usually there's enough rain to keep the ground moist and the foliage green. Before we opened the screen door to the house, I could hear my mother crying. "Mom!" I yelled as I ran into the house to find her. She was in the kitch-en, sitting at the table with her face in her hands. "What's wrong, Mom?" I asked as I sat down beside her and tried to look into her eyes. She wiped her tears and put her right hand randomly on mine, resting it there. Mom's eyes were red and she was having a hard time composing herself enough to even speak. I wasn't used to seeing her cry about anything. It broke my heart.

"Beulah, what's wrong?" echoed my dad, catching up to us in the kitchen. "What happened?"

Mom dropped the tissue from her tear-streaked face and said, "It's my brother, Leroy," and her eyes searched Dad's face. "It's Ed." She cried a minute more and we waited for her to continue. "Ed died this morning," she managed, her chest heaving with the sob she stifled in order to speak.

Dad put his arms around her shoulders and let her cry. "Jim is gone and we don't know if he'll even come home…and now this…" I thought her heart had cracked in two. I didn't know what to do or say. And…I'd been named after Mom's brother. It sounded strange for her to say that Ed died. It was him. But it was also me. A confusing pain made the hairs on the back of my neck rise up. I let go of her hand and went outside.

The smoke that had been in the distance was now looming ominously toward El Cajon. I could smell it—taste its bitterness in my mouth and feel the sting of it in my eyes. It looked like it was moving really fast, too. Crest, California, is an unincorporated community in San Diego County with dense brush and trees. The smoke we'd seen rising in tiny puffs only a few minutes earlier became a raging fire, burning so fast that I could actually see it moving our way. By afternoon, we thought we might have to evacuate because of the blaze. I was wondering just how much my mom could take that day. But she didn't fall apart. Mom always did what she had to do and trusted God to take care of us. I will always remember the day, though—February 20, 1967. A very bad, no good day.

Exactly one year later, to the day, Jim came home. Safe and sound. Our house didn't burn down and we were back to normal. And as the next few years came and went, life ticked forward. My ADHD seemed to vanish with age, and I entered El Cajon Valley High School ready to play football. I wasn't particularly interested in being on the team until I had a confrontation with the neighborhood bully the summer before. I was in the throes of a sweaty touch football game with some of my friends when Bradley strutted by wearing his high school practice uniform. I'm sure he could see me above the others because I'd gotten so big over the past couple of years.

"Hey, Buerger!" Bradley hollered as he watched me run down toward our makeshift goal line. "You gonna play football next year?" He was standing on the sidewalk with his helmet in his hand, his hair sticking up like he'd been electrocuted. I was surprised he stopped to yell at me. We weren't friends. Out of breath and only mildly interested in answering, I hollered back, "I don't know."

"Well, I just ran a five yard gain in practice, which is equal to five *touchdowns* in this puny game you're playing!" I could hear his derisive laughter as he walked down the street, his football helmet hitting his thigh as he sauntered along thinking he was Roger Staubach or something. That's all it took to get me out on the field for four years of football on the defensive line.

I was a decent student, but I wish I'd pushed myself harder. Mom and Dad weren't the kind to drive us to succeed, so I coasted through El Cajon High with average grades, but nothing more. Grossmont Junior College was a wake-up call. I strolled into English class after the first week of school, and the professor announced he was returning our first essays to us. Mine wasn't in the stack.

"Ed Buerger, would you please stay after class?" The professor didn't say it in a threatening way. He was almost matter-of-fact in his tone.

"Sure." I had no idea what to expect.

"I left your paper in my office," he said as I approached him. Then I knew he was probably trying not to embarrass me. I felt my face flush as I walked behind him to his office. I waited quietly as the professor unlocked the door and pushed it open. I shuffled through behind him. There was my paper on top of the in-basket. With a huge red **F** staring back at me. It might as well have been a scarlet **A**.

"Ed, I believe you are a very bright kid," my teacher said as he eased down into his overstuffed black leather chair and pushed himself comfortably up to his desk. He nodded at the chair I was expected to sit in. "I think you must not believe in yourself." As he handed me my paper, he said, "You're better than this."

Not much was expected of me in high school. This was the kind of paper I always handed in and I did just fine. I'd never *failed*. I was surprised. "Has someone been speaking negatively to you about yourself?" the man asked, embarrassing me further. I knew I'd made the F because I didn't put any effort into the essay, not because I hated myself for some reason. *Sheesh.* "Let's make a deal," he went on. "You work harder on your assignments from now on and I'll throw out your highest and lowest grades. Is that a deal?" he asked while I sat there dumbfounded. I hadn't said a word.

"Yes, sir," I finally replied as I folded the essay in half then fumbled out of my seat and walked through the door and down the hall. I wasn't sure I could do a whole lot better. But I'd never tried so hard in school as I did to make a better than just passing grade for that professor. It was a turning point, educationally, for me.

At the end of the semester, I received a **B** in English. The prof pulled me aside again and said, "You know, Ed, I was extra hard on you this semester. You earned that **B**." He patted me on the shoulder. "I sure didn't give it to you." He was almost as proud as I was.

For the rest of my two years at Grossmont, I worked hard and played football with that professor's words ringing in my ears. *I could do better.* And so I did.

I wanted to be a high school football coach and made Physical Education my major at San Francisco State University. When I'd almost finished my second year, my life took a turn that changed its direction. My aunt and uncle inherited a dairy farm in Santee, California, from my uncle's parents who'd refused to allow anyone to use the land for anything else while they were alive. The land was prime real estate property, and my uncle had dreams of creating a huge mobile home park on it. With his parents now deceased, my uncle finally finished the process of permitting the land for the homes and was ready to build. I was offered five dollars an hour to work for them. It was great money at the time, so I quit school. Thus began my career in construction. The park has room for three hundred fifty-five homes and is still always full.

With money in my pocket and experience in just about every facet of construction, I found my talents were in demand in the fast-growing communities in and around San Diego when the Santee project was complete. My career aspirations weren't all that had changed by the time I was in my early twenties. My religious upbringing was a thing of the past. Even though I had a unique experience in 1972, when I was in high school. Evangelist Danny Large came to our church, El Cajon Foursquare. The powerful message of this young preacher and the apparent deliverance of a girl from demons stirred up a revival that went on for a week. I attended every night. After that I was smitten with Jesus. I carried my Bible to school every day my entire junior year. But by the time I was nineteen, I started looking around at all I'd missed out on by being a good religious boy. Drugs. Alcohol. Women. Parties. All the things that had the potential to break my mother's heart. And God's. That's what I did…for years.

Though I lived in my own place by the time I was in my twenties, I still had dinner with my folks once a week or so. Never passed up a chance to have a home-cooked meal. On one of those evenings, Mom had a troubled look on her face as she passed me the mashed potatoes and meat loaf and poured me more iced tea. It made me uneasy, the look in her eyes. It wasn't sorrow exactly, but something close to it. Something heavy on her heart. She didn't ask me about what I was doing with my life most of the time, but she knew I wasn't in church. That girlfriends came and went. That I'd started drinking a while back. Like I said before, things that I knew would break her heart. I wasn't keeping anything from her, but I wasn't telling her anything, either.

After dinner, I went back into the kitchen where she was standing over the sink washing the dishes. She turned slightly to look at me when she heard my footfall. The steam from the hot dishwater made her soft round face glow and a few strands of her hair hung in little wet ringlets at the nape of her neck. I knew I was in for it when Mom shook the suds from her hands, grabbed a dish cloth and turned to look at me. Every kid knows his mom's serious face. That's the one she was wearing.

"Ed, you know I love you, honey." Mom was drying her hands and dabbing her face with the dish towel. "I wish you'd get back in church. What are you doing with your life?" The sincerity pooling in her solemn blue eyes as they searched mine for an answer made me want to hug her. I didn't know what to do but to stand there and smile at her. I loved her so much. But I had no intention of going to church any time soon. I slouched back against the wall and Mom leaned against the edge of the sink as we stared at each other for a minute.

"Your life's not going to make much sense without Jesus, Ed. You can party and drink, but that just means you're wasting time." I could tell my mother was reaching for just the right thing to say that would turn me around and I could tell she'd been rehearsing it in her head all day. "There's a plan for you that God's laid out…a dream He's dreamed for you. And your life's going to be in turmoil until you learn to pray again and ask Him to reveal His will to you." Mom cocked her head. Wiped her face with the dish cloth again to keep me from seeing she was really hiding her tears.

"Mom," I said as I reached over to her and put my arms around her, "I'm just fine. Don't worry about me. It's all good." I kissed her moist cheek. Gave her my best youngest child grin and left her there, praying, I'm sure, as she finished her dishes.

I bet we had that conversation twenty times in the next twenty years. And I did fumble around with relationships, work and purpose. I had my share of dates, had a few long-term girlfriends, but marriage seemed to elude me. "Mom, how in the world would I even know if some woman is the right one for me?" I asked over the years when she'd want to know if I'd gotten serious about someone. I didn't understand her answer until I was well into my forties. "Ed, finding a relationship is like finding a rotten egg. I can't tell you what a rotten egg smells like, but you'll know it when you find one." I hadn't smelled love. Not yet.

When life rolls along real simple, it's easy to take for granted the things you always count on. If the thought ever occurred to me that something bad would happen to my mother, I'd put it completely out of my mind. As far as I was concerned, she'd always be there, her kitchen smelling like cherry pie and her skin like cupcakes. Imagining a life in which I couldn't hear her voice or see her face was unfathomable. My indestructible mother would outlive me. That's what I thought, anyway. But I was wrong.

I was working on a job in El Centro when I got the call. "Hey, Ed. It's Daryl." My heart stopped.

"Is this about Mom?" I asked. "Is she okay?" I knew she wasn't. She'd had a lung biopsy a couple of days before. I could tell by the tone of my brother's voice it wasn't good.

"Yeah, it's Mom. She has inoperable lung cancer, Ed."

I could see her standing at the door waving good-bye to me as I carried my lunch sack off to school. I felt her big soft kiss on my cheek. I watched her pray and heard her laughter ringing in my ears. All in a moment cascading over me with what felt like panic. I couldn't live without this woman. My life shattered with that phone call. I'd always counted on her being there. Even though she'd been terribly disappointed in me in recent years, she didn't discard me. I knew I didn't deserve her love. But she *did* deserve mine. I intended to make her last days the best they could be right then and there.

"I think we should move her and Dad up to Oregon near you and Kay, Daryl," I said, trying to control the tears in my eyes. "It's just not safe in El Cajon anymore." Making a plan helped ease the shock. Fix what I could fix. That's what I wanted to do for her in the moment.

"Sure," answered Daryl. "We can talk about it."

"You know, up there the pace is slower. Mom could get out in nature." I already had her inhaling fresh high desert air into that compromised lung of hers. "It'd be so good for her, Daryl."

"I'll look around up here and see what I can find," he said. "In the meantime, take care of her, Ed. She's going to need you now."

"Sure. Yeah." And he hung up.

Grief put me into hyper-drive. I was determined to get Mom to Oregon so that her last days or weeks or months could be peaceful and beautiful. Redmond was the perfect place for that. Within only a few weeks, Mom and Dad were enjoying sunshine and a new place. Twice a month I'd drive up and stay for a four-day weekend. And when I did, it was all about Mom. Holding her hand, listening to her stories, hugging and kissing her…I wanted to make the time count. Of course, Mom didn't hesitate to remind me that I needed Jesus. Counseled me more than once that I needed to find the right girl. But as the time came closer to her departure from this world, her thoughts and conversations were more often about the next.

January 6, 1998, was the day Beulah left us to try and make it in this life without her. All of us boys were in the house, expecting her time to come at any moment. She'd been in and out of consciousness, very weak and seemingly quite far away. Her eyes seemed to be gazing into the distance when she tried to open them to see us. She was on her way from here to there, and we were gathered to see her off. Wanting her pain to end. Happy through our grief that Beulah Buerger was going to see her Jesus soon.

There was a football game in progress on the television in the den. The aromas of different casseroles from church ladies collided in the kitchen. We were uncertain what to do in our fidgeting and waiting. Then about one-thirty in the afternoon, Kay came in with a word from our Mom. "Beulah thinks it's about time for you boys to go out and feed the cows."

"What?" we all said together...all laughed nervously and looked at each other like, "What the heck?"

"Yep. She woke up a little and said you boys should feed the cows." Kay shrugged her shoulders a little and smiled. Daryl and she had some livestock on their property. Apparently, we were to obey our mom and feed them; so, we turned off the game, put on our boots and wandered, a little stunned, out the back door and toward the pasture.

By the time we returned, Mom was gone. It was just like her to go quietly without a fuss. "I think she didn't want to die in front of you boys," said Kay after she broke the news to us.

I walked over to her bed and looked down at my mother lying so peacefully there. I was afraid I'd break down...lose it. But it was hard to cry for a woman who wanted nothing grander all her life than to be in heaven with Jesus. I held her hand for a few minutes, but I had the thought she wasn't there. Beulah was in Beulah Land, and her feet were dancing. We had her for seventy-eight years. Now I had to decide how to live in this world without her. I had no idea how much my life would change in one short year.

Chapter Six

ANDI—THE BIG BLUE SKY

The doorbell rang around eleven in the morning. When I opened it, Allison was standing there with a couple of garbage bags full of clothes in her hand and a wary smile on her face. "Hi, Allison," I said. "Come in."

"Thank you for letting me stay here," she said as she stepped through the door. "I couldn't take it over there anymore." Allison set her bags down. "Where do you want me to put my stuff?"

"Why don't you go ahead and put it in the guest room now?" I offered as I began walking down the hall in that direction. "Then we'll have a bite of lunch and talk about what's next."

"Wow, this is nice," she commented once she set her bags on the double bed and looked around. Then she opened one of them and grabbed only one thing—a raggedy stuffed animal that she placed on the bed next to the pillows. Retrieved it like she didn't want it to suffocate beneath the folds of the plastic garbage bag. The act felt familiar. Squeezed at my heart a little.

Allison was disheveled and tired. "You hungry?" I asked, shaking off the déjà vu I couldn't quite retrieve.

"Yeah," she said, shyly, like she didn't want to be any trouble.

"Well, let's eat, then," I said cheerfully as we walked back down the hall toward the kitchen.

"You know you'll only be here a few days," I said as I pulled a jar of mayonnaise out of the cupboard then slathered some with a knife onto wheat bread. "When your house parents appear, you'll be able to move in and settle down in their home."

"That's totally fine," Allison replied as she pushed her glasses up on her nose and sat down on the high stool at the granite counter while I built her sandwich.

"We have some expectations of you, too, once you're there, Allison," I continued as I cut the sandwich at a diagonal and plated it for her.

"Like what?" Her eyes narrowed, the tiniest bit of rebellion glimmering there.

"Well, you'll be expected to obey the house rules, for one thing: curfews, cleaning up your room, the dishes, perhaps."

"Oh, that." Allison sighed. "That's no problem."

"Also, Beulah's Place requires you to finish high school, find a job and transportation and ultimately live successfully out on your own. We help you do that." I smiled at her as she munched the Pringles I stacked on her plate. I pushed the contract with Beulah's Place toward her. "You will need to sign this binding contract. Make sure it's what you want to do, because we will hold you to it, Allison," I said with a smile.

She took a bite of her sandwich, set the rest back on the plate and picked up the contract to better survey it. "I really want this to work. I need to finish school. I don't want to do drugs ever again," she declared when she'd finished perusing it.

"I know, Allison. Trust me, I understand. Just make certain you are willing to commit to the process before you sign your name." Ed and I know commitment is sometimes tough for kids who've become accustomed to life on the streets. They don't like to be told what to do. Surviving has taught them to be tough.

"It's definitely what I want to do." She took the pen I handed her and signed her name to the contract. Relief sparkled in her eyes as she handed it back to me. After a deep breath and the hint of a smile, Allison turned her attention back to her lunch.

"At least you won't need us to find you a car," I chuckled. "It's great that you have that Oldsmobile Ninety-Eight to get you places already!"

"Yeah," she said through a mouthful of food, "I thought I was gonna have to live in it!"

Instead of moving into her car, before two weeks had passed, Allison was given a room in the home of an older couple who lived on the outskirts of Redmond in a quiet neighborhood. Mr. and Mrs. Cordell were in their seventies and could offer Allison the exact opposite of what she'd recently come out of—peace and quiet, good food and space to heal. "When I first got there, it was kind of weird and scary," she told me when I dropped by to see her a few days later. "But now it's weird and scary...and wonderful!"

I laughed. Normal is strange when all you know is chaos.

"I just turned eighteen and I felt forty!" she said, her hands spread out in front of her, palms up, as she shrugged to emphasize the point. "The Cordells are here with me. I'm not alone. I don't think I've ever felt safe before." Allison brushed an escaping tear from her eye. "It's cool. But I'm not used to it."

"Have you talked to your mom, yet?" I asked, knowing she probably hadn't.

"No. I don't think I'm ready to hear about them being married...and I know I'm not ready to tell them what I've been through, or put myself through, these past few months." Allison sank back into the cushions of the living room sofa. "I'm just now letting myself feel secure. You know, like I don't have to be on the lookout for the next place to run."

"How are you doing with the house rules here?" I asked tentatively.

"I thought I'd hate them, but I can tell Mr. and Mrs. Cordell care about me." Allison was cracking her knuckles, peering down at her hands in order to avoid looking straight at me. "They want to take care of me. And I love to hear Mr. Cordell tell me stories...

about everything!" She lifted her face slowly and looked into my eyes. Hers were still sparkling with tears. "Do you know how long it's been since anyone gave a crap about what I'm doing?"

"I can imagine, Allison," I replied as I patted her knee. "I really can."

***

By the time I was five years old, I was infinitely aware of the fact that Leanne had absolute control of my life. There was never a moment when I didn't have to be hyper-vigilant. Joe Jr. and I never knew which of her personalities Leanne would manifest at any given moment. What was clear to me was that I was the cause of all the problems within our home—even her husband's infidelity and Joe Jr.'s constant illnesses. I heard her say to me many times, "Your days are numbered!" My understanding of that was that she'd kill me and have every right to do so. So when Allison expressed that she'd never felt safe, I knew what she meant. The only time I ever felt safe was in my bedroom lodged between the wall and my dresser where I'd sit on the floor with my knees pulled up close to my chest. I could see my door from there…if anyone came in or out. Or, when I was smaller, I hid under my bed with only my nose sticking out so I could breathe. I lived with the fear of being cursed at, beaten or violated.

Always present was the thought that I was trapped somehow. With nowhere to hide and no way of defending myself, I was at the mercy of parents who had no mercy for me. I'm sure that's why I had a childhood dream so vivid I remember its every detail all these years later. Before my eyes floated a hot pink wall that met a soft, velvety hot pink floor which extended toward me. The surface of the floor sparkled with two circles of white hot diamonds, bending the light, nearly blinding me. I thought they must be bracelets arrayed as if they were set in a jewelry shop showcase, but when I looked more closely I could see what they really were: handcuffs. *Those are beautiful and sparkling, but they are for bad people. Prisoners.* I was at once drawn to their mesmerizing brilliance and repelled by the thought that if I touched them I'd be fettered, not adorned. The vision was confusing. And the lovely diamond cuffs haunted my thoughts for years, like the dream was a puzzle I was destined to solve.

Our family found ourselves in church sometimes, as counter intuitive as that seems for such a completely dysfunctional group. There were contacts to be made there for Leanne. It was entirely social, but she and Joe Sr. knew how to play the game. We looked all scrubbed and sweet—such a nice family—smiling and shaking hands, serving up potlucks, carrying black Bibles, pretending a piety that was blasphemous. The garish pink wall and the appearance of a happy family belied the holocaust that imprisoned Joe Jr. and me. *How could that lovely family be anything but sparkling evidence of a Christian home?* The upside-down universe that was our lives was hidden from view behind the rhinestone pretense.

It was on a Sunday morning that I first saw hope in the form of a beautiful woman at an evangelical church in Playa Del Rey, California, close to where we lived. Leanne had ordered me to wait for her outside in the church's courtyard until she appeared from whatever meeting she'd attended. When I heard the woman's voice, I was leaning up against a pillar, bored and disinterested. But when I peeked around the corner to see who was talking, I saw Cinderella. That's what she looked like, anyway, with her long blond hair, ivory skin, sparkling blue eyes and perfect white teeth. She mesmerized me with her beauty. A very tall man was standing in front of her. "Why are you always so happy?" he asked her. I knew why he asked her that. She was radiant—infused with an inner light that streamed right out of her eyes, making her seem to glow. "Because Jesus loves me," the woman said, believing it was true with all her heart. I could tell. Then she said, "Jesus loves *all* His children."

Her words transformed me for a moment. Something occurred to me that I'd never dared to imagine. *I am a child. I want to be happy like the beautiful woman. Jesus must love me, too.* I didn't say this out loud. I didn't tell anyone. But I knew in my young heart that if Jesus could make her that happy, He could do the same thing for me. Though I never saw that woman again any of the numerous times we returned to that church, the vision of her loveliness and the power of her certainty that Jesus loved her would return to my heart when I most needed it for many years. It was a tiny thread of hope. Fragile, for sure. But if there was happiness and joy in being loved by Jesus, I knew someday I would find it.

Most of my days were dark, though. No one knew my pain. The bright pink wall was a picture of what most people saw. How could they know the woman beat me and cursed constantly as she called me the vilest things? Who would believe the inappropriate touching? Who really cared about a little girl with hilarious red curls and a speech impediment?

At night, I'd think about it. How I could take my own life? I wanted to stun people with it. *Why would such a cute little girl kill herself?* I imagined hearing Leanne talk about it after I died. She would figure out a way to lie about me at my funeral so she would still look good to others. She'd play the grieving mother to the hilt. Even Joe Jr. would lie to save himself. But someone might ask, "Why did that little girl run into the street?" Maybe someone would see the lies in Leanne's eyes, hear them in her voice and know...maybe.

My plan was to sit on the curb at the end of our steep rolling lawn and wait for a speeding car to come down the street. I would then run fast, out into its path, where it would kill me in an instant. I felt bad for the poor driver who would've run over the little girl, but that person didn't exist in the hell I did. The newspapers would deem it an accident. Show a picture of me in the paper. But I'd be gone, finally safe. So, I wouldn't care anymore.

My first attempt was foiled by the very person I was trying to escape. I sat out on the lawn for what seemed like hours with no cars speeding by. *Come on, somebody. Please.* But there I sat until Leanne noticed me and walked out to the curb, looked at me with those hard, cold eyes of hers, and said: "What are you doing?" Leanne hated the thought of our "doing nothing." I *was* doing something. The biggest something I'd ever done in my life. Digging my grave. Running toward the peace of darkness. I thought if I were dead, no one would move me in the middle of the night, hurt me despite the protests of my silent screams. And she wouldn't be there to touch me anymore. I would have escaped. Instead, I didn't answer Leanne but ran past her as fast as I could into the house where I rushed into my bedroom and closed the door. Next time, I'd get it right.

Only the next time, someone else met me at the curb. An unexpected visitor. With a message for me. My thoughts at the time were about what I would do if this didn't work for a second time. What else would I try? How else could I possibly get away? *"Look up!"* It was a voice speaking to me loud and clear. The voice didn't come from someone on earth. It came into my heart. Like thunder. Uncanny and confident. *"Look up!"* I felt the weight of my chin when I tried to obey the voice. Joe Jr. and I walked with our heads down most of the time. Stay out of sight. Stay out of trouble. Blend in with the scenery of Leanne's life. What I saw when I did lift my head, there above me, was the wide blue sky. For some reason, that day, it seemed immense. Too huge to calculate. Beyond imagination. *I wonder how far the sky stretches in all directions? How many people see the sky at the same time I'm looking at it right now? How many children in how many backyards see it? How many playgrounds does the sky cover in blue?* I was trying to come to grips with how big "big" is. And in the vastness of the universe I was really seeing for the first time, there was something bigger. Bigger than the woman who hurt me, degraded me, and humiliated me so regularly. The voice spoke again. *"There really is a heaven and God lives there."*

That's what I wanted. Heaven. "I want to go to heaven!" I said, out loud. I knew I had to die to get there. And I was ready! But the voice didn't seem to be encouraging me to die but instead to have a reason to live. The thought occurred to me that it was God speaking to my heart. One of the little children He loved needed to hear from Him. Maybe He talked to me because He knew what I was about to do, and He had a better plan. God met me at the curb and told me He was bigger than any defilement. Greater than any curse. Loved me in spite of how dirty and used I already felt. If heaven would have me, that's where I'd finally be. But on that day the turquoise sky covered my little broken heart like a reassuring blanket, making me believe I was seen…known and watched over…in a way that gave me uncanny resolve to live.

I got up quickly from the curb and walked back over the lawn toward the garage. I leaned against its frame and shut my eyes. Then I opened them again and blinked the sky back into focus. This time the voice was mine. Almost a whisper, it rose up out of my heart, pushing its way like a joyous stream into a promise to this God who knew me: "If You keep me alive, I'll do whatever You ask me to do in my life." Somebody bigger and I had made a deal, and I intended to keep it. I knew He'd keep His end. And the tiny thread of hope the lady at church had handed off to me grew stronger. A child's miniscule faith in the persistent love of her God would grow despite the hideous things others did to her in the turbulent years that followed.

Chapter Seven

ANDI—THE MARRIAGE DEBACLE

I was married once before Ed. If you can call it a marriage. I was working in Orange County, California, and met him at a softball game. Jeffrey Howard sang in the choir of a local church, was in his mid-thirties, single and a ladies' man. He smelled good, looked good and expected everyone to love him as much as he loved himself. The man was the apple of many a single girl's eye with his reddish-brown hair and enigmatic brown eyes. It was natural to Jeffrey that everyone else's world revolved around him, because, after all, his did.

I'd graduated from Loyola Marymount in 1983 and went on to study law at Western State University College of Law in Fullerton, California. I was twenty-six and had eight months to go to finish my law degree when I walked up the bleachers to take my seat at the ball game and found myself perched next to Jeffrey, who was regaling the other women surrounding him with stories of his own sports prowess. He was sitting on the end of the bleacher row and scooted down and edged me in, patting the empty space beside him, beckoning me to join him. From the first it should have been clear that he played the women. I was fresh meat. New to the game and actually very naive when it came to men. Had I been more worldly wise I wouldn't have dated him, much less married him. But I wanted to be loved and adored by just one man—wanted the family I'd never had. It was something I'd been praying about for years.

When we began dating seriously, I had no idea I wasn't the only one. It felt exclusive to me. Often I'd go to his condo and watch television and hang out. I was impressed that he had name brand sodas in his refrigerator and drove a Mercedes, although it was not a newer model. Jeffrey had his own business and was very good at self-promotion. He made enough money that he could afford to fly out of state to football games and come home the same day. "Just a little outing," he'd say. We went to Tahoe several times and slept in separate beds. Leanne didn't believe me when I told her that—thought I was a trollop. But I wanted to be a virgin when I married, because I believed that was the one thing I could give back to God—the only thing I could control. It had nothing to do with my past as I disregarded the abuse because I hadn't *given* myself freely then…it was taken from me.

Jeffrey made it clear he was a highly experienced lover, though. Convincing me on several occasions to nap with him scantily clad because all the other women he dated at his church singles' group—Carina, Jennifer, Tanya (of course he named them) — did the same. I, like all the other women, was desperate to please a potential mate. For someone who had never had anyone really love her in her life, the thought of losing the person who seemed to care made this concession seem almost reasonable. Jeffrey confided to me that he had a rating system by which he organized women according to hotness, potential, beauty and intelligence. I was, of course, "very close to a ten." I'm guessing, in hindsight, that the others were told the same thing. Our dates would often end early or start very late, and I wondered about that. Of course, what I found out way too late was that he rarely had just one date for an evening. Jeffrey was just too good not to spread the joy of his presence around…and around…and around.

I'd taken a break from law school about that time. When Jeffrey found out, he encouraged me to keep at it. "You're only a few

months away from that law degree?" he asked as we sat in his condo one Saturday afternoon.

"Yeah," I responded. "I'm so tired of school. It seems intermi-
nable. Plus, I'm broke and don't even know if I want to be a lawyer
at this point. I guess I'd like to finish…maybe get into politics
down the road."

"You can't quit," Jeffrey said as though he had a vested interest
in my getting my law degree. "I'll help you."

I smiled at that. How was he going to help me in law school?
"Really?" I said, rather sarcastically.

"Yes. Really." He reached down into his pocket and drew out
his wallet. "Here's my American Express card." Then Jeffrey went
to the kitchen counter and picked up his garage door opener,
walked back over to the couch and handed it to me. "Here."

"What am I going to do with these?" I asked, stunned by
Jeffrey's generosity.

"You are going to use the credit card…just don't go crazy," he
quipped and winked at me. "I'll help with school. Use the key to my
place to come over whenever you want during the day to study or
rest. I'm gone most of the time, anyway, as you know." He plopped
back down beside me and threw his arm around my shoulders as a
satisfied smiled plastered itself across his face.

It was a crazy offer. Way too generous. I wasn't used to feeling
that valued and cared for. "Are you serious?" I asked as I turned my
body toward him so that I could look straight into his eyes.

"Yes. Dead serious," he replied, and he patted my knee
for emphasis.

I took the key and the credit card and finished my law degree
while I continued to date and fall in love with Jeffrey. The over-the-
top generosity of the gift, the way I felt when this man was paying
attention to me, blinded me to the red flags that waved like Old
Glory in my face. Jeffrey would actually talk to me about other wom-
en he liked or dated. It wasn't so much a comparison as a cataloguing

of conquests. It was confusing to me because sometimes I felt like the love of his life and sometimes I didn't know *who* I was to him.

I did finish law school, which made Jeffrey proud. On his arm when he went to special events was a lawyer who could fill out a dress to the max. A younger trophy with beautiful curly hair, a big smile and a jurisprudence inspired vocabulary. It didn't dawn on me until much later why the law degree was so important to him. It added to his status. Made *him* look good. The red flags should have blinded me they were so close to my face.

Increasingly, as we dated, I grew more and more uncomfortable with Jeffrey's "naps." I didn't know what was normal and what wasn't in church relationships, and he seemed like a committed Christian. That other women had obliged Jeffrey in this way really didn't make me feel any better about it. Something down inside me cringed at the idea of it. It felt creepy. Finally, as we lay there together one afternoon, I couldn't stand it any longer.

"This makes me really uncomfortable, Jeffrey." I pulled away from him and covered myself with a sheet. "I don't care what other girls are willing to do, I'm not ready for this."

Jeffrey sat up with a half-smile on his face. He actually seemed slightly stunned—embarrassed a little, even. "Well…" he cooed as he leaned in close to me, "how would *you* like to be Mrs. Jeffrey Howard?" (Said like I had the winning Power Ball ticket.)

I wasn't expecting that. I know my face must've registered the shock of it. It took me a minute to respond because I didn't know if he was manipulating me or proposing. Finally I said, "If you really mean that, then yes." I knew in my heart, though, in a place where I intentionally hid it, that Jeffrey didn't really want to marry me. In a moment of grandiosity he'd said something he was unprepared to actually take back though he tried several times to do so over the next few months.

Wedding preparations began slowly, almost with trepidation on my part, like I had to always look over my shoulder to make sure Jeffrey was still on board. Leanne, of course, insisted that we have the reception at her house. There really was no arguing about it. She and Jeffrey were going to split the cost of the reception, and he called in favors from friends and even former girlfriends to get it all organized. Leanne thought she might be paying more than her share because she didn't have friends helping her, so she burst into Jeffrey's office one morning demanding an accounting of funds, accusing him of making her pay too much. Jeffrey's reaction? "Maybe we shouldn't get married." Dealing with Leanne in preparation for the wedding caused this response from Jeffrey on more than one occasion. I should've listened, should've heard him say he'd like to escape. But I put aside any doubts in the crush of wedding planning. I ignored his waning enthusiasm—the look on his face sometimes when I talked about marriage. I pushed down the knot in my stomach and silenced the voice in my head because I loved the man.

On August 27, 1988, at 2:00 o'clock in the afternoon, I had the dubious honor of becoming Mrs. Jeffrey Howard. As stipulated, the reception was commandeered by Leanne. I lived through it, which was something for me, but all she could talk about was what went wrong. How hard it was on her to get the yard ready. How thoughtless of people to leave trash outside—even a dirty diaper, for Pete's sake (only she didn't say Pete). There was no warm motherly congratulation or "My, you are such a lovely bride." I know by then I should have given up expectations that Leanne wasn't capable of fulfilling, but hope springs eternal.

Jeffrey and I spent the first night together in a local Orange County hotel then left for Hawaii the next day. It wasn't until the third morning of our honeymoon that things for me turned into a horror film. In my first experience as a married woman I was violated in such a way that it terrified me. Jeffrey always said, "We will always engage in consensual relations." It was a promise. "With all my experience, it will be blissful, compassionate and perfect." Instead, Jeffrey satisfied himself without regard for me at all and in a way that I never expected to happen to me. It was a perversion of trust and a violation of my body. Forever lost that day was any hope I'd ever feel safe with the very man to whom I'd just pledged my life. Locked away were old feelings of fear and desperation that I'm sure fueled the new ones into a holocaust, making me run from the room crying and inconsolable. All I could think to do was find a pay phone and call a friend in California. I had no one else to even tell me what I should have been able to expect, especially from a man who not only knew some of the heartache of my background but who also told me he was well experienced in the art of lovemaking. Crying hysterically and wanting to escape, I ran down the hallway of the hotel and into the lobby where a phone hung near the women's room. My hyperventilation made it hard for my friend to hear me. "Are you sure this isn't just first time jitters?" she asked as she tried to understand the ramifications of what I was saying.

"No!" I practically screamed it. "Something really bad happened!" I tried to find words to adequately describe what seemed indescribably awful. "Is that what is supposed to happen?"

My friend was shocked. "No! No, of course not!" It was a small consolation that what I'd just experienced wasn't what I could reasonably expect for years to come in our marriage. I would never let that happen to me again. But it also ruined my desire for further physical contact with Jeffrey. My trust was demolished. I didn't feel precious to him, but used—intruded upon in the grossest possible way. I was no more valuable to him than I'd been to others. I would have to live in a state of hyper-vigilance for the rest of my life. It seemed hopeless.

"What's wrong?" asked Jeffrey, out of breath from running through the hotel trying to find his bride. He caught my arm as I hung up the phone. "What's wrong with you?" His face was red and registered genuine panic.

"You promised me you knew what you were doing," I answered, deflated, not wanting him near me, the smell of his cologne sickening the moment. I was trapped again, this time by my new husband. I wiped the tears from my face with my hands, but they just kept washing over my cheeks. I was so ashamed and didn't even know why.

"I'm sorry." Jeffrey tried to hug me, but I pulled away. I hated him. Recoiled at his being so close. We said nothing more as we turned and walked away together in a silence that belied the subtext of our earlier encounter. At once, I had so much to say and nothing left to say. I'm sure Jeffrey's mind searched for the words that would make this all go away. It was a very long march back to our room where I locked myself into the bathroom and soaked in the tub until the water went cold. Jeffrey was sitting on the bed with his head in his hands when I came out, robed in terry cloth, averting his glance.

We had a boat ride scheduled for the late afternoon and I was relieved to have something to do that kept me from looking at him or talking to him. When we boarded, I couldn't sit far enough away from him. "You want to talk about it?" Jeffrey asked, eyes round like a puppy's, but not convincingly sad, like he was sorry he hadn't gotten away with his behavior, not that he was sorry for the behavior itself. But, I must admit, I was in no frame of mind to care what he was really thinking.

"No!" I was adamant. "I don't want to talk about what happened now or ever!"

And we didn't. Not ever again. But our intimacy was strangled. Jeffrey never really understood that the honeymoon violation coupled with the abuse I'd already suffered as a child made me less than interested in his overt wooing. And I learned in the weeks and years to come that Jeffrey's ideas of intimacy were a mangled mutation of what married love is supposed to be. It wasn't just me.

The nightmares began six months into our young marriage. Graphic and unsettling, the dreams awakened me suddenly, leaving me sitting upright in our bed in the middle of the night, trying to shake off a reality too palpable to remain in. All of them were body memory oriented. Headless people on top of me or trying to force themselves—wraith-like—down my throat. In one vivid dream, Joe Sr. was chasing me through a building set up for what looked like a play in a dinner theater. My heart was beating wildly as I ran for my life in and out of the set, around and around the building. "Stop! Get away!" I screamed with all my might. "Leave me alone! Don't touch me!" It seemed a matter of life and death that I get away from him. My mouth was dry with fear as he lurched nearer and nearer. Fueled by the outrage that stoked my body into action, I ran up onto the scaffolding that created a mock second story on the dinner theater set. I wasn't fast enough. Joe Sr. grabbed my shoulder. "I have you!" he yelled. With all my might, I jerked away from his hold and he fell, tumbling to his death onto the stage floor. The shock of it awakened me, terrified and relieved at the same time.

Because of the nightmares and the obscured memories they brought back, not only to my mind but to my body as well, I started to see a therapist. Jeffrey and I both thought it would help me cope better in our marriage. Jeffrey really wanted to heal the physical side of things, broken on our honeymoon, for obvious reasons. I wanted to not feel so crazy. My therapist used hypnotherapy on me since I wasn't always able to remember many of the horrific things done to me as a kid. She set up a scenario in which I would ride down an elevator shaft. At the bottom was a safe room where no one could hear or see me. On one particular day, she asked me to open a door and tell her what was inside.

"It's a room with many bookshelves," I said. "But someone followed me in here."

"What does that person look like?" ask my therapist.

"It's very dark. I can't tell who it is." I remember the ominous aura of the presence making me uncomfortable.

"What are the books about? Can you tell?" she asked.

I sidled over to the shelf, cautious, wary, and looked over the titles written in gold letters on the spine of each book. Row after row made no sense to me, and then I saw it. "This one says it is the story of my life," I said and I pulled it from its place on the dusty shelf and turned it over and over in my hands.

"Open it," my therapist said, gently, leading me.

The book in my hand was heavy with foreboding, like something evil might creep out of the pages and smother me in darkness. When I finally had the courage to crack it open slightly, I was stunned. "It's blank." I said this more to myself than to the therapist. I thumbed through all the pages then. *Nothing*. It's like I'd never existed—affirmed to me that I'd never mattered…to anyone. I closed the book and held it against my aching chest. The loss was confounding. *I'd never existed.* While I stood contemplating how that could be, a dark figure emerged from the shadows slithering slowly toward me and laughing insanely, morbidly, like Satan might cackle in hell. It was Joe Sr. He'd erased my life. That is what I knew in the moment. With his face too close to mine and his rancid breath wafting in the air, punctuating each syllable with the stench of certainty his words declared as they circled like a serpent around me, squeezing my breaths so I thought I might faint, the man mocked the fact that no one had ever cared about me.

"He's hiding the things he did from the world," said the therapist. "So no one will know the truth." That might have been true, but it wasn't particularly comforting. It wasn't necessarily healing. Because the truth of the matter was, I was a blank book that no one ever cared to open.

So much was coming up in counseling that I was having a hard time dealing with life in between sessions. I couldn't understand why my parents wanted to hurt me so much. Why the sexual and physical abuse was necessary to them. I just wanted to be loved… and to love them back. I wanted parents. That's not what I got.

And in my life up to the day I first sought help, that's what I felt like I deserved. But I'd learned to cope so well in my disassociation, hiding from my own consciousness the ravishing effects of the abuse, that when the memories finally flowed, I was swept up into the muddy stream with them. I needed more help than I could get in one session a week. It all came to a head one evening when I passed by a collage of my family I'd hung on the wall in our condo. For two weeks, every time I saw it I felt agitated, almost angry. There were two pictures of my brother, Joe Jr., and it was his face, I realized, that made me want to scream. In an impulsive moment, I grabbed the collage and ripped my brother's pictures from it, throwing them into the fire already burning in our fireplace. I had some peace after that. But I didn't understand why I did it.

In therapy the next week, it became obvious I had buried memories of Joe Jr.'s abuse. He'd been like all the rest. It was the last straw for me. I thought at least my brother hadn't hurt me. But my therapist identified him as a perpetrator. I fell apart. Went hysterically crying out of her office and into the restroom where I bawled for almost an hour. Grief that I was unloved and used. Sadness at the loss of what I thought was the one person who might've cared about me. Rage over the fact that I was considered useless chattel and not a precious child and sister. My therapist was worried that I might hurt myself—drive off a cliff or something. In light of that, it was suggested that I go to College Hospital in Cerritos, California, not far from where we lived. They have adult psychiatric services my therapist thought I needed. She suggested I visit it. I did. I agreed to the services provided there. What I didn't know was that I would be put into lock-up with more people more extremely challenged than I—some on suicide watch. Jeffrey agreed that I should go; insurance paid for it. So, the hospital was my home for the next two months.

I'd begun collecting stuffed animals, particularly bunnies, as a comfort mechanism during my months of therapy. Lying in the middle of their softness, holding them to me, even pretending they could hear me when I spoke to them, was reinforcing and soothing. I'd always walk past pet stores and coo over the actual lop-eared bunnies nosing around or hopping in their cages. I loved how cute and vulnerable they were. About half way through my therapy, I was allowed to go home for a weekend visit. Jeffrey said he had a surprise for me and I couldn't wait to see what he'd bought. When I walked into the bedroom to lay my suitcase on the bed, all my stuffed animals were arrayed across the comforter. And there in their midst was a pure black honest-to-goodness real bunny! House broken and adorable! "Oh, my gosh!" I screamed as I took its soft body into my arms. "Oh, my gosh! It's so cute!"

"I thought it would make you happy," he said as he stood watching me, his eyes sparkling. It was one of his genuinely caring moments.

He brought the bunny to therapy to visit me once, too. We had it in our minds that we'd write children's books. That was my initial excuse for wanting the stuffed animals. But nearer to the truth was that I felt safe with my inanimate pets; they gave me unconditional love and were always ready to cuddle with me without further expectation.

When Allison pulled the faded old stuffed animal from her suitcase the morning she arrived and gently placed it on her pillow, I understood her attachment. Someone—something—who'd always be there for her.

Chapter Eight

ALLISON—THE REST OF THE STORY

While I was living with Marge, I met Sharla. I was only seventeen at the time and she was twenty-nine. At first I didn't know about her sexual orientation. I didn't know it was why she was pursuing my friendship so adamantly. She wanted to be with me all the time. Told me how much she liked me. Bought me gifts. Took me places. I was vulnerable to her attraction to me because I wanted with all my heart to mean something to someone. The way Sharla treated me felt like love. Or at least it looked like what I thought love would be. In a few weeks, I was Sharla's partner, too. Though it was confusing in a way, I was giving love, I thought. Expressing what I felt. Only it was a trap. Just like using meth and just as synthetic a reality. Sharla was addicted to drugs—something I didn't know at first. When I couldn't help her get them, she growled at me, calling me horrible names and coercing me into compromising activities with not only her, but also selling me to others for sex in order to make enough money to get her fix. Crushed and disappointed, I turned to drugs again myself. I was so ashamed, always feeling like I deserved what was happening to me. I knew I was completely worthless. And Sharla was happy to remind me of that every chance she got. Turns out I was manipulated, not loved at all, and that further added to my shame.

Drugs and alcohol made me sick this time, though. I hated the way they made me feel. Hated that they were evidence of my deep neediness. I got quickly clean and told Sharla I was done with that scene. She wasn't happy about that. Tried to keep me interested by confusing kindness or ridiculous promises. I know it's crazy, but I still continued our relationship after this. My need to be loved was a well so deep it had no bottom, I guess. I was always hoping she'd return to the nice woman who bought me gifts and told me how great I was. In fact, I yearned for that. It took me until May, right before I met Andi, to completely break ties with Sharla. A new relationship with a nice guy gave me the strength to rebuff her further advances, but she kept stalking me, even after I moved in with the Cordells.

Sharla was the one thing I didn't tell Andi about at our first meeting. I was afraid it would be the last straw. That she'd draw the line and say, "Well, that is just too much for us. You'll have to look elsewhere for a place to live." I couldn't risk it. But by August of 2014, the stalking got so bad I had to ask Andi to help me get a restraining order against Sharla.

"What's going on?" asked Andi one afternoon when I dropped by her house. She was sitting in her office at her computer, and she was putting her phone down as I walked in.

"I was hoping she would leave me alone when I moved in with the Cordells," I said, broaching the subject as if she knew who I was talking about. I knew the conversation was going to be awkward. I sat down in the chair by Andi's desk and crossed my hands in my lap.

"Who?" asked Andi, her eyes looking intently right into mine. No way was I going to get away without telling her the whole awful story. Something about the way Andi looks at me makes me think she sees all the way down into my soul.

"Sharla." And I told Andi everything. "I wouldn't blame you if you didn't help me," I hurried to confess. "I'm embarrassed to tell you all of this." *What will I do if she kicks me out?* I held my breath, choking back my shame.

"It sounds to me like you need to end this once and for all," Andi said with a resolve that at once shocked and consoled me.

She's actually going to protect me. It almost made me want to giggle. I can't explain it, but my stomach felt just like it does when I want to laugh out loud. Maybe that's joy. It's a new thing for me. But I think that might be what it was.

Andi helped me get the restraining order. I haven't heard from Sharla since.

I wish I could say my story from there got a whole lot better, but another thing happened about a month after I moved in with the Cordells. I'm not proud of it, but it showed me something that's changed me completely. Marge's daughter and I had a fight over the phone about some stuff that happened at the house before I left. The old darkness came over me, and I wanted to run away. It's like I feel trapped in this world and have to get out or I won't be able to breathe. Ideation—suicide. Escape. I knew what was going on in my mind, but it was like I couldn't control it. I drove to Albertson's and bought some sleeping pills. Swallowed them like before along with some of my meds. Right there in the parking lot. Honestly, I don't know who called Andi and Ed to tell them I was at the hospital or who discovered me there in the parking lot.

In the emergency room, the nurses started bringing activated charcoal and pouring it down my throat. A process I'd grown almost accustomed to. I was nauseated and straining for each breath, wandering in and out of consciousness. Through the fog, I suddenly saw Andi's face very close to mine, and she was saying something I couldn't make out. I thought perhaps I was hallucinating. No one had ever been right there so quickly when I'd done this before.

"Allison. Allison, Ed and I are here," I heard her say. "The Cordells are here, too."

I tried to bring Andi's face into focus. Then I felt the warmth of Mrs. Cordell's hand wrapping itself around mine, radiating warmth, assuring me of her presence. Mr. Cordell said, "Allison, we are here for you, sweetie," as he pressed his hand lightly on my forehead. I thought I'd already died because heaven to me is that kind of love. No one had ever watched over me before. For the next few hours, one of them was always by my side. I was never alone. It was incomprehensible. Every time I opened my eyes I thought, "They've probably left." But, no. At least one of them was beside me until I went back home.

I don't think about suicide now. In fact, my problems are pretty age appropriate, I'm proud to say. I have a boyfriend and sometimes we have drama. I'm finishing online school. I have a job and have moved out of the Cordell's place and into my own. Hal is struggling with cancer and Mom is pretty sick, too. I'm trying to redefine some relationship with her that doesn't throw me into a tailspin again. Thankfully, my patterns are changing, though. I know the signposts…the things that trigger my addictions. I'm thinking differently about life, working on fulfilling "normal" hopes and dreams. I understand normal better now. Crazy, huh?

Chapter Nine

ED—A WHIFF OF THE REAL THING

In the months after Mom died, I kept hearing her say, "Ed, you can do better than this. You can get your life straightened out." It wasn't that she thought I wasn't a success in my business. She knew my life. On a deeper level, she knew I was living for Ed, not for God. It made me uneasy. Sad, really. There was a part of me that wanted to make her proud, but more than that, I was tired of the way I'd been living. Drinking, casual dating and hanging out with the guys, who weren't necessarily the best influence on my life, became empty. That's the only way I know how to describe it. I got nothing out of it anymore.

That's why I started attending Calvary Chapel Church in San Diego and gave my heart back to Jesus. It's hard to describe to someone who hasn't experienced it how clean it feels to "get right." After that commitment, even when I found myself in the position to do what I did before, I couldn't do it. My heart was changed. Mom was right.

By July of 1998, I decided to sell my business in San Diego and move to Oregon. Dad was struggling with the demands of Alzheimer's and my brothers were taking care of him without me. My friend, Kenny Lawson, had a masonry business and asked me to come to work with him. I'd never laid brick, but I learned, even became proficient at it. I began attending the local Foursquare church, Dayspring Christian Center. I wasn't much interested in dating, though I did so randomly. I'd changed my mind about the kind of relationships I'd had before. I was hoping for actual intimacy without trumping it at the beginning with the merely physical. I wanted to wait until I "smelled that rotten egg" Mom always told me about. Real love. Though I had no idea what it would be like.

Turns out, Labor Day of 1999, I got a whiff of it. John Cameron was an elder in our church and my Sunday School teacher. He'd served twenty years in the military and owned several guns that some of us guys loved to shoot when we went out to visit him and his wife, Gemey, on their property in the country outside of town. We'd spend several hours blowing things up; then we'd eat together. I loved the guy. So, I wasn't surprised or suspicious when John asked me over to his place for a Labor Day picnic. He, in fact, invited the entire church singles group. Gemey made it a point to introduce Andi to me in the living room. I didn't know her. She didn't belong to our church. *Hmmm.*

Gemey had called Andi earlier in the week. "I've got a guy I want you to meet." Andi wasn't very interested, either. Divorced and somewhat jaded by the men she'd met since, she let Gemey know that she didn't hold out much hope that this set-up was going to amount to anything.

When I caught on, I looked over at John and gave him the no-go sign by running my index finger across my throat. Andi was short and curvy. Her cropped red hair framed her pretty face, but she just wasn't doing it for me. I usually was attracted to tall blonde volleyball players. To be honest, though, she didn't appear to like me much, either.

After dinner, around dusk, the guys in the group decided we wanted to shoot things. That didn't set too well with the ladies, especially Andi. Some of the guys left then, but I sauntered inside where the others were preparing to play a Bible character game. Seemed lame to me, but I stayed. Andi was cast as Queen Esther; I was King David. I hadn't seen her animated until then. I hadn't noticed how cute her lips were. She had a mild lisp that captivated me, and I couldn't stop looking at her mouth as the queenly words of Esther wriggled free, gliding over the hot pinkness of Andi's lipstick. Not only that, she was a bundle of energy, laughed easily and was pretty darn good at pretending to be royalty. Another thing, there was this enormous bandage on her hand that stirred up a protective compassion in me. *There's a good woman.* Thought I might have smelled the rotten egg. Never felt quite the way I did when I was watching her that evening.

When the game ended, I wandered into the kitchen to find some coffee. I could see Andi where I'd left her on the couch in the living room. I didn't know what came over me. I felt giddy, like a kid. As I poured a cup for myself, I yelled in her direction, "Hey, Hot Rod, how do you like your coffee?" I know it wasn't brilliant, but at least she knew I was talking to her because she wandered toward me with a huge smile on her face. In the full light of the kitchen with the insects outside singing their night songs and the heat of the day cooling down with the dark, Andi seemed to sparkle in her emerald green shirt, her short red hair shimmering as if to hypnotize me. There was an energy when she was in the room. It bounced off the walls and seemed to swirl around me. And she was so smart! We weren't *really* Queen Esther and King David, but you could have fooled me that night as we sipped hot coffee and chatted.

When the picnic ended around nine that evening, I walked Andi out to her car, opened the door for her, closed it as I told her good-bye, then sauntered toward my Mustang. But I couldn't let her leave. There was a ridiculous ache in my heart that drew me back to her car where I knelt beside her open window. Suddenly I wanted to know everything there was to know about this feisty redhead. It seemed like only a few minutes had passed when John yelled from his front door, "Hey, it's almost eleven and I'm turning off the porch lights, you two!"

"You need an escort home?" I asked, thinking she might have trouble navigating the winding country roads back to Redmond in the dark.

"Sure," she said with that adorable crooked smile of hers.

Oh, man. I was hooked. Never felt like that before. It was the hardest thing I ever did to say good-night. "Can I see you again this Saturday?"

"I would actually love that," Andi replied, her eyes twinkling in the starlight. I was sure hoping she was feeling what I was feeling. Saturday could not come fast enough.

When the weekend finally arrived, I took Andi to Sweetwaters, a local coffee house. We talked about everything possible—religion, politics, family, past, present and future. I wanted to talk my head off and at the same time hear about every hour of every day Andi had been alive. I was completely wasted—absolutely smitten. I had to keep myself from asking her to marry me that night. I waited an entire week. For our next date at the Pine Tavern Inn, an historical landmark restaurant in downtown Bend, I showed up with two dozen red roses, and even put on slacks and a polo shirt. I was forty-four and didn't want to fool around with the dating crap, pardon my language, anymore. *This woman has it all!* I knew, like Mom had always told me, that I didn't have to look any further.

We ordered steaks, but I forgot I was hungry. Being with Andi seemed to curb all other appetites. It was enough for me—sitting there with her. While our steaks sat lazily on our plates, lounging in their cooling white fat, I picked up the white linen napkin that still lay impeccably folded beside my dinner plate. I'd been thinking about this since our last date: *Why is it that people have to wait so long to know they are right for each other?* I devised a plan mid-week and couldn't wait to brilliantly lay out my own answer to this quandary in a way that would dazzle Andi…and, maybe, convince her, too. I drew a dot on the napkin. "Most people start dating here," I said as I pointed to the dot I'd drawn. "Then, as the relationship grows, they move on to talking about marriage." Here I drew a line from the first dot to another one. "Then they become engaged."

Another line. Another dot. "Ultimately," I said, as I drew a line to the final dot, "they get married."

Andi studied the lines and dots as though I'd come up with a new theory for the creation of the universe. "So," I said, "we are here." I pointed to the very first dot I'd drawn. My heart was thumping against my chest cavity. I knew it was very early in our relationship to be so bold, but there it was. "What do you think about getting married?" I skipped a few dots.

She looked up from the napkin, laughing with incredulity, and saw I was serious. I'm pretty sure I didn't breathe for a second while I watched her face. "I think it's perfect!" she exclaimed, clapping her hands lightly in front of her, then kissing me lightly on my lips.

"When?" I asked, ready that moment to call a preacher and set the whole thing up.

"I've always wanted a June wedding," Andi said.

I love this about Andi. She's in the moment with me.

"Okay, June it is." It was the second week in September. June was a long way away, but I'd sewn it up. Found my woman. I could wait.

My next task was to study up on diamonds. I had no idea how to purchase one. I'd worn a ridiculous gold chain for a while in the seventies after *Saturday Night Fever*. That was the extent of my experience with jewelry. I read up on color, clarity and cut. I wanted to get Andi something amazing. But amazing I couldn't afford from the local jewelers. There was a very reputable pawn shop in town. I went there and found a gorgeous diamond. About a carat in weight, and it sparkled like fireworks. I had it mounted in a gold setting, and I couldn't believe how beautiful it was. Without much fanfare, I went to see Andi. I pulled the ring out of my pocket. "Well, here's your engagement ring," I said, too excited to hold off any longer. "What do you think of it?" A stupid grin slapped itself onto my face that morning, and it was still sitting there as I waited for her response. I couldn't have erased it if I'd tried.

"Wow." That's what she said. Exactly what I was hoping for. "I love it!" she exclaimed as she slipped it onto her finger. A perfect fit!

I can't tell you how much I loved Andi. Bowled over and "smelling" the aroma of love. I wrote her a long email on September 22, 1999, that read in part: *I feel so overwhelmed with His grace and so blessed that He showed me the way to you. It did finally pay to hold out for the best, forty-four years of wondering: "Okay, Lord, I'm a man and still alone, and You even said Yourself that this is not good nor is it by design. So Lord, what about me? I'm not getting any younger. Okay, I got it, trust in You, believe in Your word and remember that all good things are in Your perfect timing. I so vividly remember You telling me, 'Get your heart right, Eddy.' But for nearly twenty years I had to do it my way. What a fool I was! I had no idea that when I finally aligned myself with You that You would reward me so handsomely! Really! You've been holding Andi for me all this time! You're such an awesome God, You knew all the time, Your perfect plan, Your perfect timing, the perfect will. You rewarded me with the perfect girl! Wow! I'm so humbled."*

Andi, you are truly my precious angel who I feel responsible to protect, hold, comfort, cherish and love like there's no tomorrow! You are like a precious gem…If I lost you I couldn't replace you!

I'm not a kid anymore. I know what I want and I know where I'm going. Hey, will you go with me? My arms are open and waiting. I hope this isn't too heavy. You know I'm a light guy who knows how to have fun, but there are also times when a person must seize the moment and express what's going on inside."

Andi didn't read the email until the next morning, so I had to wait to see if she was going to think I was out of my mind. I kind of was, actually. This was her response:

My One and Only Prince,

Yes, I will walk with you. I can't imagine being with anyone else.

Woke up and had to see if there was a message from your castle. So glad, and what a message! If you can take a Princess with temperamen-

tal insides on occasion, that works for me! I see the green lights too and want to go for the life ride together. We just need to remember that we both have "challenge" areas to discover because no person is perfect. But I think if people want to, they can commit to living through the discovery process. My insides keep saying, "Boy, wait 'til he finds out we're human! Then what?" I'm trusting "then what" is that we just work through it, eh?

WOW! Now it's my turn to say, "Is this real?"

Yeah. Okay, in the ensuing months before our wedding, I discovered Andi is a real, live woman with her ups and downs. I'm just crazy enough about her to say it only made me love her more.

Chapter Ten

ANDI—THE RUCKUS ABOUT THE RADISH

The lights on the answering machine were blinking when I got home from running my morning errands. I set the groceries down on the counter top and punched the PLAY button.

"Um...my name is Evelyn." There was a long pause. I'd become accustomed to this nervous first call from an anxious young woman who is out of options. "A friend gave me this number to call." I could hear the rustling noise of her fumbling with something, and her breathing sounded like little puffs of wind crackling in my ear. "Will you call me back?" And she left her cell number.

It was a gorgeous sunshiny day in May of 2014; the air was dry and hinting at summer's heat. I thought it ironic that there was a young woman in trouble on such a beautiful day. We'd just placed Tabitha, our newest teen, with a family who had two children of their own. It seems that just as we get one young woman placed, another is in line. Ed and I are constantly trusting God's timing for each phone call, each home into which they transition. When the phone rings as it did that day, it is the fact that we give hope, thin as it may appear to the teens at first, that makes us push forward. A part of me still responds to the little girl on the curb who had no way out. I never want another child to feel that hopeless. I punched in Evelyn's number.

"Hello?" It was a question. I could hear it in her voice.

"Hi, Evelyn! I just got your message," I said. "My name is Andi Buerger...from Beulah's Place."

"Oh, yeah." Silence.

"So, what's going on, Evelyn? I'd like to hear a little bit about your situation. When can you meet with me and I'll treat you to coffee?" I could hear Evelyn clearing her throat. She wasn't expecting things to go so quickly. I could tell.

"Uh…how about tomorrow?" she asked tentatively.

"Sure. Tell me where." Evelyn gave me an address and we settled on eleven in the morning.

I emptied the grocery bags and pulled out the fresh vegetables I'd bought at the market. As I took the veggies from their plastic bags and rinsed them in the kitchen sink, I couldn't shake the palpable fear and isolation I'd picked up in Evelyn's voice. It was familiar to me on a level I'd buried over time, on purpose. Abuse is isolating; it creates a wariness that makes trust almost impossible. Standing there in my kitchen that afternoon, I flashed back to me as a five-year-old in Leanne's kitchen… and it was Christmas.

It was about a radish. One single radish left on my plate before Christmas Eve guests came to dinner. Joe Sr. invited his relatives from Chicago to join us that year without giving Leanne much notice, clearly not asking her permission, so she was already angry at the imposition of hosting such a large group. Leanne decided that I would eat in the kitchen alone and not with the guests when they arrived. While she bustled about baking pies and slicing ham, her apron soiled from wiping her cranberry stained fingers on it and her hair tousled from pushing it back with her hands, I slowly ate everything on my plate…everything, that is, but the lone radish. I just couldn't eat it. I don't remember it being a test of Leanne's authority. I just remember thinking there was no way I could choke that thing down. She was scurrying in and out of the kitchen getting things ready for her guests while I sat there looking at the enormous red, peppery, disgusting vegetable staring back at me, its long thin root lying across the plate like the tail of a dead rat.

When Leanne noticed that I was still sitting at the table, silent and apparently done with my dinner, she glared at me, screaming, "You will not leave this table, young lady, until you have eaten everything on your plate!" As she walked back toward the kitchen counter, she stopped, looked over her shoulder at me, and added, "You will pay the consequences if you don't obey me this minute!"

I don't know why I didn't just toss the nasty thing into my mouth and eat it, but I didn't. Perhaps it was the fact that I was often force-fed even after I was full that made me resist. I knew this would make Leanne rage; but, I also thought it might make me throw up, an act which had its own special consequences. I was trapped. There was so much commotion in the house that I slipped from my chair, thinking she wouldn't notice, and sneaked to the garage because it was the closest place to the kitchen. Once there, I tried to think what I would do—suddenly realizing I was trapped in the semi-darkness with no way of fleeing except back through the door that led back into the kitchen. *I should have taken the radish with me.* After what seemed to me to be hours, I thought maybe if I went back into the kitchen, the plate and its lone occupant would be gone and all would be well. That maybe Leanne wouldn't beat me with all the company coming over. I slinked back through the door, bent over at the waist like a thief trying not to be seen. I was thinking I'd just eat the radish… or that it was ground to a pulp in the garbage disposal by then.

"Where have you been?" Leanne screeched, stomping her feet as her face turned beet red. "Did you think you could run away from *me*?" At that point I was aware of the voices coming from the living room. Guests had arrived. "Did you think you could defy me and not eat everything on your plate?" The decibel level rose with each word. I knew Leanne was going to go over the line with me. I wished for a knife so I could end my life before she did.

"How dare you disobey me! Eat that radish right now or I'll shove it down your throat!" Her finger was in my face, waving back and forth like an uncontrollable snake about to strike. The whites of her eyes were red with fury. My heart beat fast with fear and anger.

I reached to retrieve the radish. "It's too late," she screeched as she slapped the vegetable out of my hand. "You're gonna wish you were dead!" She stomped off to get Joe Sr. from the living room. "You need to take care of this when I'm done with her!" Which I knew meant whatever penalty I was going to pay with her would be doubled with him.

Leanne caught me by my dress collar and began dragging me toward my bedroom past the living room full of Christmas guests. As she walked, she pummeled me with her fists and slapped my face over and over again, humiliating me, cursing me. When we reached my bedroom, Leanne threw me across my bed and beat me with her tightened fists. I could see the craziness in her eyes. The tension mounting. The need to escalate the beating. Her breath was coming in great heaves. Then, for a moment she stopped. Looked around like a wolf for its prey, and ran to her bedroom. When she returned, she had a belt in her hand. I cringed and screamed against the pain as she wielded the strap as a weapon and slapped my legs, arms and back over and over again. The more I screamed the more invigorated the woman became until she'd exhausted herself.

She must have realized she'd been away from the relatives in the living room for too long, so she called down the hall to her husband. "Joe!" she hollered. "Come in here now!" By the time Joe arrived, Leanne was red and sweating, panting like a lion after its kill. There was a fierce light in her eyes, like she got high from the exercise of completely subduing me. Joe took over then. I was curled up in a ball on the bed, my hands over my face, every inch of my body red and burning from the beating. I have no idea how much longer he continued the abuse because it seemed to be forever. I just wanted it to end. *Didn't anyone in the living room hear my screams? If they did, why didn't they help me?*

Finally, I was alone. I could hear the television in the living room, where Joe Jr. and our cousins were watching the movie, *The Wizard of Oz*, with the sound turned up really high. Everyone was enjoying Christmas Eve while I lay in a bludgeoned heap quivering in my room. About the time I was catching my breath and wishing that God would let me die, I heard her footsteps pounding ominously down the hallway toward my room. The door to my bedroom flew open, and Leanne started in on me as if the first two beatings were not enough. I don't know what made her come back in. What impetus there was to further abuse me. I lived in a horror movie that never ended.

I was semi-conscious when she left me there on my bed, swimming back and forth between munchkins singing and blackness. I don't know how long I was in the isolation of my room, but, eventually, I tiptoed down the hallway to hear what was happening there. I peeked around the corner just in time to see the Wicked Witch in *The Wizard of Oz* melt and remember thinking, *I wish the witch who beats me would melt like that.*

"We showed her who is boss," Leanne was saying to the relatives assembled on the couch and scattered about on dining chairs set around the room. "If she even thought she'd get away with not doing what I said, she certainly had another thing coming!" Only she was cursing. Still high from the fix of beating me. Aglow with the conquest over her five-year-old daughter.

Little wonder I can't stand *The Wizard of Oz*. I hated the flying monkeys, and the witch scared me. My witch, the one who called herself my mother, would never, ever melt away. Family celebrations often make me anxious, even now. Afraid of my own shadow and filled with anxiety, every holiday was fraught with volatility that overwhelmed me with dread. I was small for my age and lacked coordination. I was helpless and alone, completely at the mercy of the monsters controlling me. What I would have given for a way out.

I wondered, as I chopped the fresh vegetables I'd just purchased into salads for Ed and me, what in Evelyn's life had created the reticence I heard in her voice—the loneliness that wafted through space as she called me for help. Deep calls to deep, I guess.

Chapter Eleven

EVELYN—FROM MAYHEM TO SEATTLE

I didn't know what to expect the morning I met Andi. I'd been sleeping in my car or trying to bum a few nights with friends when I met Lynn, this really nice guy that seemed to care about me. Worried that I was alone on the streets in my car, he made a plan. Since he had a paper route that took him out early in the mornings, he suggested I ride along with him, then go back to his house afterward to sleep until his mother got home from work late in the afternoon. I'd leave through the back door as she came in the front. That way I wasn't alone for very long at a time, and I had a safe, comfortable place to sleep. It's a long story, but his mom had only recently discovered I was sleeping over there. I was in his room when I overheard their conversation.

"Whose things are these?" she asked as she held up a pair of my shorts.

"Uh…I don't know…" Lynn stammered.

"Of course, you do!" his mother said, her voice steady. She knew her son. "Who is she?"

"This girl I met, Mom," he replied. "She's…well, homeless, I guess."

"And you felt sorry for her…" She finished his thought. Because he couldn't. Because, of course, I was listening and didn't want to be felt sorry for.

"Yeah, I guess," he said, almost in a whisper—conciliatory and contrite.

"I'm really disappointed in you that you didn't tell me your friend needed a place to stay instead of sneaking around behind my back. I wish you'd been man enough to tell the truth." Then I heard a door shut, like his mom went into her bedroom, ending the conversation.

That night Lynn told me his mom said I had to be out in two weeks. That's when I called Andi. A friend of mine contacted me on Facebook when she found out I was going to be homeless again. Told me I should try this nonprofit called Beulah's Place. I wasn't sure it was a good fit for me. Nothing in life up to then had been.

My parents were both in the military, stationed for years in Alaska. Dad left us when I was ten and moved to Portland, Oregon. I have two older brothers and a younger one. We were left with a mom who couldn't cope with the fact that Dad didn't love her anymore. Drugs and alcohol took her away from us—dulled her pain. We were left to fend for ourselves most of the time, except for the random occasion she'd choose to assert herself—like making me go to summer school every year so I'd graduate early. So caught up in the throes of her addiction that she couldn't function, I had to make decisions that my mother should have made. The older boys left home and joined the service as soon as they turned eighteen, leaving my little brother and me with a mother so caught up in her grief and her drugs she barely noticed the two of us were there.

The summers when I was a kid were spent with my grandmother in Bend, Oregon. My younger brother and I were shipped off as soon as school was out and we didn't return home until school started again. I think my grandmother resented the fact that her daughter was an addict unable to cope with her own children. It wasn't only that it was embarrassing; it was an imposition for her to care for us as a vicarious summer mommy. By the time I was in my early teens, the visits had stopped. Grandma wasn't enabling her daughter any longer.

The year I turned fifteen, Mom and I had it out. I came home from school one afternoon to find her just where I'd left her that morning, sprawled across our dirty old couch, the television blaring, her eyes bleary and a cigarette drooping from her bottom lip. There were piles of dishes in the sink, dirty laundry was strewn across the house and she hadn't bathed in days. This was home and the spectacle on the couch was my mother. In that moment I became an impartial onlooker, an observer of the mayhem, and I wanted to be taken out of the picture—a scenario in which I no longer wanted to function.

"You know what, Mom?" I screamed as I picked up a pair of dirty jeans from the floor and waved them at her, "You need to step up!" I was so tired of her drug addled life bumping into mine. Tired of being the mother to my mother.

"Or what?" she asked, her voice snide and slurred from the drugs. She didn't even look at me.

"Or send me to someone who will!" I couldn't believe I was saying those words. I'd thought them for years, but never until that day had I dared to express the threat for fear she'd actually send me away, assuring me once and for all that I was as invisible and worthless as she made me feel. My pounding heart was shaking my chest and angry tears streaked my face while I stood there nervously wringing the jeans still hanging from my hands.

"Okay." Mom slowly unfolded her body from the couch and sat up lazily, tenuously, to get a better look at me from her hollow, red-rimmed eyes. The hair on the back of her head stood up in a matted wad like a peacock's crown as she took the cigarette from her mouth, blowing a long stream of smoke into my face. "Okay." She reached for me and I stepped back from her. "I'll send you to your grandma." Mom waved her hand dismissively, glowing cigarette poised between her fingers, like she was the queen and I'd bothered her beauty sleep.

"Fine!" I screamed and threw the jeans to the ground as if they were a bomb that might explode and stop this war. A physical gesture of my inward implosion.

"Fine." That's all she said. "Fine." Waved me off again. Smoked her cigarette and looked over at the television.

"I mean it, Mom! I'm sick of you, and I don't want you to be my mother anymore." I got into her face, wanting a response, something that even looked like she cared. "I'm going to get emancipated from you!"

Mom had to look at me, but I really don't think she saw me. Not like people who are really listening to you lock eyes with recognition, with depth of understanding. I might as well have been yelling at the walking dead. "You don't care about me, anyway. All you care about is getting your fix!"

Mom looked stunned, then. That seemed to wake her up a little. But what could she say? It was her life now. Drugs. Her love for her addiction was who she was. And in that moment all the anger drained out of me. It was too pathetic—she was too pathetic. And I was not only wasting my breath, I was ruining my heart.

I handed Mom the phone. She crushed the butt of her cigarette into the ashtray that already overflowed, picked a piece of tobacco from her tongue with a fingernail and dialed Grandma's number. The conversation wasn't pleasant, but in the end my grandmother reluctantly agreed to take me in. It was a small victory for me. Grandma wanted me only slightly more than Mom.

Once in Bend, I was under the control of my grandmother, who I am sure was hell bent on my not becoming like my mother. On the other hand, I was accustomed to fending for myself, so when she started telling me what to do, I balked. "Make something of yourself or leave," was Grandma's motto from the very first day I arrived. Words to live by, for sure, but I was hoping she'd at least help me catch my breath. I'd just been delivered from hell; I was hoping for a bit more compassion and support. But it wasn't in her to mess around with talking about all I'd been through. I needed to get on with accomplishing something with my life.

I did finish high school there, a year earlier than most. By the time I graduated at sixteen, I was legally emancipated and ready to start making my own decisions—at least, that was my plan. I had absolutely no desire to go to college. I wanted a job and my independence. Grandma had other ideas about my future. She'd given me a car for my sixteenth birthday, making me less dependent upon her for my transportation. But it seemed that she rarely did anything for me that didn't have controls attached to it. I'd told Grandma many times over the course of the year I was there that I didn't want a college degree. I was sick of school. I wanted to make my own way. She saw that as a deadbeat life. It all came to a head one early summer afternoon right before dinner.

"Let's talk about what you're going to do this summer. And where you'll be going to school in the fall," Grandma began. "I know you didn't apply to four-year universities, but there is always Central Oregon Community College." She was standing at the kitchen sink peeling potatoes with her back to me. We'd had similar conversations before that hadn't ended all that well.

"I've been going to school straight through for three years now!" I replied for what I thought was the thousandth time. "I want to get a job and make money." My back was to her as I set placemats on the kitchen table. I was glad I didn't have to look at her right then.

"And how do you think you're going to do that?" Grandma asked as she turned to face me, drying her hands on a dishtowel she'd grabbed.

"Some of my friends and I from school are thinking about moving to Washington and getting jobs," I explained. "We can all live together there." I was arranging napkins beside our plates, and when I looked up she was glaring at me.

"Well, you just think you have your life all figured out, don't you?" she spewed, like I was an idiot. Like I'd not put any thought into what I wanted to do.

"I know you want me to be a lawyer, but I don't want to do that." I was adamant. I was sure I could do life better than Mom…and Dad. I hadn't worked so hard to finish high school to have someone else tell me what to do. And while I appreciated Grandma taking me in, I didn't think it was fair for her to control me.

"Well, then, go do your own thing. You go to college…or leave." Grandma folded her hands over her chest and set her jaw. It was her way or the highway. Right now. This minute. No further negotiations.

So, I packed up my car and left. I thought my friends were serious about going to Seattle, but it turns out, I went alone. Lesson learned: most people don't do what they say they will. I drove the whole way thinking about how I would make it. I had no money, no place to live, no job. And…no one who really cared what happened to me. Grandma didn't even say good-bye. I was on my own, and she could sleep at night, she told me, because she'd done her part.

My first night in Seattle, I slept in my car. It was summer, so it wasn't that unpleasant, though I discovered Bend is much warmer. I knew I had to get a job quickly, so I found the local Supermart. They hired me right away to stock shelves. It took me a month to make enough money to be able to afford rent, so I slept in my car and washed up where I could. At the time I didn't realize what a risk I was taking. It was my only alternative. I made the best of it.

With my second paycheck, I was able to afford a small room in the basement of a boarding house. My life became about work and sleep. I made a few new friends, but generally, I was surviving. I'd been at the Supermart for six months when the manager hired a new supervisor to replace the one who'd been working with me. I hated the woman. All of us did. She didn't know how to manage people or schedules. We were all better equipped to do her job than she was. One day I just had enough.

"Look, Mrs. Grange," I explained to the supervisor, "this woman is making life miserable for all of us."

"You need to work together with her," Mrs. Grange replied. "Get along."

As she was walking away, I touched her arm. When she turned around, I said, "It's not just me, Mrs. Grange! No one can stand her!"

"Well, you're the only one complaining." She said it like it was a question. Her voice went up at the word "complaining." It made me furious. *No one takes me seriously. No one listens to me.*

"You need to fire her." I said. She just stood there unresponsive. "Or me."

"You, then." It wasn't mean. Just matter-of-fact. I'd drawn a line in the sand…again. And lost…again.

So I left. Got in my car and felt the weight of what I'd just done. Seattle was lonely. I didn't really know anyone. On the way to my room at the boarding house, I decided to go back to Bend. At least there I knew people. And way back in my mind I thought there was the tiniest possibility Grandma might take me back in again. I packed up my few belongings, put gas in the car and headed back to Oregon. I played out scenarios in my head as I clicked off the miles toward Bend. Grandma was my number one hope, but if that didn't work, I thought maybe one of the friends who hadn't gone with me to Washington would let me stay with her. It's about a seven-hour drive, so I had time to get my bearings before I stopped at the edge of town and called my grandmother. She didn't pick up, so I left her a message. Asked her if I could stay there. I waited. Nothing. She clearly didn't want to speak to me. I got an email from her the next morning telling me where all the homeless shelters were in Bend, suggesting I choose one.

My friend, Maggie, answered when I called her number. "Yeah, Mom and Dad said you could stay here." I knew it wasn't going to be a convenient situation. Maggie had a two-year-old son. Her parents were already stretched taking care of the two of them. I wasn't a great addition to the mix. Room was scarce. Tensions ran high. After a couple of weeks, her parents wanted me out.

That's how I met Lynn. He was Maggie's friend. We hit it off right away and began seeing each other. I really liked him. He became protective of me. So when I had to leave Maggie's, it was the next logical step that I stay with Lynn. By the time I spoke with Andi, I was desperate. I had nowhere to go if she didn't find a place for me.

Andi picked me up at Lynn's house around eleven in the morning. I didn't know what to expect. I was nervous about the encounter. Ashamed that I needed help. My emotions were all screwed up. When I opened the door after she knocked, what I saw was disconcerting. Andi is this pretty little woman with a huge smile and short dark red curls that fringe her face with a frothy halo. Seriously. She, like, bubbles over. She seemed too happy. I wasn't sure she was for real.

"Hi, Evelyn," Andi said, her face beaming as she held her hand out to me. "I'm Andi Buerger."

"Hi," I said as I sized her up and shook her hand. "Thank you for coming to get me."

"Not a problem," she said. "Let's go talk."

We got into her car. I was still feeling awkward, but Andi is very chatty. I think she was trying to make me feel comfortable as she talked about herself, the other girls at Beulah's Place, her husband…just easy stuff. She didn't ask me about my situation until we were seated at the coffee shop at a local strip mall. I didn't have any money, but I didn't know how to tell her I could only afford water. As we stepped up to the counter, Andi ordered for both of us. Paid, too. I took a deep breath. *She's really nice. I wouldn't have done that for anyone.* Andi handed me my drink and I followed her to a nearby table where we pulled the chairs back and sat down.

"So…" she said as she looked into my eyes. Honestly, I felt like I was transparent, as if she could see through me. It scared me. The thought that she might know me was so terrifying that I didn't talk for the first several minutes. I was unsure of what... how much...to share with her. I wondered if there was a specific thing Andi was waiting for me to say that would clue her into the fact that I was the kind of person she'd help. Or if there was something I might say that would make her write me off. When I finally opened up, I thought I shared way too much...thought I might be going down a rabbit hole. Andi just listened. Her expression didn't change no matter what I told her, so I ended up telling her everything. When I was finished, I still wondered if this was all going to be another major disappointment. I couldn't help but wonder what I was getting myself into.

"Okay," Andi said, again with this disarming cheerfulness, "I'm going to find you a place to stay." She pulled a piece of paper from her purse and handed it to me as she said, "Here's a list of food banks you can go to if you get hungry." While I was looking over the list, Andi began texting on her cell phone, already in the process of locating housing for me. "It might take me a few days," she said, "but we'll get you taken care of." Andi put her phone back into her purse. "Okay?" She looked at me again with that same confusing ability to see too much, the big smile on her face and the curls freefalling over her forehead.

"Thanks," I said as we walked out of the coffee shop and to the car. There was some small talk on the way back to Lynn's. My mind was churning so fast that I don't remember much of what was said. I wasn't so much worried that Andi wouldn't find me a place as I was about how long it would take. I was creating a back-up plan in my mind so that if I was disappointed in the outcome with Beulah's Place, I wouldn't be devastated by it. My best plan? *Beg Grandma to take me back.* That's all I had. I was hanging over the edge of a cliff just waiting to fall off.

Chapter Twelve

ANDI—THE BIG BLACK BIBLE

Evelyn is petite. Her short dark hair is tamed by bobby pins that hold it back from her forehead, but the unruly curls always seem to be trying to escape their confines as they loop around her ears and lay in playful random patterns at the nape of her neck. When I met her that morning in May, her wide-set brown eyes gazed into mine with a directness that surprised me. I could tell she was reading me as I chatted with her over coffee and a muffin. She was still so young, but there was more life swimming in her gaze than her years hinted at. I eased into the conversation about her situation. Though she was hesitant at first, Evelyn finally revealed the chaos her young life had become. About the mother in Alaska living in drug-slogged agony, too wounded and addicted to care for her. And I could hear in Evelyn's voice a distant yearning even so. I could feel the wall the young woman had built in order for her to survive, stacked stone by stone, seemingly too high to climb.

Mothers. So often it's about the mothers of these young women. There's either too much control or too little—a narcissistic whirlpool that either spins the daughters out or sucks them in, leaving them damaged and insecure.

The woman who gave birth to me wasn't a drug addict. Her issues weren't that obvious to the outside world. Leanne got her rush from her perversions, one of which was draconian control. When I was eleven, she was in college to become a teacher; so, in the summer Joe Jr. and I were in lockdown in our Culver City, California, apartment. During the few hours a day Leanne was at school, Joe Jr. and I weren't allowed to go more than five feet from our front door if we wanted to be outside. Leanne actually measured it. Set the boundaries. If we didn't immediately answer the phone when she called, we would be in serious trouble. Though these rules may seem natural to others because mothers want to protect their kids, we knew there were more noxious overtones. We had no friends because of our restrictions. We couldn't explain it to people, and we were ashamed of what happened behind the closed doors of our home. But the most pressing reason we were friendless was because Leanne liked it that way.

In the apartment complex that summer there was a single mother with six children of her own. She noticed me languishing on the porch day after day, and took pity on my plight. Came over to me as I sat on the porch step one morning before Leanne left for school and asked me to a birthday party for one of her kids.

"Kayla is having a skating party today. It's her birthday," she offered with an empathetic smile. "Would you like to come?"

Yeah, I would! "I can't. My mother won't let me." This I knew without doubt. And I didn't want to pay the price of *actually asking*.

"Well, would you mind if I ask your mother?" she said, maybe thinking I was simply shy.

"Okay." And I let the woman into the house to ask Leanne if I could go skating. I knew, of course, that she'd think I put the neighbor lady up to it. That it was at my suggestion that the woman begged my mom to let me go skating.

"Fine. She can go to the party with you," Leanne said condescendingly to the lady. "But she can't ice skate, she can't watch the other kids and she can't have any ice cream. If she even asks you for a quarter, I'll beat the crap out of her." At this, Leanne shoved me toward the horrified neighbor, who put her hand on my shoulder and led me outside toward the van where her kids were patiently waiting. I heard the door of our house shut authoritatively as I climbed into a seat next to a kid I didn't know.

For the next four hours I sat obediently beside the neighbor mother who couldn't skate herself because I wasn't to be left alone, the only one at the party who was told *not* to have fun. When I got home, Leanne was waiting. I'm sure I had a pouty look on my face because what twelve-year-old wants to go to a birthday skating party ordered to refrain from enjoying it—to sit on the sidelines, humiliated in front of my new friends? "Well, you got to go ice skating," she said with the snide whine to her voice that sounded like the wicked witch from *Wizard of Oz*. "So, shut up."

I know it sounds a bit Cinderella to be believed, but I still remember the satisfied look in her eye as she realized she'd ruined something for me. That she had that much power. When Leanne really wanted to drive a point home, she'd use her black Bible. It was the ultimate controlling device because in her eyes, the Bible gave her permission to brutalize us. It was very confusing. I'd had my own sovereign revelation of a Jesus who loved me personally—who was aware of my circumstances and promised to deliver me from them. But Leanne's particular brand of Christianity was a weapon.

I'd trespassed against her somehow one morning. I could see it building up in her, this eruption that started with the seed of what I'd done to make her mad that so often grew into a full-blown cyclone of anger which culminated in her beating me mercilessly with her fists until she'd gotten her fix. The look in her eyes always terrified me. Made my heart race and my mind devise any possible way of escape. Only there wasn't one.

"Come here, young lady!" the woman screamed. "Right now!"

I didn't know what I'd done. I often didn't. Leanne would get it into her mind that I was the "little pig" that needed a whipping. I don't know. I often felt like she hit me because I existed. No other reason. But I went to the den and stood before her like a convict before her executioner. "You know what you did!" she bellowed. Held aloft in her left hand, with the golden-edged pages flopping against the black leather cover, was Leanne's Bible.

Desperate, I whined, "No. I don't know what I did." *I didn't.*

"God told me, right here in this Bible, His Word, that I must correct you when you are bad!" She sounded like a demon-possessed preacher, screeching heresy as she prepared to beat me for I-didn't-even-know-what. That my punishment was "righteous" often made it even more severe.

I don't own a black Bible. And I won't own Leanne's god. My belief in Him was fragile, at best, but the Jesus I'd seen in the beautiful woman's eyes loved children. Loved *me*. I squeezed my eyes shut and thought of Him while Leanne defied His teachings and defiled my body.

Shortly before I married Jeffrey, Leanne made an effort to talk with me about those beatings. "Do you understand why I *had* to do the things I did to you?" she asked, interrupting a conversation about plans for the wedding reception at her house.

The question left me in stunned silence. There *is* no reason for her horrific treatment of me. Before I could say anything, Leanne went on with her justification. "You are too much like your father, you know." I locked eyes with her. "I couldn't let you grow up to be like him!"

So you beat me. With Bible held high in the air, tried to make me believe God would flail me, too. I didn't say it. What good would it have done? Leanne was too far gone.

I understand Evelyn's motherless heart. How she has to throw up barricades and act tough. We must survive the knowledge we are our own mothers. That if our hearts are going to be nurtured, we will have to feed them ourselves. It made me determined to find her a place where she felt loved and cared for. Although Carina already housed one of our young women, I called her to see if she could take on Evelyn, too. Their family lives on a farm with animals and chores. The two daughters love Tabitha, the young woman already there. When I asked if they would take on Evelyn, too, the entire family agreed. If they hadn't, Evelyn would've been back on the streets.

Chapter Thirteen

EVELYN—SETTLING INTO PEACE

I got the phone call from Andi three days after we met for coffee. She found me a place with a lady named Carina and her family. She said Carina would be picking me up the next morning to take me home. I was nervous, still not sure this was going to work out. I slept fitfully. The next morning, Lynn sat on the bed while I packed up my things into my banged up suitcase. I don't remember us saying much to each other. I was pretty sure that our relationship was going to end when I walked out the door that morning. I didn't know what to do about that or what to say that would change anything. We stood together by the window peeking out between the curtains, waiting for Carina to drive up. My car had broken down, so I didn't have transportation now. I felt wholly at someone else's mercy, and I balked at the vulnerability of it.

Around eleven, a van pulled up in front of Lynn's house. As Carina was opening the van door, Lynn was grabbing my suitcase. No hesitation. Not like he was ready to get rid of me so much as we had to do this thing. He took it straight to the door, opened it with determination and set the suitcase down on the front porch. *Good-bye, Evelyn.* My heart was pounding. I hugged Lynn as much to hide from Carina as to tell him good-bye. *What have I gotten myself into?*

Lynn disengaged from me and turned me toward the tall, thin woman walking toward us. Just like Andi, Carina had a huge smile on her pretty face. Her hair was dishwater blond and cut in a modified mullet. She moved easily in her blue jeans and waved me to the minivan. "C'mon!" she called as she ran to open the hatch back for my suitcase. I took one longing look back at my boyfriend then tossed my suitcase into the van and climbed in beside Carina for the ride to my new home.

"We have two daughters," Carina began as she turned on the engine and pulled away from the curb. "Priscilla and Angie." She gave me a sideways glance. "Do you have sisters?"

"No," I replied. "Three brothers." She laughed at that.

"Well that must be interesting!" she said. "The only girl."

"Two of them are older, so they've been in the armed services for a while. My little brother is still home in Alaska." I hadn't thought about it much, but I sort of missed him when I said that.

"The girls are going to love having you at our house," Carina said, glancing my way again. "Priscilla is the oldest and never met a stranger. She might bug you to death with questions. Angie, on the other hand, is much more introverted. More of a watcher. They are as different as night and day."

"And which one will be my roommate?" I asked.

"Priscilla." Carina's whole face lit up. "She can't wait to meet you." I could tell from the tone of her voice that her older daughter was going to be an experience. But talking about her kids and family, where I'd be living and knowing I was welcome calmed my nervousness. I could even feel excitement bubbling in my stomach. A home. Sisters. A huge relief.

Priscilla was, of course, waiting for the van when it pulled into their driveway, her straight blond hair hanging in braids against her white cotton shirt and her feet shuffling impatiently as we pulled up beside her. She was already talking before I could even get out of the car. It was her job to show me our room, where for the moment there was only one bed. The room was small, painted a light pink, and the soft gingham curtains on the windows rose and fell with the cool breeze wafting in. "They are going to bring us your bed this afternoon," Priscilla chirped. "For now, you can put your things over there in the corner."

After I set the suitcase down, Priscilla opened the closet. "Look," she said, "we made room for your clothes right here." And she pointed to the section of empty closet rack that would belong to me. "And…" she said, "I emptied my drawer so you could have room for your clothes here, too!" Priscilla stood proudly over the drawer.

"Wow. Thanks." I wasn't used to people accommodating me with such enthusiasm. I was usually more of a burden, so Priscilla and her family blew my mind. I spent about an hour arranging my things in the room while she sat on her bed and asked me question after question about my life. It might have annoyed me except Carina had already prepared me for the deluge.

The bed for me was delivered in the middle of the afternoon. We assembled it then Carina let Priscilla put the new bedding on it. She'd helped choose it and couldn't wait to spread the flowery comforter over the new pink sheets and fluff the pillows into the lace trimmed shams. A bed of my own. A family. A drawer for my things. I dared to hope a little, I must say.

The Supermart in Seattle called to tell me I could have my job back. I was right, they said, about the manager. They'd fired her. But I told them I was already settled in Bend, where another Supermart had hired me. And, for the most part, I embraced my new situation. Carina was also housing Tabitha. We have pretty opposite personalities, so sometimes we'd clash, but we usually worked it out. Carina and her husband had rules: midnight curfew, do your own dishes, keep your space clean. Nothing I didn't understand the merit of. And there was no real drama. Ironically, it took a while to get used to peace.

Chapter Fourteen

ANDI—THERAPY

Shortly after Ed and I married, a pastor friend of mine in Redmond pounded Ed's back and said, "We have been praying for you for years! We don't know how she's made it this far, but we're so glad you found her!" My man chuckled and drew me in close to him. At the time, he had no idea.

Both of us were raised in Southern California so you'd think God could get us together there. But, no. The delicate thread of God's love that kept me moving forward against all odds led me to Eagle Crest Resorts in Redmond, Oregon in 1995. Jeffrey dumped me there and went back to Orange County, California. A long story I will, for the sake of my current sanity, shorten.

Marriage didn't bring healing to my hurts and insecurities. Instead, they worsened. Jeffrey didn't understand me any better than I did; and, he was impatient with his desire for me to become the marriage partner of his dreams. Always churning in me was the knowledge I wasn't good enough for him, or at least not what he wanted. My weekly therapy made me dig down deeply so I could be fixed, but I became even more miserable because there was so much to excavate. But God was working with me all the time, even when I didn't recognize it. Preparing me for what awaited at College Hospital. That's the only way I know how to put it. Cutting into places so damaged, filled with so much scar tissue, that I had to be further wounded in order to heal correctly. I would've never consented to hospitalization without the events that preceded it.

Through his work, Jeffrey had contacts with a few celebrities in Los Angeles. That's how we came to discover The Little Chapel in Tarzana, California. A former actress, Sara O'Meara, who had given her life to helping abused and orphaned children, fell ill herself with terminal cancer. From her hospital bed one day, Sara heard the mesmerizing voice of faith healer, Kathryn Kuhlman, wafting from the television set in her room. "If you want to be healed," Kathryn was saying, "come to the Shrine Auditorium this Sunday." Sara says she had nothing to lose by going, but she had to convince her doctor to discharge her early from the hospital. She was told to go straight to bed, as her stitches were not healed and her body very frail. But Sara went to the healing service and was miraculously, immediately healed of the cancer she was told was destined to take her life. Her healing was so dramatic that Ms. Kuhlman contacted her, then featured Sara on her own nationally televised show. They became not only fast friends, but Sara began helping with the services, learning to discern when God was going to heal or deliver. Ms. Kuhlman knew, even before Sara did, that God would use her in a ministry of healing others.

That is how Sara came to be at the Little Chapel. She and her dear friend, Yvonne Fedderson, met while they were playing the girlfriends of Ricky and David Nelson on the "Ozzie and Harriet" show years before. Yvonne was with Sara the night she was healed at Kathryn Kuhlman's service. Took her to the doctor the next day to hear him proclaim in amazement that not only was the incision wound from her surgery healed, but the cancer was gone. The two women were inseparable, experiencing together the wonder of what God was doing through Sara. With the help of donations from many of those who'd been healed, Sara and Yvonne established a chapel that seated up to one hundred people at a time. The Fedderson family commissioned a statue of Jesus from an artist in Italy. It took a year for all to be ready for the meetings. The artwork stood in the center of the chapel, Jesus reaching out His arms in love. Sara held healing meetings there, and taught about Jesus. Because the women were also busy with their charitable work at Childhelp USA, the services at the chapel were not held every week. It was, therefore, a unique privilege that Jeffrey and I found ourselves there one Sunday.

There were no seats available except at the very front of the chapel when we arrived. Although there were noted celebrities there, I couldn't take my eyes from Jesus standing there fashioned in marble with His hands reaching out to me. Compassionate, caring, wanting to embrace me. *If only He would materialize. Be flesh, not stone. Talk to me. I really need Him to talk to me.* I had trouble believing He was interested in my situation—my nightmares, my marriage, my past abuse. Agonizing questions were swirling around in my head. Tears were irritating my eyes. *Jesus, do You hear? Will you ever fix this awful pain in me? How long?* I wanted to stand and leave, but we were in the front row. I was uncomfortable in my skin, fidgety and anxious. *You just have to wait and stick it out. Pray for the service to be over.* Self-talk. Trying to settle myself until I could flee.

"God said someone here has been crying out for years," Sara O'Meara began. "God has heard. He wants to restore and is healing you now. It will take time, though, He said. It will take time, and He will heal you in layers." Then her eyes caught mine and rested there a moment.

That must be me, Lord. The thought of it touched a place in me, dammed up for years. I couldn't control my tears. Hadn't I just asked if God heard me? Hadn't I just been praying, "How long?" My heart thought to hope again. That same glimmer that always pulled me along, gave me some grace to take another step.

Sara finished her talk, prayed for people and maybe spoke into the lives of others who were there. I heard nothing after she said the Lord would heal my heart…in layers. I was stunned to be singled out. After all the years of abuse, I was, for a thrilling moment, the center of God's attention. When Sara left her place and stepped down toward me from the podium, I thought my heart would pound out of my chest. I didn't know what to expect—was still overcome with emotion. She sat down beside me, put her arms around me, and rocked me. She actually rocked me back and forth, like I was her child, hurt by the world and in need of condolence. I couldn't help but think, *This must be what it's like to have a mother comfort you.*

I don't remember Sara saying much to me in that moment. I was sure Jesus hugged me when she did, because, for two days afterward, I felt a warmth, a brightness, that was inexplicable but for that. A bright light seemed to have settled in next to me, brighter still when I was alone. I felt its warmth, like the radiance from a glowing fire, wrapping me in a peace for which I had no earthly explanation. Later it would be clear why I needed this encouragement.

I was still in weekly counseling sessions. Still dredging up all the buried debris, sunk to the bottom of my consciousness, a pile of detritus that I lived over until I couldn't anymore. Marriage to Jeffrey challenged my ability to disassociate…brought up familiar reactions. I wanted so much to be the perfect little wife—do it all right. To do all the things I felt the church dictated I do. I was trying so hard. All by myself. And, just like so many things in my life, I felt I was failing miserably. Or so Jeffrey told me. My damage, his damage—all dammed up.

Barbara, a friend of mine, invited Jeffrey and me to a church in Toluca Lake, thinking we'd enjoy the service. It was a beautiful structure, with the feel of a cathedral. The pulpit was raised and behind it was a striking stained glass window of Jesus placed so that when I looked at the preacher as he spoke, it was impossible to miss Christ in the window in the background. The mid-morning light poured through the multi-colored panes, causing the colors to collide in prismatic rainbows onto the ceiling and walls of the church. I was enthralled by it. Felt the heat from it. Couldn't take my eyes off Jesus on the wall behind the preacher. Captivated by a single tear—a red one—coursing down Jesus's cheek as He held a little lamb in His arms. *Why is the tear red?* I could taste it on my tongue—the bloody tear. It was destined, of course, to drop onto the head of the lamb cradled there. Stilled, though, for now, in the moment, never to actually dampen the sparkling white wool of the Shepherd's pet. Jesus would become the Lamb. I understood that. The sacrifice for all the flock once made to pay for their own misdeeds. The compassionate tear mingled with blood so that no more sheep would bear the weight of the world on sacrificial altars. So, I must be the lamb, cuddled in for safety. The thought of it was so foreign. Feeling safe wasn't my normal. The glowing window made me yearn for a thing I couldn't adequately define, never having really experienced it before. Still. I could taste it…the tear and its promise.

Suddenly the speaker was saying, "Someone here today has been the victim of great abuse." The man stopped for a moment. Looked around the congregation. "I think it's a woman."

I thought, *Given the crowd, that's a safe assumption.*

But then the man went on. "God is still healing you. Layer by layer." My face went hot. I felt electrified. Again. God speaking to me. I didn't know quite what to do with the incident, but I carried the palpable comfort of its revelation into the very challenging months that followed.

Therapy was one such a hurdle. Recalling abuses I'd put away in an interior vault gave me nightmares. Sapped my energy. Almost disabled me, and made me angry. Trying to sort out my spiritual life was a challenge all of its own. Where had God been? Where was He now? Some days were so black. Some days it would have been easier to quit. And God knew.

Jeffrey and I went back to the Little Chapel a few days before I was voluntarily admitted into the College Hospital psych ward… only a few hours before I was headed for the edge. It had been weeks since the last time we visited the church, so I had no expectation of Sara remembering me. We sat back in the crowd this time, instead of front and center. I felt shielded from the exposure of another emotional encounter. Mingled in with the celebrities and those in need of divine healing, I slid comfortably down into my chair and let myself feel the atmosphere that was always punctuated by the presence of Jesus, His compassion forever carved into the arms reaching out to us as He stood in all of His marble elegance. I'd been slowly coming to grips with my fears—especially of abandonment and trust. I had no paradigm for security. I was lost.

Sara was speaking. As always, her words were reaching places in people that only God could've known about. I could tell. I wasn't expecting anything since I was singled out by God that last time. That was a miracle in itself. I was stunned when I heard her say, "Someone is here today who's been here before." She didn't look at me. I doubt she'd have remembered me. So many people wandered in and out of her life and her meetings. She wasn't singling me out because she recognized me. It was God Who knew I was there. She was aglow with an ethereal aura as she said to me, "God is giving great healing to you," Sara continued. "But it will take some time as there are many layers." That word again. And tears came so fast I couldn't control it. "He'll never leave you or forsake you."

And Jesus held me in His arms through the weeks that followed—hour after hour of peeling back the pain, one thing at a time, one awful incident at a time, until I could go back home to Jeffrey and cope.

After my two months of therapy at College Hospital in Cerritos, the staff surprised me one Friday morning, telling me I could go home a few days early. They felt my coping skills were exceptionally strong and said there wasn't much more they could do in the cloistered atmosphere of a hospital.

I phoned Jeffrey. "Hi! Surprise! I can come home today! I'm good to go!" Thinking, of course, he'd be delighted. He worked from home and we lived only a few miles away.

There was silence on the other end for a breathless moment. "Uh…I wasn't really expecting you to come home so soon." Then nothing. I wasn't quite sure what he expected me to say.

"Well…" I stammered. "You don't have to come get me, but I have to be out of here by midnight." The old worthlessness surged in. Left me holding the phone in my hand, looking at it as if it held the answer to my fate.

"No." Jeffrey stalled. Sounded annoyed. "No…I'll come get you."

"Okay." All the joy of the moment wilted. "See you when you get here."

During my first few days home, I felt more empowered to express what I needed and wanted. Also, since I knew Jeffrey expected me to come out of therapy all fixed in the marriage department, I decided to be more experimental in trying to please him. This often only made him laugh. Those of us who have managed to escape horrific abuse are not fixed overnight and especially if we are living with someone impatient for us to perform. Though I now know the perpetrators of my past abuse, there was still much to cull through, to overcome or at least begin to understand. But there wasn't enough room in Jeffrey's world for me to explore my healing. I was supposed to be fixed and raring to go. That proved to be difficult…again.

Jeffrey's solution to this was a surrogate wife—someone who could meet his seemingly endless needs *for me,* an ironic solution presented with no irony whatsoever. I didn't know it then, but he'd already picked her out. A woman he worked with whose own marriage was on the rocks. She was a sexy blonde; a former pin-up girl who was ready for some fun. She'd told Jeffrey her husband was also the victim of childhood abuse whose issues were, apparently, similar to mine. It seemed a paradoxical pairing of souls for them to find each other and want to hook up. The subject of his interest in a sexual companion came up one night in the middle of a terrible fight which had deteriorated into a lengthy litany of my inadequacies. We were sitting on the couch in the living room, each of us on either end. Jeffrey looked like a puffer fish, blown up in his disgust, cheeks exploding with unspoken subtext. I was poised on the other end, defensive and wanting to smack his insipid face.

"You know," Jeffrey began, trying to lower his voice to a more normal pitch and adjusting himself closer to me on the sofa, "the Bible has all kinds of stories about men having surrogates when their wives can't have children."

Of course, this took me aback. *What on earth?*

"So," he continued, trying on a pious face and sounding very serious, "it makes sense that I should have someone who can meet the needs you can't...or won't." He was staring at me, then, smugly, as if he'd made a tremendously salient point about how to fix our floundering relationship.

Seriously? I was very confused and momentarily tongue-tied. Did the Bible actually sanction my husband finding a concubine...some woman to meet his manly needs? Jeffrey was much more familiar with scripture than I was then. But it didn't feel right. "That doesn't sound right to me," I said as I arose and left him and the conversation right where it was. I honestly didn't even think to be mad. It was too preposterous...and Jeffrey tended to be overly dramatic when he wanted to make a point. Of course, at the time, I thought this was a theoretical concubine, not the woman from his office.

A couple of weeks later, Jeffrey walked into the kitchen while I was making dinner. "Let's go to Tahoe," he offered. As he reached into the refrigerator for a can of soda, he said, "And Teresa, my assistant, is going with us."

That didn't seem unusual at the time. She worked for him. We'd gone to Vegas with her before. Usually the two of them got hammered and I'd find myself driving through the desert on the way home with them lolling awkwardly across the car seats in varying degrees of consciousness.

"Okay." I'm appalled now at my naivete. I'd forgotten all about Jeffrey wanting his own biblical Hagar.

"And you might just want to get used to the idea that she'll be going with us a whole lot more." Jeffrey strode from the room and sat casually on the sofa in the living room while I finished preparing dinner.

I know he assumed I'd connect the dots. Surrogate. Teresa. Inadequacy. Satisfaction. But I didn't. So, I was surprised when Teresa called me over to the adjoining room at the Tahoe hotel that weekend to have a chat. She patted the bed beside her, inviting me to sit down. "Are you sure you're comfortable with this?" she asked, ically rather tenderly "I...uh,,,wanted to make sure you are really okay with this before we do it."

My mind had to catch up. Had to put two and two together. Had to think surrogate. Had to think Oh, my God! Had to think son of a gun! I wanted to throw up.

"Jeffrey explained it to me," Teresa was saying, taking my silence as acquiescence, maybe. "But I don't want you to be hurt by all of this." Her face was so earnest; not the face of a woman who is trying to get your tacit approval for sleeping with your husband. I felt upside down. Stupid, really. Like there was something missing in this formula, and I was the one who couldn't process the common sense of the arrangement.

"All of this" dawned on me as I sat in deflated wonder beside the buxom blonde who made me feel like a little kid who knew nothing of the world. "Oh, yeah," I choked out, trying not to let my voice break with the hysteria I felt rising like a geyser, ready to explode all over the woman's pretty face. "I got it...you mean you...and Jeffrey...here in this room right next to ours..." It was a statement, not a question. I felt like I was looking right into the sun. The light had dawned bright and unrelenting. That son of a gun! The idea was disgusting, demoralizing, ridiculous and tawdry. I'd married a real piece of...work.

I stood up from my place beside Teresa, straightened my dress, took a very deep breath and said, "Okay, yeah, sure, you and Jeffrey do whatever you want to." I ran my fingers through my curls, testing myself to see if I was still me, then walked as uprightly as I knew how from the room, feeling utterly humiliated and childishly naïve.

On the other side of the adjoining door was Jeffrey, who'd arrived back just in time to see me fly into our room like a careening wounded bird. I ran into him but pushed him away brusquely, the smell of his after shave, which clung to him, reminding me of the sweetness of carnations at a funeral. I was nauseous and couldn't look at his insipid face. "I'm going to go somewhere," I said with as much class as I could muster. "You do what you need to do." Then I retrieved my purse and walked out the door, into the hallway, going I didn't know where.

I had no sense of self. I felt completely lost—almost out of body. *What the heck just happened?* I wish I'd hitchhiked home. I wish I'd slapped Jeffrey's vapid face. I wish I'd gone Bette Davis on him, screaming my pain and shame, beating his chest with closed fists, crying the tears that didn't come pouring, in torrents of confusion and anger, until I was well out of sight. I walked all over Tahoe until I thought they might be done with their tryst. I didn't know what else to do then but to go back to the hotel.

"Where were you?" he dared to asked when I came through the door of our room. He was lying across the bed, his head against the pillows, still wearing his shirt, dress pants and tie. He'd put a book down onto his chest to speak to me. "Why did you go off?"

Really? I overreacted? I was disgusted by him lying there. I wanted to knock the stupid out of him. To let fly all the rage of the evening so that he'd be bruised physically the way I was emotionally. But passive-aggressive was all I knew. "I thought you wanted to do your thing" was all I said as I set my purse on the dresser and sat down to remove my shoes.

"Oh, that…" said like it was only a passing thought. Never really intended to follow through. "I decided not to do that."

By then, I didn't care. Do it or not. I felt stuck with my choice of a husband. I didn't have Christian counsel to discover how out of the box and into hell he really was. *Did other husbands act like this?* I honestly didn't know who to ask and was embarrassed about the relationship we had.

Though I should have known what kind of man he was by the time he asked my permission to be a sperm donor, I have to admit I was surprised. Not long after the Tahoe trip the phone rang in our condo. It was an old girlfriend of his who seemed to specialize in having affairs with married men. This left her childless in her mid-forties. Her latest boyfriend decided, as all the previous ones had, that he would go on back to his wife. So she came on over to my husband. Didn't want *him*. Just wanted a baby with brown eyes, nice hair, a good mind and, you know, one who would grow up to be amazing, like Jeffrey. That's what *he* heard. I knew: *She just wants a kid before she's too old.*

"That was an interesting call," Jeffrey began as he sauntered over to the sofa and sat down. I was reading and barely noticed until he went on about the gist of the conversation. "Remember Molly?" he asked.

"That was her…just now…on the phone." Jeffrey was smiling like he'd just been given the Man of the Year award. "You'll never guess what she wants."

I put the book down. That Molly wanted something piqued my interest. "What?" I asked. "What does she want?"

"A baby." Jeffrey laughed then, but it was mirthless. Like Captain Hook laughed at Peter Pan. Supremely haughty. "Mine." And he spread his arms out across the back of the sofa, smiling a self-satisfied smile. I should take for granted, as all who knew him would, that to carry the spawn of Jeffrey Howard was to procreate with the gods. "So, what do you think?"

"What did you tell her?"

"I'd think about it." The smile still plastered across his face.

"So," I began, "the word *No* didn't cross your mind?" I asked this, of course, of the man whose world spun with him as its axis. "You seriously want me to consider allowing you to give another woman your sperm? A woman who will raise your kid any way she pleases? Without any input from you besides the obvious?"

Jeffrey knew he'd put me in a catch-twenty-two. If I said yes, go ahead, he could take the moral high ground and say, "I don't think that's the right thing to do." I was pretty sure he'd go ahead with it, though. The thought of another little Jeffrey gracing the world was too heady to resist. If I said no, I'd be a witch. I took the witchy road.

When the Berlin Wall went down in 1988, Jeffrey thought we should take a European vacation and go into East Berlin. We hadn't been married long at the time, so I was thrilled. It would be a second honeymoon. Just the two of us on a great adventure. It wasn't until we landed that I discovered the real impetus for the trip was to follow one of Jeffrey's old flames all over Europe to hear her sing. He'd been in a vocal group with her in Orange County for a short time. An exotically beautiful mixed race woman with an amazing voice, she'd been in love with Jeffrey for a time…or so he said.

After taking several train trips, eschewing our previous itinerary for opera houses in various countries, I drew a line. We were sitting in a German restaurant in a part of Berlin with which I was unfamiliar. I didn't have the slightest idea where our hotel was in relation to the eating establishment. If I'd decided to storm out of our dispute, I wouldn't have recourse. Because of this, when we began to argue, I mostly sat quietly and listened to Jeffrey rage at me, belittling me for my insecurities and selfishness.

"You're never satisfied! I bring you to Europe and all you do is complain!" His voice grew so loud he was attracting negative attention from the other patrons.

"Calm down," I said, patting him on his right hand as it rested on the table. "You're too loud." It was like Leanne all over again, raging at me, shaming me, with everyone looking, judging, thinking I'd done something terribly wrong.

On and on it went until the server walked over to us. His vivid blue eyes popped out from beneath bushy white eyebrows and narrowed angrily on my husband. I was impressed with how large and sturdy the man was. Jeffrey looked like a toad next to him. "Miss, are you all right?" the man asked, turning a more tender face toward me. "Is this man bothering you?" *Well, yes…for years now.*

I smiled at him. "No, we are just arguing."

The big German server didn't believe me any more than I believed myself. He gave Jeffrey one last *you better behave* look then returned to waiting tables. For the first time in years I felt seen, even protected. And Jeffrey was cowed, if not embarrassed. But only for the moment. It was startling how well he kept his hubris preened.

Life was simply a maze I felt stuck in most of the time. I lost all affection for the man I married, but I didn't really know what to do about it. I prayed and prayed that we could somehow reconcile our relationship. This was the man God gave me, and I was stuck. I made the best choice I could, I thought, based upon my very specific prayers for a man who could show me the world, take me to fine restaurants and the theatre. I didn't want to be the one to destroy our marriage, so I put up, naively, with some pretty horrific stuff.

Jeffrey decided to run for public office in the early nineties in Southern California. I helped with the campaigning. It was a bust, and he lost huge amounts of money on the endeavor. And, his business wasn't thriving. I needed a job that paid well. In 1995, I was offered a good position with Eagle Crest Resorts in Redmond, Oregon. The company liked my resume, especially the fact I had worked in training and development with the Disney Corporation. I was just their cup of tea. They hired me and gave Jeffrey and me a new condo to reside in during my first two weeks with the company. Jeffrey loved the idea of living on a golf course and enjoyed our little vacation on the company so much he decided we should buy one of the condos. He signed the paperwork, then went back to California to live…effectively dumping me.

I didn't understand this fully. Jeffrey told me that for vague financial purposes I failed to comprehend he was going to file for a legal separation. But he continued to visit me occasionally at Eagle Crest, confusing my heart and intentionally allowing me to misunderstand his motives. I had several conversations with the paralegal who was processing the paperwork. When I'd call in, I'd say, "This is concerning the legal separation." She'd always say, "Oh, the Howard divorce." *It's not a divorce. Why does she keep saying that?*

I didn't think to ask her more, or if I did, I sublimated it. Jeffrey came up one weekend for a visit after I'd been working at the resort for several months. He was in bed already and feigning sleep when I crawled under the covers. I'd worked a twelve-hour day and was completely exhausted. I'd just laid my head against the pillow when Jeffrey popped up to a sitting position. "We need to talk." His tone was urgent.

"Okay," I said, yawning. I drew the covers up around me and struggled to a sitting position against my pillows.

"I'm going to bring the rest of your belongings from California next weekend," Jeffrey announced much too abruptly. He was frantically raking his hands through his hair like he was panicked about something.

I tried to read his expression. "No rush," I said. "It's not like we're getting a divorce or something." Jeffrey didn't say anything then. He became very still and just looked at me. His eyes were sad with the kind of remorse one might have when dumping a stray cat—he didn't want me, but he felt guilty about it. The cold chill of realization froze me for a second. *Oh, my God, he is divorcing me. Oh, my God.*

I got up and walked to the closet because there wasn't anywhere else to go. I heard it then. "Yes...yes. I'm divorcing you."

I stood in the closet, my emotions attacking me, cascading
over me in such a way I couldn't sort them properly. Relief. Anger.
Shame. Hurt. I wish I'd thrown him out. I wish I'd had the presence of mind to speak all the disappointment and anger welling up
in me, but I didn't. I simply felt empty. I went back to bed, turned
out the bedside lamp, huddled in the fetal position as far away
from Jeffrey's body as I could get, and went to sleep. I had a busy
day the next day. I would cope.

Our divorce was final a year later. I was safely placed in Oregon, alone and waiting for my prince to arrive from La Mesa,
California. He would appear soon, not on a white horse, but in
his Ford F150, rumbling up the highway in search of the princess
whose Cinderella life was in full swing.

Chapter Fifteen

ANDI—CINDERELLA MOMENTS

Speaking of Cinderella, though I had no wicked step sisters, I have to wonder over the miracle that I made it out into the world in one piece. We have our similarities, the fairy tale chimney sweep and I. By the time I hit college, I was so accustomed to being told I am nothing, that it affected just about everything I did. However, I was down, but not out. Always pulsing through me, whether I was conscious of it or not, was the knowledge that God loved me. That He was bigger than all that I was going through. And there were some small victories that let me know He'd not let me down. My college ballet class was one of those.

Ms. Yeager was a petite woman with long, light brown hair that she wore pulled back into either a pony tail or a tight bun on the crown of her head. Her almond shaped eyes seemed to slide from hazel to brown like the colors of a kaleidoscope when the light hit them and were accentuated by the severity of her hairdo. She wore leotards and tights, and she had those dance socks that scrunched up from her tiny feet, slouching down from her knees—the ones like Jane Fonda wore in her exercise videos in the early eighties. They always looked to me like caterpillars were trying to eat her legs. The other would-be ballerinas in my college dance class were decked out in the same Fonda-esque regalia. Everyone but me. I wore jeans. And sneakers. The thing is, I always wanted to be a dancer—to be graceful, swan-like in a pink tutu gracing an enormous stage as I glided on the tips of my satin-covered toes to the strains of *The Sugar Plum Fairy*. But the truth of the matter was, I was too short and coordination wasn't my strong suit. I had the heart of a dancer without the body, or the experience. *Ballet 101*. I needed the elective credit.

There was a great deal of eye rolling about me in that class. In my mind I could dance. In my heart, I wanted to succeed. I needed better than a C in the class, but half way through I had to have a skin cancer removed from my back at the school health center and missed out on some necessary classes. I had to take a make-up class with the teacher who taught the professional dancers. She was horrified at me. Never wanted me back in her class. So, when I returned to regular class, I was humiliated enough to give myself two alternatives: Do the minimum and get the C or go for it on the final dance. I went for it. I told myself I could think like the most elegant prima ballerina ever to grace the stage. I could pretend in my head that I was tutued up for *Sugar Plum,* and dance my butt off, forgetting what anyone else said. The ballerina in my head could do it for real.

The final was a ninety second ordeal. Ms. Yeager watched each student dance while she made marks about us in the notebook that rested on her forearm. It was intimidating even for the better dancers. When she came up to me, I *did* believe that I could be the most amazing prima ballerina ever. I thought God had made me just that fabulous and fluid—a glory to behold.

"That was so wonderful," she said, surprised and obviously taken aback at my performance. She'd even forgotten the notebook in her hands as she gaped in wonder at my newly found confidence.

The next day the grades were posted. With some trepidation, I thought maybe a C+. When I looked at the posted pages, trying to push past the other ballerinas, I started with the D column. My name, *Whew!*, wasn't there. Then to the C page. By then I was thinking maybe I'd flunked. Crowded around the A and B pages were the other girls in the class. The ones who'd gawked and chuckled at my jeans'n'sneakers ballet form. Astounded, I found myself on the A page. A-. The other girls shrieked when they saw it. To be fair, so did I. Ms. Yeager had written: *For those ninety seconds, you were a ballerina.*

Cinderella acknowledged by the fairy godmother because the Prince had anointed a dance. I was allowed the limelight. A coming out of the little girl who'd been told all her life she wasn't good enough. For ninety wondrous seconds, I knew who I could be when I was set free.

It's that way with the girls who come to Beulah's Place. They have no idea who they really are. They have been defined by abuse their entire lives. No one has ever said, "You are beautiful and you matter." Nevaeh was no exception. She was working at a local fish house in Redmond. She'd been living with her boyfriend, but he dumped her. The young woman was barely making it when she got in touch with her ex-stepmom, Stella. Stella had seen the interview for Beulah's Place on television. Told Nevaeh to call me. I answered the hotline phone in my office one day in January of 2014. I have set the phone to a distinctive ring so that day or night I'll know it's a call I need to answer.

"Hello…" came a voice from the other end, interrupted by a deep, gurgling cough. "Hello," the girl said again, "sorry about that."

"You sound very sick," I said.

"I am…" A long rolling cough interrupted us for a minute.

"You've called the hotline for Beulah's Place. Did someone give you the number?" I asked.

"Yes, my ex-stepmom. She said maybe you could help me." Another fit of coughing. "Are you Andi?"

"Yes, I am. What is your name?"

"Nevaeh," the girl offered.

"Where are you, Nevaeh?" I asked.

"I'm living with some guy in Bend. I don't have any other place to go…I've run out of options." Nevaeh stopped to breathe. Words came out in puffs, like steam from an engine, not in a steady stream. I could tell it hurt her to talk.

"How old are you?"

"Eighteen. I just turned eighteen." Nevaeh hacked into the phone, coughing and wheezing. "Can you help me?"

"Tell me where you are, and I'll come now."

Nevaeh gave me the directions to a rundown apartment complex in south Bend, forty-five minutes away from my house. It was clear from the outside of the building that the inside was decrepit and overcrowded. Broken down cars slumped in random disarray like patients awaiting care in an overly busy hospital emergency room. Too sick to move. Some past hope of a cure. Just outside of the apartment where Nevaeh was staying were plastic toddler toys lying broken and forsaken in the dirt beneath the windows. *She didn't tell me she had a kid.* I didn't know what to expect when I knocked on her door.

"Come in." The voice beckoning me through the door was thin, almost inaudible. I'd picked up some medicine, food, blankets and juice on my way. I set my packages down on the front stoop and cracked the door open to peek in. The room was dark, and wafting from the slightly open door were the rancid reminders of last week's Chinese food and dirty laundry. I could barely see as I said, "Hello. Nevaeh?"

Then I saw her there. On the couch. Nevaeh's body curled up under a filthy blanket—a tiny bird alone in an abandoned nest. I came closer and saw how beautiful she was as her long dark hair flowed over her neck and chest like a mermaid's. I didn't know what to do with the groceries in my hands—where to put the basket of clean clothes and towels I'd brought this sick young lady. The floor was covered with unwashed laundry, household items, used food wrappers and containers and other debris I couldn't identify.

"I brought you some juice," I said as I tiptoed past Nevaeh and forged my way through the piles of clutter and into the kitchen.

Several boxes of cereal and their contents were strewn all over the countertops as if people walked through and poured some into their mouths whenever. No point in putting them away or cleaning up the mess. An unidentifiable slime filled the kitchen sink, its odor like pond scum in a marsh. Just finding a clean glass for juice was like foraging for treasure. I picked up one that wasn't stuck to the counter and rinsed it out. I filled it with orange juice and moved toward the refrigerator to put the container there. But it was crammed full of inedible leftovers that were brown and green or spotted with mold, spoiled milk, and, really, God only knows what. I shut it and took the glass to Nevaeh where she lay on the couch.

The stench of stale cigarette smoke and body odor that permeated the cushions of the couch drifted toward me as the young woman rearranged herself in a sitting position in order to drink the orange juice. While she sipped it, I brought over a basket I'd left by the door and showed her its contents. My Bible study group put it together: toiletries, wash cloths, some clothes and warm socks and a Christian devotional book. I'd thrown in a clean new purple blanket that I'd found on sale in December. Somehow, I don't know, I felt purple was Nevaeh's color. "I love this!" she exclaimed as she threw off the ratty coverings of her couch bed and drew the blanket over herself. "This is my favorite color!"

"It's yours," I said. "To keep." No strings. No one exacting anything from her for the gift.

"I'm really embarrassed about the place," she said, wheezing the words so they sounded as if they were coming from the back side of an oscillating fan, pushed out by lungs too filled with fluid to keep much air. "I was on the streets. This friend of mine knew this guy, the one who lives here." Nevaeh blew her nose on the tissues I'd brought. "He has a kid. But he lets me pay rent...just a little...to stay here."

I had all kinds of questions, of course. Like, *What else do you give him besides rent?* Her cough was so deep it shook her body. I thought she had pneumonia. "Have you been to a doctor for that cough?" I asked.

"No," she managed over the rumbling noise that was her breathing.

"Well, we have to get you to one," I said. "And I can get you a place to live."

"I have a boyfriend." Nevaeh's eyes narrowed on me. It was a question, really.

"We aren't set up to house couples, Nevaeh," I said. "Does he live here, too?"

"No," she said as she lowered her eyes, "he's in jail."

Beulah's Place doesn't take couples. It's too distracting. The young people who come to us are already so broken, so damaged by the trajectory of their young lives that we want to focus on each one individually without the drama that comes with relationships formed out of mutual need. "I can help you in every way, Nevaeh, but I can't get you lodging if you intend to bring your boyfriend along when he's out of jail."

"Okay." Used to fending for herself. Used to going it alone. The word came out on the stream of a sigh.

"But, I will help you get well!" I said, changing the direction of the conversation. "I can help with a job, with transportation, and with your finishing school, if you haven't yet." I wasn't sure she'd live that long. She might have weighed ninety pounds. The dark circles under her eyes and her labored breathing worried me. "I'll be back tomorrow. In the meantime, are you going to be all right here with this guy?"

"Yeah, I think so," she said hesitantly. "It's just that…"

"Yes?"

"It's…well, he's been walking around here naked the past few days." Nevaeh searched my face for a reaction. "He even does it around his four-year-old daughter."

"Well, that's not good," I said, understating my fears. "Has he asked you for favors?"

"No," she said, "but it wouldn't surprise me."

"Okay, you need to get out of here, and I need to get you to a doctor." I hugged her and left, promising to return the next day. I heard the scuffling of a rat in the walls on my way out the door.

While I drove home, I mused at the distorted picture I'd just seen. The beautiful young woman, fragile in her illness, doesn't know what she's worth. Doesn't know who she is. Stuck in a stagnant hell hole while waiting on a boyfriend of dubious origins to come to the rescue. No handsome prince riding on a snow-white steed. Maybe because Nevaeh doesn't know she could be a princess. *God help her. You are her best hope.*

Chapter Sixteen

NEVAEH—THE IRONY OF ESCAPE

The woman who gave birth to me in Albuquerque, New Mexico, was a schizo-druggie. She and my dad weren't married. He left her before he knew about there even being a "me." It was just the woman and me until I was two-and-a-half years old. That's when she shoved car keys up into my private parts in order to rid me of my demons. When Child Protective Services found me, I was covered with new and old cigarette burns, bruised up and obviously violated. I was put into foster care—the only white kid in the family—while they tried to contact my father. It took a year before the man came and got me. He didn't believe I was his. He'd told CPS: "That woman slept with several other guys. I'll need a paternity test. I doubt she's my kid." I was. His kid, that is.

Dad came all the way from Fredericksburg, Virginia, to get me. Took me home and showed me to his wife and her two sons. It was all smiles...until Dad left for work the next day. The woman put me outside in the back yard. Had her sons bring me lunch. Didn't let me in until my dad got home from work. He was in the car business. I guess he was pretty good at it. But he was gone a lot. My life to that point had been such a disaster I didn't know I was being particularly mistreated. It wasn't until my stepmom started beating me that I realized how sick she was.

Shawna was a tall blonde woman, thin in a wasted sort of way—shriveled, hollow-cheeked and unhappy. And her eyes weren't right.

It's like you looked into them and saw nothing. A Stepford wife—some scary version of a mom. Shawna's sons could do no wrong. She coddled them, stroking their heads or patting their cheeks, fawning over them like they were pets or something. I knew early on that I was in her way. Dropped into her little world in order to wreak havoc on the family. The first time I crossed her, I'd only been living with them for a few weeks. She found a toy I'd left out. I was in the bathtub when she came rushing in with a hair brush and beat my little naked body with the bristles and the hard plastic handle. I was terrified, screaming into a void with no rescuer in sight. When the woman was done beating me, she washed off the blood, towel dried me and pretended it had never happened. My pajamas covered the welts. I didn't tell Dad. I wasn't used to being believed, anyway. And I thought he might blame me.

Over the next few months, Dad understood at least to some extent that his wife was abusing me. They had a few fights about it, but I was still too young to recall much of what went on. Then one day I went to find Shawna in her bedroom. The hair clip she'd used to pull my hair out of my face had broken. I had the pieces of it in my hand.

"What the hell happened here?" she screamed with such ferocity you'd think I'd murdered one of her sons. "Why did you break this clip? Were you trying to pull it out of your hair?" Shawna was in my face, hers red and sweaty in front of mine, hot rollers dangling like skewered white sausages from her head. I didn't understand her anger and tried to move away. She grabbed me then. Shook my shoulders until I thought I'd break in two.

"I'm asking you a question, you little snot! How did you break this clip?" Then she slapped me hard across the face. And the sting of it made my eyes water.

"I…I don't know." Tears streamed down my face. Not because I was sad or angry, but because I was scared to death.

There was an open window in her bedroom. The breeze made the cotton curtain fill up then suck out like it was snoring. The woman was dragging me toward it, so I made my body go limp and my shoes scraped the floor as she pulled me along. I realized in a horrifying second she was going to throw me out from two stories up. Her high-pitched hollering made her eyes bug out, and random hair that had escaped the rollers was flying in greasy wisps around her face as she lifted me up with her sweaty hands in my armpits and pitched me forward out the window. I landed on a hedge of boxwoods or I'd have probably died. I looked up to see her leaning over the window sill. Sorry, I'm sure, that I was still in one piece.

Dad didn't leave Shawna because of how she treated me, though. He left because she was crazy. Tried to kill herself with pills. Her kids weren't his kids. He didn't need the drama in his life, so it became him and me. We moved into an apartment for a while. I loved him. I was Daddy's little girl. I rocked preschool. He was proud of me. It was heaven until he met Stella. Not that she was a bad thing for him. It's just that it changed the dynamics for us. At least she didn't come with two kids she adored. We moved into her house and settled down.

The first time Dad hit me I was maybe five. It was a stupid reason, too, which shows how unpredictable angry people can be. I'd found some pants in my drawer that didn't match the top I was wearing. I wore them around the house thinking I'd done a pretty good job of getting dressed. Dad hated them. It felt like he hated me *in them* when he picked me up and threw me down on the couch. He was choking me and yelling, "Take those things off now!"

Stella stood there for a minute watching then turned and left the room. It would be her habit whenever Dad raged and hurt me. To leave, that is. And I never knew when his fits of rage were coming. Sometimes we would go for weeks without an incident and I'd think he'd never hit me again. I was always wrong.

When I was six, we moved to Salem, Oregon, to be closer to Stella's family. I was enrolled in the first grade there though I test-ed well enough to start second grade. Dad and Stella thought I was too immature for second grade, and they didn't like the idea of my being with older kids.

Dad became the service manager for a car company in Redmond, so we moved there soon after. He was well liked in the community. He's a tall man, over six feet, and slim. Skinny, really. He keeps his brown hair neatly combed and sprayed down so it doesn't move all day, wears lots of men's cologne, and smiles at the customers and coos at their babies. No one knew what went on at our house. And no one would believe it.

One day in the restroom at school, while hiding in the toilet stall, I started crying. Dad had freaked out the night before and beat me. I never knew when he was going to blow up over something I did. It always felt like it was my fault, but I honestly didn't think I was that bad. Then he would be so nice for a while that I'd hope. The cycle was crushing, even for a six-year-old.

"What's wrong?" Another little girl had ventured into the restroom. "What's wrong? Why are you crying?" Then her face appeared from beneath the door, her curly blond pig tails falling like corn silk onto the dirty tile floor.

I put my face in my hands, stifling my sobs, and tried to control myself. "Are you okay?" she asked.

"Yes," I said as I got up from the toilet and released the lock on the stall door. But I couldn't stop crying as the little girl touched my shoulder and put her face close to mine. She really wanted to help me. I could see it in her crystal blue eyes as they watered up, tears waiting on the rims to cascade down onto her cheeks. No one ever asked me what was wrong. No one really cared. "My dad hits me."

The little girl wasn't expecting that. "He does?" Incredulous. She brushed the tears from her own cheeks. "Why?"

"I don't know." I really didn't. Except that there was something hideously wrong with me. I wasn't beyond believing that could be true.

"Doesn't your mommy stop him?" She said this with such fervor that I knew she'd never been hit.

"I don't have a mommy." *Stella. That's all.*

It seems the little girl went home and told her mommy. Her mommy told the principal. The principal called Stella, who told Dad. Dad said, "Tell the principal you lied." So I did.

It was like someone put a hand over my mouth. There was no one I could escape to when Dad became violent. No one I could trust. Both Stella and I were accustomed to being hit when Dad was in a mood. And, like I said, he knew everyone in town because of his position at the car company. Big schmoozer. Starched shirt. Plastered down hair. Who knew?

Stella and Dad went out to dinner one night, leaving me to fend for myself when I was ten or so. Around eight in the evening, I turned the water on in the tub then went back to my room for a few minutes to finish watching a television program. The thing is, I forgot I'd turned the water on until it was overflowing onto the bathroom floor. I panicked. Pulled the plug, gathered every towel I could find, and still didn't have all the water swabbed up when I heard the key inserted into the front door. *They were home already!* Quickly, I got the hair dryer out and turned it on full blast, hoping the hot air would lap up the water that was left on the slick linoleum. The bathroom door was open when Dad came strolling in. "What the hell happened in here?" He was taking in the scene: sopping wet towels, water standing on the floor and me looking stupid, trying to air dry the mess with a towel around me. Before I knew what happened, Dad jerked the dryer from my hands and began beating me with it. "How stupid are you?" he screamed. I could smell the dinner still on his breath. The wine, too. He pulled my hair when I tried to get away. It seemed to take forever for him to stop. I covered my face with my arms so he beat my back and legs. "Finish cleaning this up!" he hissed as he finally dropped the hair dryer and walked out of the bathroom, his fury spent, now just tired. "I'm going to bed."

I would hide the marks when I could. When I couldn't, I stayed home. Like the time Dad came in really drunk. It was pretty late on a week night. I'd had some ice cream. Left the container out on the granite counter top. I forgot it. Fell asleep upstairs in my room while the ice cream made a sticky mess in the kitchen. "What the hell?" Dad yelled, waking me up. "What *the hell?*"

I heard him stomping up the stairs sounding like thunder heading for my room. "Nevaeh!" My stomach was tied in knots. Awakened too quickly. I didn't know what I'd done. "Did you leave the ice cream out?" My door banged open. I could smell the alcohol before he switched on the light, making me squint and cover my eyes. "I *said*, Did you leave the ice cream out? Answer me!"

"I don't know…" I was already tearing up. I knew what was coming. His fist was in my face before I could defend myself. He pulled me out of bed and onto the floor where he pounded my body so mercilessly that I kicked myself free and ran. Somehow, and I don't remember to this day how, I found myself downstairs by the front door. He was chasing me. I was so scared, I peed all over the marble entryway floor. He stopped then. But I was so badly beaten Stella guided me back upstairs and put me to bed. She brought bags of frozen mixed vegetables and piled them on my mutilated face, trying to keep the swelling down. I didn't go to school for three weeks…until the bruising was mostly gone. Stella helped me put makeup on to cover the greening skin around my eyes and nose. Dad never said he was sorry. Maybe he didn't know that every time he beat my body, he also broke my heart. Maybe he didn't care. I don't know.

I remember going to a slumber party when I was twelve and telling the kids there that my dad beat me. They called me a liar. Like I would make that stuff up. So I began running away. At first it was to the houses of friends of mine. A safe distance from home. I'd stay overnight if they'd let me and go home after Dad was gone the next day.

One night my parents sent Officer Claire Hendrickson over to the house I was staying in. "You're coming with me," she said, trying to force me to go with her as she grabbed my arm.

"No!" I pulled away. "I'm not going home! Dad beats me up!"

"Well, you can't stay here," said the officer. "Get your stuff. I'll take you to The Loft."

My friend's parents looked confused. Didn't try to stop me. So, I went to The Loft where all the runaways and throwaways crash. Stella came and got me. But I didn't stay home because the more I fought against the abuse the more it escalated. I'd rather be on the streets and take my chances than to live at home knowing beatings were a sure thing. That's how I came to be at a friend's house the next time I met up with Officer Hendrickson. My friend's mom saw the bruises on my neck from Dad's latest chokehold. She called the police when I told her how I got them. Enter Officer Hendrickson.

"Oh, does it hurt? You want me to call an am-bu-lance?" Officer Hendrickson asked, taunting me—sarcasm dripping from her chapped lips and her dull gray eyes narrowing in accusation.

My friend's mom was flabbergasted. She pulled me to herself, drew my hair from around the nape of my neck, and pointing to the bruising there, made Claire Hendrickson look. "Do you not see the marks on her neck?" Like, *Are you blind?*

"I don't see anything," Officer Claire Hendrickson said, off-handedly, shaking her head as if to say my friend's mom was blind. We all stood there looking at her, dumbfounded, until she finally ended the awkward silence. "Look, Ma'am, if I take this girl home, she's just going to run away again." And that was the point all along. I was a waste of her time.

"I'm not asking you to take her home. I'm telling you someone needs to do something about what's happening to her *at* home!" My friend's mom nearly yelled this, the incredulity she no doubt felt making the decibel level of her voice arc and her cheeks brighten in blotched circles as she stared a hole through the cocky officer.

In the end, I was taken to the Becky Johnson Center, which offers family counseling. I talked to someone there then I was taken to school, where Stella picked me up. Of course, Dad told me to say I lied. That was the standard response. The same principal who accepted the excuse that I'd lied when I was in first grade was the same principal when I was in sixth, so he dismissed my stories as a ploy for attention when I was taken to his office the next day. My dad was a good old boy. Couldn't imagine him hurting his little girl like that. He blew me off.

No wonder I started smoking weed when I was thirteen. The person I was staying with at the time offered it to me. I was in and out of school by then. Running from my Dad. But, also running from myself. I know that now. It's just that everywhere I went, there I was. I started hitchhiking. Mostly to Portland or Eugene, at first. I'd meet drug users downtown in Portland and we'd get high. Then I'd spend the night under the Burnside Bridge. It's a huge drawbridge that spans the Willamette River. It's not just a homeless hangout, but lots of runaways end up there and sleep in groups. I never really felt unsafe. And someone always had weed. One night a homeless guy found some beer and was randomly handing it out to us. I took one. Drank it. Then threw up. There was blood in it, though. I'd noticed a nauseating ache in my belly from time to time, but dismissed it. Something was wrong. But I washed the worry away with another warm beer.

For the first year or so I was a runaway, I'd be caught and the police would bring me home, creating a rap sheet a mile long. I'd change my appearance with piercings and pink or green hair hoping to look different enough that the police would leave me alone. It rarely worked.

I actually tried to stay home and get my act together once. I did odd jobs to make a little money. I really wanted to learn to play guitar, and that motivated me to lay low and go to school. I bought a Fender Stratocaster with my own money. Though I went to school, I wasn't very interested in succeeding there. I was surviving. That's all. School smacked of a future I wasn't connected with. Today was all there was. So when Dad jerked my backpack off my back one afternoon after school and started pulling papers out of it, he came across a test I'd failed. And to make matters worse, I'd doodled on the back of it. Obviously I didn't give a rip about my grade—hadn't even tried. His punishment was to calmly walk over to my guitar and smash it to bits in front of me. *That'll teach you.*

I left the house that night and hitchhiked to California. I was fourteen. I'd met this hispanic guy on the streets in Bend a while back. I was smoking weed with some of the other homeless teens when he and his roommate approached me and asked me to give them a joint. Hector was his name. He wasn't homeless, but he knew he could get high if he hung around us. He and his roommate lived in Bend at the time, but he'd moved back to California. I had enough of a relationship with him that he gave me his phone number when he left, and we'd talked a couple of times. He knew about my dad and our situation and was sympathetic toward my plight. I got as far as the California border and called Hector to see if he would come get me…from Fresno. I had no idea what I was asking—how far it was. Just, "Will you come get me?" He did.

Hector lived with his sister and her little boy. They were part of a large, conservative Catholic family. He thought I was eighteen and just needed a place to stay, so he told his family that I was his girlfriend so that my bunking down there made sense to them. Because he was religious, he didn't try anything with me for a while. Then after about two weeks, he cornered me in the kitchen and grabbed me by the waist, pulling me into him so tightly I couldn't breathe. I was frightened as he kissed me and pulled at my clothing. "Stop!" I screamed. "What are you doing?"

"Aw, come on," he said, breathlessly. "You owe me." And he grabbed my arm as I struggled to get loose from his grasp.

"I don't owe you anything!" I yelled at the top of my voice. "Let go of me!"

I lunged away from him just as he lost his grip. I fell to the floor, scooted along it as fast as I could, and ran out the front door, leaving what few belongings I had at the house. I wandered aimlessly around Fresno late into the night and found myself on a deserted side street.

"Hey, honey, nice hair." I couldn't tell how old she was, the lady walking up to me. "You're out here kinda late, aren't you?" The teeth she still had were brown, making her half-smile look like a checker board. She could have been thirty or fifty. She had the eyes of an addict, dull like warn platinum. Bottomless and empty. "You got someplace to go?"

"No." I offered, though I felt a little uneasy telling her the truth.

"Come on with me," she said, gingerly touching my arm. As she did, I noticed her ragged fingernails, nicotine stained and dirty. "You can stay with me tonight. It's not safe for you out here."

The woman lived in a shed behind this house not far from downtown. It wasn't locked. I guess there wasn't much anyone would be interested in taking. As the woman opened the door, the smell of dirty sheets and rotting leftovers escaped into the night air. It was overly warm inside. California nights are cool, even in the prairies of Fresno. I was hoping she'd leave the door ajar to get breathable air inside, but she didn't. I was closed in with her for the night. I'd have to make the best of it. I didn't know where I'd sleep, though. The shed was one room consisting of a kitchenette and a couch. The toilet was behind a door in the area she called the kitchen. That was it. Barely...barely a liveable place. I slept on the couch. I don't know where she slept.

Very early in the morning, before sunrise, a guy came to her door delivering meth or crack to the woman. She put a condom on him and favored him for his efforts. I waited for it to be over. There wasn't someplace she could hide this from me, and she didn't even try.

Later in the morning, another guy came by and took us into town. Turns out he was a dealer who wanted the same thing from the woman the other guy did. Her drugs came with a price. While they were in one of the back rooms of his house exchanging favors, I was given some pills to take. Ecstasy, I think. I lobbed them into my mouth and swallowed them without water. For some reason, it didn't feel careless so much as dangerous—exciting. And, I was so uncomfortable with the weirdness of the place—the meth, the sex, the filth—I saw the drugs as an escape. The pills didn't waste me, though I waited for a high. It felt more like I'd just taken a dose of cold medicine, making me drowsy but still in control of myself.

When the two emerged from the back room looking glassy-eyed and somewhat disheveled, they headed for the front door. "C'mon," the woman said then waved me toward the door as she opened it. The sunlight streamed so brightly into the darkened room I thought maybe I'd died and was going toward "the light." But it wasn't heaven that awaited me. I got into the old sedan sitting out front, and as I was closing the door, my acquaintance asked, "Can we drop you off on the corner there?" pointing to an obvious place for pick-ups. I knew what they were asking me: Did I want to be pimped out? *No.*

Instead, I had them drop me off where the woman had found me. I wandered around the corner into the downtown area where other homeless teens were congregated, smoking pot and huddling together talking. When I joined them, they were talking about going to a place called the Rose Motel where this guy rented one of the rooms and was making money helping some dopers bag marijuana. They were also using the motel as a place to dispense it. We went to check it out, and a couple of us decided to stay and work there. I made a few bucks over the next couple of weeks, but the area was dangerous and I wasn't comfortable.

Though I was only fourteen, I told everyone at the Rose Motel I was much older. No one knew I was a minor, or if they did, they pretended I was telling the truth. I knew I had to get out of there one night when a group of us were waiting outside the motel for a ride to a party. A huge black Cadillac Escalade drove slowly by us, its chrome rims spinning and shining in the street lights, and loud music and the pounding of sub-woofers shaking the ground, making me feel like the car was about to blow up. We didn't think anything of it until the sight of a rifle pushed its way out of the passenger side window that was slowly and ominously gliding downward. The sound of it firing made us jump. One, two, maybe three shots. Then we heard the squeal of tires and saw the flash of taillights as the Escalade swerved down the street. There on the sidewalk was a man bleeding to death from gunshot wounds to his stomach. We were right there. Maybe ten feet away. And nobody...*nobody*...did anything to help him. Not even me.

For days, I couldn't stop thinking about the dead guy. Or the fact that we didn't treat him like he was human. We left him there like we'd leave a dead possum that had been run over. I wasn't quite sure what I'd become, but I was sure I didn't like it. I didn't know how to change myself, though. Going home never seemed to be the answer to anything. But at least I would have a safe place to sleep. I just didn't know how to get back to Dad. Someone suggested there was this guy named Omar who could help me. The man owned a chain of gas stations and was nice to runaways. A middle-aged, middle Eastern man with a nondescript past and present. I don't know if he was married or had kids...nothing really except when I got in touch with him, he took me to McDonalds for a burger, to Burlington Coat Factory for a coat and some shoes and when he dropped me off near the motel, Omar gave me one hundred dollars and his phone number. That was enough to get me through a week or so, but things turned really, really bad.

It's hard to talk about it even now, but after this one night, I knew I had to get home. I guess I'm lucky it only happened once since I spent so much time hitchhiking and walking the streets. I'd spent time with this guy who lived in a shed behind his friend's house, and he was having a few friends over to hang out, drink, smoke weed and listen to music. It was dark by the time I headed there alone. The shed he called home was at the end of a long alley way. I remember thinking how weird it was there weren't any stars in the sky...or any moon, that I remember. It was as dark as a black crayon as I moved along the alley. The funny thing is, I hadn't thought to be afraid. I'd been to this guy's place before. But this time, an arm came out of the blackness and grabbed me. Then a hand was over my mouth, pressed tightly against my lips to keep me from screaming, I'm sure. The man turned me around so that my back was to him and slammed me against his body. I could hear his labored breathing, smell his rancid breath and feel his full weight on top of me as he threw me to the ground, stripped off my underpants and held me down while he raped me. It was probably pretty quick, but it seemed to take forever. The attacker didn't say anything, and in the surreal darkness of the alley, I couldn't see him. I don't know who he was. Then he ran away and left me there. Like *we'd* left the guy who'd been shot. And no one came to help me, either. I got up quickly, terrified he'd come back, wiped the tears and smudged mascara from my face with the back of my hand, straightened my clothes, smoothed my hair, and careened in the pitch black toward the shed. I was unsteady, wobbly, feeling like a zombie wandering toward a vague sense of safety in an apocalypse. And no one was going to rescue me. My knees were bloody and my elbows scraped; I was shaking all over and in a daze. I was no longer a runaway. I'd wandered into a soulless jungle and been devoured.

I spent the night in the shed with my friend, but I was too shattered to sleep. Early the next morning, I called Omar. "Hi, it's me, Nevaeh," I began. "The girl you picked up the other night."

"Yes…yes, I remember you," Omar said nonchalantly.

"Well," I said, but didn't know exactly how much to tell him. "I…uh…I want to go back to Oregon."

"And you want me to help you." It sounded like he was gulping coffee while he spoke to me.

"Could you?" I was so desperate. I know he heard it in my voice.

"Meet me at five today at the food store near the Rose Motel, and we'll see what we can do." Matter of fact. No drama. Sounded very good-Samaritan-like.

"Okay. Thanks." And I took a deep breath. There was a little glimmer of hope that things might get better.

Omar tried to get me some identification, but since I was a fugitive and had been detained as a runaway, I used a fake name. Then he handed me off to another middle Eastern man who was supposed to take care of me or something. "You won't be able to call anyone or see anyone, do you understand?" asked the new man, Rafi, as he walked me to his late model Mercedes.

"Can I call my boyfriend, then?" I wanted to let the guy in the shed know I was okay…wanted to tell him good-bye. He'd been nice the night before. Sorry for me and all. "Could you take me to Target so I could see him for a minute?"

Rafi let me use his phone, gave me money and took me to Target where I met up with my friend. Rafi waited for me then took me to his house. It was small and under furnished. There was a stench I didn't recognize. Maybe gasoline…chemicals, anyway. I didn't question anything, though. Rafi wasn't like Omar. I didn't really trust him. I went to the bathroom, he showed me the bed and I slept for two days.

It was mid-afternoon when the sun peeking through the slats in the blinds woke me up. I felt drugged…groggy and disoriented.

I sat up in bed, trying to remember where I was and why I was there. I stumbled to the bathroom, splashed water on my face and dried it with a dirty towel. *I wonder where Rafi is?* I slowly opened the door and looked up the hallway toward the kitchen. I didn't hear anything. I slipped into the clothes I'd left on the floor of the bedroom and tiptoed down the hall to see if I could find the man. He was nowhere. I was alone. When I tried to use the land line to call my guy friend, the phone was dead. I felt trapped. And scared. Like I wanted to flee. When Rafi came home, I sort of freaked and called Omar.

"I don't want to be here anymore." I didn't sound as frantic as I felt, but Omar got the picture. I'm still not sure what his plans for me were, though I have a good idea. "Come get me, please."

Omar took me to a nice hotel. Checked me in and I thought he'd left. I really needed a bath, and the luxury of a tub with essential oils shampoo and conditioner and soap that smelled like lavender seemed heaven sent. It wasn't until I walked out of the bathroom naked to get my clothes that I noticed Omar had let himself into the room. "You'd make a great belly dancer," he said, eyeing me in a way that made my skin crawl. I didn't know what he was thinking or what he was about to do. I grabbed my clothes and put them in front of my body and went back to the bathroom to dress. I was hoping Omar would be gone when I came back out, but he wasn't.

"I will pick you up tomorrow," Omar said as he rose to leave. "Take you to the bus station." He stood looking at me for a minute like there was something else he wanted to say, then turned and left the room.

The next morning, I was on a Greyhound bus back to Redmond, relieved to be getting out of California, but wondering what I was going to do next. I really didn't plan to go home to Dad. I just wanted to be back on familiar ground. Hours later, the squealing of the brakes and the whining of the exhaust as the bus entered the station awakened me. I was back in Oregon.

Chapter Seventeen

ANDI—FINDING PRINCE CHARMING

It's what all we women want to know: we are beautiful, precious, loved unconditionally. It changes us. But abuse robs us of this knowledge. Defines us as someone else sees us through a distorted lens, smeared with the abuser's fingerprints. I had no real sense of self from my parents any more than Nevaeh did. If God hadn't met me on the sidewalk that day when I was five, I wouldn't be here now. I'd most certainly be someone other than His hand guided me to be. If I hadn't heard the beautiful lady say that Jesus loves all His children, I'd have believed for a lifetime that I'm not lovable. To walk out of the effects of abuse is a process. For me, it was possible to regain my equilibrium after Jeffrey left me because God didn't. Not that it wasn't a struggle. Not that I traipsed on into the rest of my life with aplomb. But God was always there—the thread that sewed me back together one stitch at a time.

I was still working at Eagle Crest Resorts the first two years after Jeffrey left. I had a roommate to help with my bills. I was busy, if not happy. I hadn't dated. I didn't really know how to keep from getting myself into the same mess I was in with Jeffrey, so I was safer keeping occupied with work, church and friends. But one night I agreed to meet up with my friend, Robin, at the golf course where she worked. I got there early and sat at the bar in the club house restaurant. I was playing with a drink when a man sat down beside me, ordered a cocktail then said to me, "I haven't seen you around here before." When I turned to look at him, I was shocked by the brightness of his eyes, aqua like the ocean, and unnerved by the way his sandy blond hair fell across his forehead. My heart did a little jig that surprised me.

"I *haven't* been here before, that's why," I said with a grin. "I'm waiting for a friend."

"Well, isn't she lucky," he said, then smiled. My God, his teeth were white!

Eric was his name. He played golf at that course often, when he came into town. Robin showed up pretty quickly, but not before I discovered Eric had been married before. Visited Redmond often. Before I left with Robin, Eric wanted to know if I'd see him next time he came into town. I pretended my little heart wasn't racing like mad and calmly said, "Sure." That was that.

But it wasn't. Eric did come back. We went out on several occasions. He thought I was funny and pretty. He made me laugh. I felt beautiful and vibrant with him. He's the first man who'd wanted to please me—to do the things I wanted to do. It felt really wonderful, I'm not going to lie.

One night he met me at the clubhouse after he'd been drinking. It should have been a red flag, but I was so attracted to him and so happy to be in his company I went with him to a nice restaurant in Bend where we had dinner and more drinks. Because he was too impaired to drive, Eric suggested we get a room in a local hotel and watch movies and hang out for the night. I knew in my head that he wanted more. Maybe I did, too, initially. But I decided to believe that we'd stay up and watch television. It was midnight before we checked in. I felt awkward. Didn't know exactly what to do once we were alone together. Eric took off his coat and drew me to himself, clearly thinking I was thinking what he was thinking. I pushed away. He tried again. I acquiesced a bit, but this wasn't what I wanted. I wanted to be loved. Forever. Not taken for one night.

"Andi," Eric said finally, understanding the rebuff. "I don't want to get married again."

I smoothed out my clothes. Tried to smile, but I knew what he was going to say next.

"You want happily forever after, Andi." His blue eyes went soft and his smile loosened.

He was right. So, when he fell asleep across the bed, I lay beside him and prayed. It seemed to me there were two angels, then, fluttering above my head. I could feel the brush of their wings as they hovered over me. And between them, a throne on which I knew Jesus was sitting. The angels wanted to lift me up out of the situation, but Jesus was looking at them like, *Wait and see what she'll do.*

I was conscious then of the need for me to make a decision about my life in terms of men. I'd made a huge mistake the first time. Chosen what I thought was best. I never wanted to do that again. "I choose You, Jesus. You choose the man for me," I breathed, then dozed off.

The next day, Eric left. I've never seen him again. But I'll never forget that he was the first man to help me understand my value. No pressure to please him. No taking advantage of me. He respected what I wanted. Thank you, Eric, wherever you are. But...I did feel wrong about having gone to the hotel with him. About putting myself in that position. I struggled with guilt as I drove home. Then I received three phone calls. On that particular day, God had a particular message for me.

"Hello, Andi," said Penny, an older lady who attended my church.

"Penny!" I said, surprised that she would be calling.

"You know, Andi, I've been thinking about you lately and I wanted to see how you're doing...and, I feel like you need to know that the Lord loves you. I think He wants me to tell you that today," she said.

Penny couldn't have known what had happened the night before. I thought the Lord was telling me that I was still on His

Christmas list. That He hadn't written me off. Though I'd dangled my feet in waters too deep for me, God cared about my life.

The second call was from a friend I'd not heard from in forever. Her message was the same. "God wants you to know He loves you."

Never in my life had I been given grace for my mistakes. This was new to me that God could offer His love on the day after I'd come so close to the edge. Growing up, I was punished for things I didn't even do, and more so for what I couldn't control. Who was this God Who could love me with such mercy?

The final call brought me to my knees. A good friend of mine from whom I hadn't heard in a long while called out of the blue to say, "God has just been pulling on my heart. I had to call you today to see if you're okay. I want you to know God loves you." Tears I couldn't control ran in little rivulets down my cheeks, dripping from my chin, washing me in humility. It was too much to understand that God would woo me in this way—love me for Andi, flawed and imperfect.

I went to a local jewelry store the next day and, for $19.95, bought myself a little gold wedding band. As I walked out the door, I put it on the ring finger of my left hand and promised God I wouldn't take it off until I met the man He had for me.

I kept the ring on until Ed gave me an engagement ring. Within a couple months of marrying him, I heard from a friend of mine named Angela. We'd met through business associates, but I'd lost track of her until I heard she was going through a messy divorce that was similar to my road with Jeffrey. I was so touched by her struggle that I felt impressed to go find the ring I'd worn for all those years until God sent me my prince. I'd put it back into the box it came in, so I packed the ring up and mailed it to Angela with a letter that read something like this:

Dear Angela,

I bought this ring after my divorce from Jeffrey as a way of promising God that I was His until He gave me to the man He wanted for me. I chose for myself the first time, and I've found out it's better to wait on God than to wish you had. I know God loves you so much. I understand that some of the things you are going through I've experienced, too. Since we both know what it's like to not wait for Him, I want to give you this ring. May you wear it until the right man comes along.

Love, Andi

Angela wore the ring until she met the man to whom she's been married for many years. She passed the ring on to another young woman who passed it on to others. It's been on the hands of at least six other women.

Even though I decided to wait on God, I did get a little antsy a couple of years down the line and found myself dating Dave, the George Hamilton of Central Oregon. Skanky isn't any prettier on a man than it is on a woman, but I thought of him as just a friend. We wound up one night going to see *The Thomas Crown Affair*. He wanted to take me on a real date. I knew the evening could change the dynamics of our friendship but risked it anyway. Some of the scenes from the movie were provocative and made me nervous. *Dave* made me nervous. I decided that night that dating this guy put me in a compromising position. I'd stuck my toe in the water, just barely, once again and was reminded of why I wore that gold ring on my finger.

I'd met a woman named Gemey from church and we'd become good friends, but life had gotten in the way. It had been a year or so since we'd spoken when she called the day after my date with Dave. "Andi, I've never done anything like this before, but I think

I've found the man for you. God's just put this on my heart. I'm
going to make a way for this to happen."

Oh, man. I was so done with men in our town. I couldn't believe she'd be able to deliver anything better than I'd already been
stuck with. "Okay. Let me think about it and I'll call you back."

Two months later I rang her up. "Who is this guy, anyway?"

"His name is Eddy, and he's a mason," Gemey said. "A really
nice guy."

"A mason?" I thought that meant he belonged to the lodge.

"A brick mason, Andi. He lays brick." Gemey chuckled. "He
doesn't belong to a masonic lodge, for crying out loud. He's kind
of a workaholic. The only thing, he's maybe forty-five or so. Never
been married. Would that bother you?"

I was thirty-seven. That didn't seem to be such a reach. "No. I
don't think so."

"Okay, then," said my friend. "Monday night. Labor Day. Can
you bring the cake and salad?"

"Sure, I'd be happy to."

I had a plan at eleven o'clock the night before the picnic. I was
going to the deli for a cake and I decided to make a salad from
scratch just in case I really liked this guy and wanted him to be impressed. When I got home, I spread all the salad fixings out before
me on the counter and began the process of chopping everything
up…only I sliced open the end of my finger in the process. Blood
spurted everywhere, ruining the salad and my good intentions. I
wrapped my finger in paper towels and waited for the bleeding to
stop. While I was waiting, the tips of all my other fingers on that
hand turned blackish, like they were blood deprived. I'd had some
medical issues with my heart over the past couple of years, so it
freaked me out. I called a friend.

"Are all the fingers on my hand supposed to turn black when
I cut one of them?" I asked. "I don't think that is supposed to
happen."

"What?" she was appalled. "I'll be right over."

That's how I found myself in the emergency room of the local hospital at midnight. Turns out it wasn't all that bad. But it took the bloom off the rose as far as meeting any erstwhile prince the next day. By the time I arrived at the party, all I wanted to do was throw down the steaks and get home to bed. I'd managed to create the salad and already had the cake, so I'd done the minimum I'd promised. I had a bandage that looked like a finger puppet of Casper, the ghost, on my left middle finger and couldn't do much with my hair and make-up with one hand out of service. *Just get it over with.* That's what I thought. I'd promised the cake and the salad, and I didn't want to disappoint my friend.

The first person I saw after Gemey greeted me was a large giggly woman who was hovering over her potato salad and talking about this guy who was coming to the party. She was obviously infatuated with him and had made her special dish because she just knew he'd love it. I sidled past her and set my salad on the table already loaded with sides and drinks. The barbeque grill billowed white smoke as the breeze hit the glowing charcoal embers. The party was about to get started. Only Eddy Buerger was bringing the steaks, and he was nowhere to be found. I sat down in the sunshine on an outdoor folding chair and talked with Gemey, my bandaged finger aloft and pounding with my every heartbeat. "He's not here, yet," she whispered. "He's bringing the steaks." *Oh, the late Eddy. Not a good sign.*

Meanwhile, the giddy woman, Mindy, with potato salad on her list of lures, was talking about how she thought this Eddy guy was the one for her. Mr. Right. He was the target of the enormous bowl of salad, or, his heart was—the way to a man being through his stomach and all. If that was the case, I'd just as well go home. My salad was minimal, just like my attitude.

When Eddy Buerger finally appeared, I was mildly impressed. But I have to say, he *was* handsome in a Patrick Swayze sort of way…okay, he was beautiful. But already attracted to Miss Potato Salad, to hear her talk. And, I've been more in the mood to flirt than I was that afternoon.

"Eddy," called Gemey to him, "come here. There's someone I'd like you to meet."

He strolled over with the steaks still in his hands. "Eddy, this is Andi, my friend I told you about."

"Hi," he said, smiling. Blue eyes twinkling. White teeth sparkling. Dark curly hair tousled about his forehead like some Greek god's. Made me think for a moment that I should've made potato salad, too. "I'd shake your hand, but…" and he looked down at the steaks. "I need to get these over to the grill." With that he walked away.

I wasn't much impressed. Apparently, neither was Eddy. Mr. Right strolled over to the men who'd grouped themselves around the grill, followed by the woman who'd peeled potatoes for want of him. "Are they an item?" I asked Gemey.

"Only in her mind," said Gemey, winking at me. "I don't think Eddy's really noticed her."

"Hi, Eddy," the woman cooed, putting her hand on his back and leaving it there a little too long.

"Oh, hi, Mindy," he said, smiling then turning back to the men.

She turned to glow on all of us. She'd connected. He'd said, "Hi." And there was a glitch in my gut. *Honey, he's just not that into you.* I think we all thought it. I looked down at my feet, uncomfortable with her naivety.

After dinner, the guys announced they were going shooting. Well, I hadn't given up my Labor Day to sit around the table with a bunch of women or do the dishes whilst the men walked down to the pasture to indulge in their ancient primal rituals of smoking, joking around and shooting stuff. "We're starting the game now," said Gemey to her husband. "Can't you do that later?"

He shrugged, looked at her like a kid who was about to disobey his mom, and walked out the door.

"So…you're going to bail on us to go shoot?" I called out to no one in particular—maybe a little too loudly and a might too bossy. I couldn't believe it! After all I'd been through, the men weren't even going to sit in the living room and play the game.

Eddy turned around as he trotted toward the back door with the others and looked back at me, like he was noticing me for the first time. "Gemey went through a lot of trouble to put this game together and you men need to stay," I said, sounding like the mother they were all disobeying.

Eddy stopped then, obviously making a decision based upon my smarty-pants demands. There was a look in his eyes I couldn't really read. I was hoping by then that he might just think I was spunky. Turns out the games were fun. He stayed and played then walked me out to the car when the party was over. I got into my gray Honda, and Eddy went over to the door of his red muscle car. But, he didn't get in. Instead he walked back over to me and hunched down to talk with me through my open driver's side window. For forty-five minutes. We couldn't talk enough. There was so much life to share… past, present and hopeful future. "Hey, you guys, it's eleven o'clock and we're turning the lights out," yelled John.

"Okay. Okay!" yelled Ed, waving his hand in the air as he stood to his feet.

"I guess I'd better go," I said with a chuckle.

"When can I see you again?" Eddy asked. "I want to take you to coffee."

I couldn't tell him in the moment that I was heading up north the next day to meet another man a friend had set me up with. "How about Saturday?" I asked. "That's my next free evening."

"It's a date!" Eddy said with that smile of his slathered across his tanned and shining face. "I'll call you!" And, of course, he did. My prince had arrived. I was no longer "pig," "stupid," "klutz," or "idiot." In true fairy tale fashion, the handsome one who rescued me called me "heart throb," "sweetheart," and "my dear princess," as he claimed to be "destitute without me." Never. Never in my life. Not even once had I been so loved, cared for and adored. It took a while for me to believe it as I pinched myself for months to be sure this lovely man wasn't just a dream.

***

The night after Jeffrey told me he was indeed divorcing me, I was alone in our condo at Eagle Crest Resort. The day had been another long one. I hadn't had much time to decompress and synthesize what was happening. But I felt as though someone had dropped a boulder into my stomach and I was weighed down by the heaviness of it with each step I took. I dug for the house key in my purse and wandered through the door, kicked off my shoes and threw myself onto the couch. When I looked around, the place seemed different, somehow. Like it was someone else's. Always before I could project Jeffrey into the kitchen or living room. That's his big chair over there. In the pantry are things he likes to eat. He'd lived there on and off in spectacular color that I had to erase, leaving the picture bland and uninteresting—and me alone in black and white. Although our marriage was an incongruous mess, the shame of it ending fell like a landslide on me that night, crushing me beneath its weight. It was all my fault. I wasn't good enough. And the rock in my stomach dislodged itself, forcing out a sob so loud it scared me. *What would I do? How would I live? What had I done? Would I ever love a man again?* No one at work knew my marriage had crumbled. I had no mother or father in whom I could confide. I was utterly and completely alone. It was just too much. The tears soaked my dress, bled out my heart, and poured in a seemingly endless stream of desperation.

I threw myself onto the floor and prayed. Always my only hope. Jesus, my only confidant. "Please don't leave me!" I yelled it through my sobbing. "Take my marriage! Take this house, my job, whatever You want!" I was throwing up my life, ridding myself of the baggage of it, handing it over. "Just don't leave me because then I'd die. There would be nothing!" I couldn't stop the wailing sorrow. It shook my body. But after a while, somewhere in the deepest part of me, a song was playing, like it was coming from an interior stereo, and the volume was being turned up ever so slightly as my body calmed to hear it. *Alleluia.* That was the song. It means praise Yahweh. It seemed counter intuitive to praise God as I lay there prostrate and spent. *Was I supposed to sing?* But the strains of the interior orchestra were calming me. "Please forgive me, God, for my failed marriage. I have confused my priorities. Made a mess of things." I took a deep quivering breath. "I've lost all respect for myself." Then I began to hum the song. It quieted me. A peace surrounded me that I can't explain. Like my God wrapped me into Himself, assuring me He loved me. There was joy then…the knowledge that Jesus totally accepted me, cared for me, sat and cried with me then held me tight. It changed me in an inexplicable way.

I slept soundly that night for the first time in years. Jesus gave me what I so desperately needed: His love. It would carry me through some very dark times and finally lead me to Eddy Buerger. I wasn't ready for a prince before Jesus was more important to me than anything else. Before my God showed me that I was so valuable to Him that He'd take care of me. I didn't need a man. I had a Father Who loved me and Who would never leave me alone. "Alleluia."

Chapter Eighteen

ANDI—THE ROCKY ROAD TO BEULAH'S PLACE

I checked in on Nevaeh the next day as I'd promised. When I arrived, she was already in the process of packing her things up, getting ready to move out. Her cough, however, was no better. She didn't have insurance coverage. Ed and I didn't have the funds to get her the Urgent Care help she needed as the costs for those services were prohibitive. Nevaeh found lodging with a forty-year-old divorced man who lived in a trailer park. Again, not ideal, but she'd lived under a tree, in a car, beneath a bridge and with many unsavory people and was accustomed to making snap decisions that she'd live to regret. Driving her, always, was the need to survive.

I took on the task of getting her well. I'd heard of City Care Clinic, which is a free clinic staffed with volunteer doctors and nurses, so I called. It was a week before we could get an appointment with them, but we had no choice. It was a forty-five-minute drive for me the day I went to Nevaeh's place at the trailer park on the outskirts of Bend to pick her up. Standing on the porch when I pulled up was a man whose thin body was slumped forward in a saggy u-shape. There was a cigarette hanging loosely from his lips, and the smoke from his puffing hung like dense fog around his head. The scruffy tan whiskers that flecked his chin and cheeks were in stark contrast to his over-long dark hair that was swept back from his face as if he'd used his hand to comb it. Faded tattoos decorated the man's arms, which dangled from his tattered blue t-shirt in flaccid repose.

I was hesitant to get out of the car, but I'd come to rescue a teen in need, after all. I mustered my courage and headed toward the porch. "Hi," I said with more cheerfulness than I felt. "Is Nevaeh here?"

"Yeah, she's in there," the man answered, pointing toward the busted screen door that hung loosely from its hinges.

"May I go in?" I asked, uncertain as to whether I really wanted to or not.

"Suit yourself," the man answered as the ashes fell like snowfall from the cigarette now attached to his lower lip.

The door banged closed behind me, signaling my entrance. Nevaeh was standing in the living room, coughing and wheezing. She looked dreadful. The days of waiting to go to the clinic added to the depth of the young woman's cough. She'd dropped a few more precious pounds, too, from her fragile frame. I was worried. And, I didn't trust the guy she'd moved in with. There was something creepy about him that I couldn't put a label on. The house, however, wasn't the hell hole the other had been, and Nevaeh had her own room, at least.

The clinic was only open one day a week, and our appointment was primarily to fill out the paperwork so that Nevaeh could be seen by the staff. I'd prayed all the way there that we could get a same-day appointment for her. I was so thankful when we were told a doctor could see her in two hours.

"You hungry?" I asked, rhetorically, really. Of course, she was.

"Yes," Nevaeh answered, "thanks."

"Then let's go to Walmart while we wait for your appointment." I was already on my way to the car with the keys in my hand as she padded behind me, looking a little lost. At the McDonalds inside the store, we both ordered something to eat and found a table pushed up against a wall in the crowded luncheon area. There was so much I still didn't know about Nevaeh. At eighteen, she already looked tired and used up. The youthful light that should have danced in her eyes was dimmed by cynicism. The beautiful long mane of dark hair was dull and in need of a good haircut, and her body was ravaged by her years on the street. *How did she get here?*

"So, Nevaeh," I began as we munched on our food, "tell me how you came to need us at Beulah's Place." It was non-threatening, my tone. Matter-of-fact.

"Well, my boyfriend went to jail, and my dad moved to Portland." Nevaeh reached into her sweater pocket for an old tissue and blew her nose.

"Why is your boyfriend in jail?" I asked as I picked up a French fry and dipped it into ketchup.

"For stealing guns from Dad," she replied while chewing her bite of hamburger. It was a nonchalant reply that seemed to assume this was all the information I needed.

"How did you meet your boyfriend?" I asked. By then I was disturbed that Nevaeh might be in some trouble herself.

"Well, when I first came back to Oregon from California, I wound up at a party. I'd just gotten off the Greyhound bus a guy named Omar in Fresno put me on, and I wandered around until I found this house where a friend of mine used to live. There was loud music and a crowd of people I didn't know, but I went inside anyway. Everyone was too drunk or too stoned to notice I'd come in, anyway. Then this really drunk girl freaked out—probably stoned on meth or something—ran outside and started screaming her head off. Some neighbor called the police. I was on my way outside with my suitcase in my hand when the police car pulled up. "Are you okay?" one of the cops asked.

"Yeah," I said. But I really wanted to get away from there. I was a runaway and I knew I'd show up in their system if they asked my name. Which, of course, they did. So, they put me in the back of the police car. Found out about my warrant. Eventually, a judge sent me to Oak Creek Correctional Facility." Nevaeh looked at me then. "Do you know about that place?"

"I do," I said. "How long were you there?"

"Nine months." Her eyes were trained on her Big Mac; her fingers were pushing her fries around in their paper holder. "That's where I met my boyfriend. He'd come in every once in a while to see his cousin."

It was making sense to me now. I was listening, wishing I could help her rewrite her story. Erase some of the pain that lined her face already. Oak Creek Youth Correctional Facility is an all female facility that combines behavioral therapy with eastern meditative principles. I knew they tried to integrate family back into the lives of young female offenders. "Was that helpful? The time at Oak Creek?"

"Yeah," she said, "I guess. They gave me dialectical behavioral therapy. It helped me, I think. Because, you know, I needed to stop making some pretty bad decisions, especially about drugs and always running away in hard situations."

"What made you start running away in the first place?" I asked.

"My Dad." Nevaeh took a deep breath that rattled in her chest. "He started beating me when I was a little kid, and no one believed me when I told them about it. I guess I just decided not to take it anymore."

"So…running away…did that make things better?" I leaned into her and put my hand on her arm, which radiated with the heat of her fever.

"No," she almost whispered. "But when I got out of Oak Creek, I wasn't about to go back home. I was put into foster care because I was only sixteen, but Dad wanted me to live with him again. I told the counselor about how my dad beat me. When the counselors went to the house to interview Dad, he told Stella to lie about the abuse. Stella was his wife then. She'd seen all the stuff Dad did to me over the years, but she always lied for him. He beat her, too. This time, the counselor didn't believe her. The court gave Dad six months of probation. And I was eventually sent to the Pathways

Program in Eugene. It's this transition program that's supposed to help people rethink their lives…in my case, my abuse…and my drug use."

"How long were you in Eugene, then?" I asked as I lifted my empty food tray and set it on the table beside us.

"A few months." Nevaeh brushed the crumbs from her mouth with her napkin and dropped it onto her tray. "Then Dad convinced me to come home. Said that he wouldn't hit me anymore. It was an okay time. I didn't do drugs for a while. But I was still involved with the guy I'd met. He still used—meth and pills. Peter was his name. He's still my boyfriend, by the way," she said, defensively, looking me straight in the eye.

"The one who's in jail?" I asked, trying not to sound as judgmental as I felt because I was beginning to love this young woman deeply.

"Yeah. He…uh…stole my dad's guns from the house. Dad pressed charges. Dad caught Peter with the guns, so there wasn't a way out for him. It scared Peter enough that he quit using for a couple of months before he was sentenced to prison. I stayed with Dad for a while longer. Stella and he were divorced by then. Dad was mad that she snitched on him, so it was just him and me. Then, a couple of weeks before my eighteenth birthday, Dad said he was moving to Portland. He'd always said the day I was old enough, he was moving away. He lives in Portland now, I think."

"And where is Peter?"

"He got out of prison after nine months. Got in touch with me and we moved in together. We found a room for rent on Craig's List and I got a job at McGrath's Fish House. It was good until November first when he dumped me for this rich blonde girl who's in his out-patient therapy group." Nevaeh sniffed and threw her head back, pretending tears weren't sparkling in her eyes.

"Do you hear from your Dad?" I asked.

"Every once in a while," she replied as she blinked back the tears and leaned forward with her elbows on the table. "He came through town recently and said he's moving to Texas."

"How did you find out about Beulah's Place, then?" I asked as I handed her a clean napkin from the table dispenser so she could dab the wetness from her eyes and blow her nose.

"I called Stella," Nevaeh replied as she crinkled the napkin in her hand then played with it as she continued. "When Dad left, I started talking to her. I mean…you know…she's the closest thing I have to a mom. They were married since I was a little kid." Nevaeh shrugged as she said this, as if apologizing for her weakness. "She couldn't take me in…didn't want me living with her. But when she saw an interview about you guys on KTVZ, she called me up and said I should check it out."

"I'm glad you did," I said as I patted her arm. "But can I ask you something?"

"Yeah."

"Is the boyfriend you are going to live with now, Peter?"

"Yeah, I'm thinking he'll be back. I got a better job after he left. He's coming around again." Nevaeh's head was tilted wistfully to the side as she looked at me with eyes that said something different than her hopeful words.

"Did you finish high school?" I asked, changing the subject on purpose.

"I got my GED right after I left Pathways. I want to get enough money saved so I can go to junior college. I have enough already to get started with a couple of classes." Nevaeh's face brightened then, and she shifted purposefully in her chair. "I want to study criminal justice."

"That's a great plan, Nevaeh," I said. "But let's get you well first!" And we rose to gather our lunch trays and head out of McDonald's.

Back at the clinic, the diagnosis was that Nevaeh had severe allergies and a respiratory issue that would require some pretty expensive drugs. The two of us worked our cell phones for an hour or so finding a pharmacy that would give her a discount. It took her a few weeks to get well enough that I could help her find a new job and a new place to live. It's the first truly stable life she's ever had. She's smart and capable, but the road isn't smooth. Abuse is a thing to live through and then live past.

Chapter Nineteen

ANDI—DEATH OF A REASONABLE FACSIMILE

Fathers. Nevaeh's story is a haunting reminder that fathers are important to daughters...that we need them. And if they have abused us, the road to healing the scars they leave is long and arduous. I was still married to Jeffrey the last time I saw Joe Sr. He was lying in a hospital bed with tubes careening from his fragile white arms as intravenous fluid flowed from the bag hung high above his bed. I hadn't even known he was ill. Aunt Ruth, Leanne's sister, called one afternoon.

"Hi, Andrea," she chirped. "This is Ruth."

"Oh, my gosh," I said, surprised to hear her voice. "How are you?"

"Good, good," she said. "Just wanted to give you some news... about your dad."

I thought my heart stopped. Joe Sr.? I actually had to catch my breath before I could respond to my aunt. It had been a long time since I'd even thought about the man, much less heard about him.

"Joe is in the hospital...Cedars, Leanne said," Ruth continued, filling in the silence with this latest news. "I thought you'd like to know. It's very serious. Heart and kidney failure."

"Oh," I said, lamely. My mind rushed toward some vague clarity—my heart, toward an appropriate emotional response. Wasn't there a well down in me somewhere that could generate a flow of compassion for the man who lay dying...the man Ruth called my father? I'd spent my life trying to get away from him and Leanne—trying to live after the molestation and beatings. Now I was invited to participate in what was likely his death.

"And your mom would probably like to hear from you." That was almost a question. Ruth knew. I'd told her years before about what went on at our house, or, at least, hinted strongly enough that she assumed much of the rest. She was aware that we kids didn't live a normal life with Leanne and Joe Sr. I hadn't been as fully aware at the time I confided in her about what had happened to me. My dissociative disorder masked that pain from me until my time in College Hospital. But Aunt Ruth knew enough. "I'll meet you there if you want to see her," Ruth continued, knowing I'd probably need a buffer for that encounter.

"Thank you." My mind was reeling with the thought of having to see *both* of them. "I'll have to think about it, but, again, thanks for calling."

After we ended the call, I stewed about the possibilities for the rest of the day. When Jeffrey arrived home that evening, I told him about Joe Sr. "Do you want to go?" he asked, as surprised as I by the news.

"I don't know. I think I need to sleep on it." My stomach was churning, stirred up by the ferocious encroachment of images I'd suppressed for years. Just the thought of Leanne and Joe Sr. made me queasy. "But I doubt it," I said as I wandered to the bedroom and lay across the bed on my tummy. "Dear God," I asked in cringing sincerity, "do I have to do this thing?"

The night brought fitful, intermittent sleep as the need to make this difficult decision barraged my thoughts with a hundred different scenarios, possibilities for closure or opportunities for even more collateral damage. I was very close to tears when I awoke the next morning, frustrated and unresolved.

"So," asked Jeffrey as he poured a cup of coffee for each of us when I wandered into the kitchen in my robe and slippers, "are we going to see your dad?"

"First things first," I sighed into the steamy cup and took a sip. "I need to call Leanne."

"Really?" Jeffrey knew we hadn't spoken in several years. "Well, that will be awkward at best."

"No kidding," I said as I picked up my coffee and padded over to the phone. "Wish me luck."

In the night as I prayed about the call and played the scene over and over in my mind, I thought hearing Leanne's voice would make me anxious—even somewhat scared. But in the moment, all I wanted was to get it over with. "Hello." Her voice was raspy and high-pitched, and she sounded as though she'd run to the phone to answer it—like she was out of breath.

"Hello." My own voice sounded thin and faraway. But I'd rehearsed this into my pillow in last night's darkness. "Hello," I repeated, "this is Andrea. I'm sorry to hear what has happened."

"Oh, my goodness, it's so good to hear from you!" shrieked Leanne as if I'd been the daughter of her heart for all these years and good fortune and a happy life were all that separated us from speaking sooner. *Psycho woman...* deep breath.

"I thought I might go see Joe Sr.," I said, hesitating to encourage her.

"He would absolutely love that!" she exclaimed. "Yes, your father would be so happy to have a visit from you." Her laugh tinkled like crystal when it's hit lightly with a silver spoon. Too light and thin to be real. I wasn't unfamiliar with the sound of it, which came from the mother who was ever so sweet and gentle—the personality saved for special occasions.

"Okay, then." The conversation was making me nervous. "Well, Jeffrey and I will visit him later today. Ruth told us where he is."

"Wonderful!" There was an awkward pause. I could hear Leanne's breathing and imagined her face against the receiver, eyes narrowed, almost daring me to go on.

"Okay." I cleared my throat. "Bye."

Whew!

Jeffrey heard the short conversation. "So, we *are* going to the hospital?"

"Yes," I answered. "When I was praying about it last night, it seemed like a small thing for God to ask me to do. He's done so much for me. So…yeah, we are going to go visit the man."

Joe Sr. was alone when we got to the hospital. He'd always seemed so big to me when I was growing up. After all, he had the power to humiliate and hurt me—a fearsome presence from which I was always trying somehow to flee. But there he was, deflated from his illness into a ghostly phantom of things past. His eyes were closed, his breathing shallow, pumping out of him in little puffs of acrid air. Joe Sr.'s hands lay white against his chest, the blue-green veins that patterned them plumped beneath the cellophane thinness of his skin. The dark hair that used to furl around the man's face in magnificent abandon was now thin and gray, protruding like porcupine quills from his crown. I'd come to visit the man who'd hurt me, but this was a facsimile of that father. I inhaled courage.

"May I ask who you are?" It was a nurse hovering near the door to Joe Sr.'s room. Her presence surprised me.

"His daughter." I replied, slightly annoyed.

"Oh," she replied, looking over the chart on this sick man's wall. "We don't have you on the list. We didn't know he *had* a daughter." The nurse didn't stop me from moving gingerly toward the bed where machines were whirring and beeping signals I didn't recognize. Before I moved so close that Joe Sr. could see me, I stopped and measured my response. In that moment, I changed places with this man. I had the power now. I could choose, so that when my body lightly touched the bed and my birth father opened his eyes to look into my face, I knew what I would say. What I wasn't prepared for was the sudden burst of tears from his eyes, for the feeble reach of his hand toward me, the clench of his fist holding onto me for dear life, for the depth of sorrow that comes with the end of a life ill spent.

"Don't try to talk to me," I said as I stood over him, looking down upon his grief. "You need to concentrate on whether you decide to stay here or go on to what's next…and don't worry about *her*…" It's what he and I called Leanne in order to declaw the woman. *Her.* Even she had no power over this situation.

The tears were unstoppable, forging a river from Joe Sr.'s face and onto his pillow as his emaciated chest quivered with stifled sobs. I wasn't feeling anything in particular. Not even pity. It was as though I'd been set down into this drama to say my lines. "Whichever way it goes with you, I forgive you." His body relaxed as he closed his eyes, rested from the emotion of it all, I suppose. I stayed a few more minutes then left.

Joe Sr. died the next day. Several massive heart attacks in a row took the Chicago boy wherever God saw fit. After Ruth contacted me, she called my brother, trying her best to get him to come to the funeral. Leanne was begging everyone to get Joe Jr. home. He adamantly refused. In the meantime, my brother called me from Northern California where he lived alone—no wife, no dog, no kids. Though he had a good job, Joe wanted nothing to do with anything that remotely smacked of family. I was surprised when I answered the phone and heard his voice on the other end of the line. I hadn't seen him for years, so I had a difficult time picturing his face as we spoke. At first there was just small talk. Then I told him about seeing Joe Sr. About his crying and clutching my hand. About Leanne's overly gracious telephone conversation with me the day I visited Joe Sr. at the hospital. I'm sure my brother rolled his eyes as I heard his mirthless chuckle. I felt understood by him and connected to my brother in a way I thought impossible. Our conversation was so natural that I ventured a deeper thought. "I'm sorry you hated me all those years, Joe."

"I never hated you." The words jolted me—choked out a little wad of shame. Something in my stomach settled. There was a minute when we didn't say anything—when we both dared to look back. "Dad deserved to die!" Joe repeated it. "He deserved to die, and I wish *she'd* die, too. I can't stand to be around her. She's always trying to touch me." He was breathing hard, worked up. Just the mere thought of Leanne sent him into a rage. "It was unnatural... the way she was with me!" My brother tried to compose himself. "I won't be coming to the funeral."

"I didn't expect you to," I answered. "I'm glad you didn't hate me, though."

"I didn't even *see* you for the first year of your life," Joe said. "Mom and Aunt Judy were always in your room. I wasn't allowed in there. I don't know what they were doing to you."

"But you can imagine," I said. For a sickening moment, my mind took us back there, my brother and me, to the glint of the butcher knife as it caught the kitchen light, hoisted in the air by the woman who birthed us—and once again we feared for our lives.

"I don't want to talk about it," Joe replied.

And there it was. A conversation about what really happened in the perfect little household. The secrets no one told. Joe Jr. acknowledged his abuse. "But, it's over. I'm done with them. Have been since I left for college back east. I've gone on with my life." And just like that, he put the horror movie that was our childhood into his back pocket and said, "Well, I've gotta go now."

Leanne was "terribly disappointed" that Joe Jr. wasn't coming to the funeral. That's what she said when Jeffrey and I went over the day after her husband's death with a casserole and a cake. She'd fixed up for the party, as others from the church she'd been going to dropped in with food and consolations. When we arrived, the pastor was there nibbling on cake and sipping fresh coffee. He looked at us like we were from outer space. "This is my daughter and her husband," chirped Leanne. It was clear the pastor had no idea she had children, much less the obviously successful and handsome couple standing in front of him. Before we could speak to the man, Leanne took us on a tour of her home. "Look what we've done to the house!" she exclaimed as she walked us through the living room. I had to keep remembering that her husband had just died. It was as if the world absorbed him into the greater cosmos without a whimper. It wasn't until Jeffrey and I were instructed to take out the trash an hour or so later that we understood just how limited Leanne was. There was barely room for the accumulated garbage from the day in the large trash cans that lined the stucco wall beside the garage doors. Stuffed to the brim, they overflowed with her husband's belongings. There was a shoe lying on the ground, solitary and soiled, lacking its partner...like she was. Somewhere in the depths of the aluminum barrel was its mate, smothered in dress pants, plaid shirts and underwear the man would never wear again. It seems Joe Sr. was as easily discarded as his clothing. Leanne was ready to move on to the funeral, where she would be center stage, munching pot luck fare and regaling anyone who would listen with stories of her suffering.

"Is your brother coming?" she asked when we sauntered back in from the garbage, her eyes glowing with that particular passion saved only for her son.

"No," I said. Nothing more.

We took her to the funeral home the next day to make arrangements for her husband's body. Jeffrey was patient and kind. I was simply being available. Doing what was next in a robotic daze.

At the funeral later in the week, Jeffrey sang, my mother sat stoically as if the love of her life lay in the casket at the grave site, and I was awash in the confusion of the moment. Though I didn't wish Joe Sr. dead, I didn't embrace his living, either. I wondered what it would be like to have actually loved and been loved by the man now asleep in death.

After the burial, I mingled with friends I hadn't seen in years. Many of them had been kind and decent to me, and I was proud to show off my husband and tell them of our mutual successes. There were years to catch up on with friends I'd lost track of. Jeffrey and I found ourselves at the center of a growing number of people interested in our lives. It lifted my spirits in a way it's hard to describe, except to say there was joy in it. I talked and laughed, reveling in the comradery.

The phone rang back at Leanne's house late in the day when we'd gathered there to eat the casseroles and pies people had been kind enough to bring. Relatives and a few friends were still lingering over coffee and dessert, so I answered.

"Hello, this is the American Transplant Foundation calling," said the thin-voiced woman on the other end.

"Yes?" I said, wondering *what the heck!*

"I'm calling to let you know that we have donated the organs of your father, but we have a question regarding the donation of his eyes."

I didn't hear anything else she said. *Oh, my God. Really? She couldn't just let the man rest in peace!* I know he had to sign his own donor card, but I was sickened by the idea that someone would have that man's heart, someone his skin, and someday I might look into his heartless beady eyes staring back at me from a different face! I needed air! I dropped the receiver before the woman could finish her courtesy call, and I ran outside as the coiled phone cord bounced like a bungee up and down. On the way out, my aunt caught my arm. "What happened?" she asked.

"She had him cut up and farmed him out to other people!" I nearly screamed it as I ran out to the front yard where all the men were gathered smoking. I don't smoke. But if I ever were to start, it would've been that very moment. I wanted to tell them, "Smoke one for me!" I was trying to make sense of the irony: Out of the goodness of Leanne's heart she was giving away *his* heart…and neither beat with any compassion for another living soul.

As I wandered around the yard, inhaling second-hand smoke and vaguely hearing the inane conversations the men were having, a growing emptiness welled up in me. Somewhere in all the drama a father lurked, and I was trying to find him. To feel something— grief or compassion. Something worthy of a death. Instead, my mind wandered back to my memories of the man who now lay in an everlasting satin-lined bed beneath the earth, and to the sum of my years in his home.

There was the night I realized Joe Sr. was ogling me. I was twelve and in my cotton nightgown. He was watching television and as I passed the screen, I realized I could see through my clothing in that light—the womanly form of my body, new to me. In the reflection was also my father's face noticing the same thing I was. I turned to see him leering at me. He knew I noticed his eyes on me. I didn't know why then, but it made me feel dirty. I was ashamed of my emerging figure—that I was wearing something that made him look at me that way.

There were also the years of over-kissing and over-hugging— lingering with his hands on my body, his lips on my face. There were nights when I would close my eyes against the touching about which I was to keep silent. "Don't tell your mother." The man's dewy breath warm against my ear. The insinuation I was somehow complicit in his midnight secret.

And, of course, there were the beatings, shameless and unnecessary, that left me cowering when Joe Sr. came near, my hands in front of my face to shield me from yet another pounding. Even if he reached for me affectionately, I'd flinch. I could never trust his intentions.

As I grew older, Joe Sr. would say things like, "You need to lose weight in your butt," or "You sure fill out that dress nicely." Things daddies don't say to their daughter. Fathers shouldn't have eyes that dance with lust. Daddies shouldn't make their girls feel shame.

Because Leanne championed their son, Joe Sr. used me as his ploy. It would be us against *her*. That's what we called Leanne—*her*. It was a game with them. Leanne pawing and perverting—Joe Sr. making me the object of his overt affection. My brother and I, pawns in a chess game that no one ever won.

When I was in College Hospital for therapy to work through the effects of those years of abuse, I put my parents on the DO NOT ALLOW list. However, as we progressed in counseling, Dr. Dean, my psychologist, thought it might be helpful to speak with my father, as he kept coming up in my sessions. Besides, Joe Sr. wanted to know "what was going on over there" with Andrea and the psychiatrist. I'm sure he was wondering what awful things I was saying about the family. He walked in Dr. Dean's office as Chicago Joe and took a seat.

"So," he said, "my daughter had a breakdown." A statement made with absolutely no knowledge of why I was there. A judgment, of course.

"No," said Dr. Dean. "Andrea is here to better understand things that have happened in her life that have brought her to a place where she is courageous enough to work through them."

"I know what happened to her," Joe Sr. offered smugly, sitting back in his chair, crossing his legs.

"And what is that?" the doctor asked, already beginning to understand this less than winsome father.

"*I Never Promised You a Rose Garden.*" And the man tapped the arms of the leather chair with his hands for emphasis as a supercilious smile smeared itself across his face...like he'd just correctly answered the million-dollar question on *Who Wants to be a Millionaire?*

"Pardon me," said Dr. Dean. "Do you mean the book?"

"Yes. Yes, the book," Joe Sr. answered. "She read it. Andrea. And it made her think crazy stuff." He leaned forward into the doctor's face. "That's what did it to her."

"Meaning what?" Dr. Dean was, by then, fascinated by his ignorance.

"Meaning she had expectations after that...and the girl in the book, I think she was crazy, too." A matter of fact. Those who read *I Never Promised You a Rose Garden* will become mad like the girl, Deborah Blau, a schizophrenic who'd created a make-believe world. It's essentially a book about the child's mental illness. I don't remember reading it, but I certainly know I didn't *catch* a mental illness from reading a novel.

"So, there weren't things in her childhood that might have affected her more than reading a novel?" Dr. Dean, who *had* read the book, knew Deborah's horrific experiences as a child were very much a part of the story.

"Well, I think she should have had more sex." Joe Sr. shrugged his shoulders as he said this. Like it made perfect sense. "With a lot of different guys."

"Excuse me?" Dr. Dean was taken aback by the surprising arrogance associated with such a ridiculous assertion.

"Yeah. She should've had sex with a bunch of different men. Her mother was too protective of her." My father's fix for me was sexual promiscuity. It was certainly good for him. Who couldn't see that?

The doctor needed to hear no more. By the time Chicago Joe arose from the tufted leather chair on which he sat, Dr. Dean was thoroughly exasperated and even more understanding of my life.

And this was the man for whom I was to find a place of mourning. A way to grieve. Like many of the young women who come my way these days, I was searching in vain for a daddy who simply didn't exist.

For a few months after Joe Sr.'s death, I tried to normalize my relationship with Leanne, hoping as adults we might be better able to communicate with each other. I would call and check in on her, or drop by for a short visit. Nothing too intimate—just casual connections to test the waters. I thought we were making progress—slow, but it was endurable. That all ended with a phone call from Joe Jr.

"Have you heard from Leanne?" he asked.

"No, not for a month or so," I said, curious, as the familiar knot tightened in my stomach. I couldn't imagine Joe, my brother who never called to chit chat, would be phoning me up with good news.

"Well, she's been saying really ugly things. She's been lying to everyone about you." Joe Jr. sounded tired. Like Sisyphus, who rolled the same ball up the same hill only to always watch it roll back down again. Sick of the same old thing.

"What would she lie about? What have I done now?" *Sheesh!*

"She said you were on drugs at the funeral." He let it sit there.

"What?" *Honestly, where could she have possibly gotten that?*

"Yeah, she said you were laughing and talking and too happy after Joe Sr. was buried. Inappropriate behavior at the funeral, I guess." Joe sighed.

"I just talked to some old friends! Good grief!" My head was spinning. "I can't even enjoy being with people I've not seen for ages?" I stifled an angry scream. The woman wasn't weeping and wailing, either! All Joe Sr.'s clothes were in the trash the afternoon he died, and *I* wasn't sad enough when we lowered the man into the ground!

"You know how she is, Andrea. I just thought you should know." And that was it. He said good-bye and we hung up the phone.

I sat there in a daze. I had so much on my plate. A marriage that was beginning to fall apart. A job that required a sixty-hour work week. A broken heart and a tired body. I'd spent thirty years of my life being kicked like a can down the street by a woman who clearly despised me. It was then I remembered a few years back when she needed surgery and scheduled it on my birthday, knowing that Jeffrey had already made reservations for dinner and had purchased tickets for us to see a play. We dropped by before the evening's activities out of sheer guilt. She was alone in the room, but awake and alert, reclined on the hospital bed, adorned in her blue hospital nightgown. Jeffrey and I looked at each other, sighed and strolled in.

"Oooohh, how *sweet* of you to come," Leanne cooed from her perch. She said the word *sweet* like it had fourteen *e*'s in it. I was already sorry we'd made the effort.

As we neared her, she reached out a hand. "You know, I was really hoping to die in surgery today so I could go home to heaven." She left out...*on your birthday, of course.*

I didn't know what to say. I'm sure Jeffrey ameliorated the quiet with some non-sequitur just to have said something. Leanne was hoping to die on my birthday so I could forever remember it as a day of mourning? Happy birthday to me.

"You know," she continued with a mawkish grin that seemed stapled to her face, "it's all good now, though. The nurses are just waiting for my bodily functions to normalize, and then I can go home."

It seemed in the case of Leanne, heaven could definitely wait, and it's not like I didn't understand why. We'd done our duty and shown up, so we wished her luck and left shaking our heads. *Who was this woman?*

I could never win. Leanne was incapable of relationship. Time after time, no matter how hard I tried, she and I arrived at the same uncomfortable and punishing impasse. After Joe Jr.'s call, I was done. I sat down at my desk after work that night and wrote the woman one final letter.

Dear Leanne,

Your son told me what you've been saying about me since the funeral, and I'd like to respond. First of all, if you're truly a Christian you would be rejoicing that your husband is in heaven. I don't know about your god, but mine is happy when His children come home. So I don't think my behavior at Joe Sr.'s funeral was at all inappropriate given what we are supposed to believe. Secondly, I have been trying since the funeral to have an honest relationship with you, but it doesn't appear that you are capable of having one with me. If that is the case, then we don't need to communicate anymore. If you choose to have an honest relationship where you can go through a period of time without lying, manipulating or causing hardship, then great. Otherwise, I wish you the best in life.

Andrea

And that was it. The last time I communicated with the woman.

Chapter Twenty

ANDI—ELIJAH

We were eating dinner together one night in my apartment in the weeks before our wedding, and Ed asked, "How do you feel about having kids?" The fork he held with his thumb and index finger was suspended over his plate of food. "Because I think I'm a little old for that now, and I know I'm probably being selfish."

"You know, I've never really felt my biological clock ticking away…and, no I don't think you're being selfish. I think you're being realistic," I said, smiling. "I've never really had a strong desire to have kids. Maybe because my own childhood was anything but pleasant."

"You wouldn't feel like you'd missed out on something?" Ed asked, his eyes searching mine, flickering blue sincerity.

"You know, Ed, if they come along, that's great, but I'm not going to feel like I'm not a real woman or that I'm not accomplished if I never have children," I said as I patted his shoulder. "Besides," I continued while I moved the chicken on my plate around with a fork, "since I was nineteen I've always wanted to help other kids. Especially those who struggle like I did."

Then a strange thing happened in February of 2005. My clothes began to shrink, my mood began to swing and my body felt like it was betraying me on every level. I didn't think too much about it as I planned for a business trip I was to take. I hadn't mentioned these changes to Ed. The fact that I might be pregnant didn't occur to me. I was simply uncomfortable. Maybe too tired from my two jobs. I wasn't even aware that I'd missed my period…until it came late and was very painful. It vaguely reminded me of a miscarriage I'd had when I was married to Jeffrey, but I didn't put the two together. I was unnerved by the changes, though, enough to see my doctor before I left Redmond on my trip.

"Yes," my gynecologist said, "it does appear that you were pregnant and miscarried. I'd say you were about six weeks along." Then the doctor sat down on the stool in the examination room and took a more serious tone with me. "Andi, I'm not sure you can carry a child to term because of your health issues. And my concern is that if you do carry a baby for any length of time, and we run into the trouble I think we would, you'd want to save the baby, Ed would want to save you, and I'd probably end up losing both you *and* the baby."

Six weeks before, those words wouldn't have bothered me, because there was no baby that was the culmination of my love for Ed and his for me. But I'd just lost what now was the only hope of my seeing our child. An unexpected grief crept up on me and settled there.

I didn't talk about this with Ed until we were on our way home from the airport when I returned from my trip. There in the car, holding each other's hands, I told Ed about the miscarriage. He drove in silence for a while, lost in bewilderment and surprise. The thought on which I'd ruminated for days was new to him: there was a child, but now it's gone. It was one thing to talk of hypothetical children; it was another to lose one, however early on in the pregnancy. When Ed was finally ready to speak, we both recognized the magnitude of the loss. We grieved the loss of the home we thought before to be impossible. Let go of a dream we'd only caught as it trailed off into the distance, leaving us with a vague reality, empty arms, and lost hope.

I went through with a tubal ligation to prevent another pregnancy. Life picked up where it left off, but the baby was in the back of our minds. "It would have been kind of okay to have a little guy around," Ed mused one afternoon a few weeks after the miscarriage. I hadn't known he was thinking about it like I was.

"I know," I said. "I would have loved seeing you in him...or her." And that ache tugged at me again. Loss. I know I never saw our child, but our child was still within me for those few weeks. It changed my body, and it also changed my heart. I missed not having held the baby in my arms. I wondered how I could love someone so much—someone I'd never even seen.

On a late spring afternoon of that year, I climbed the stairs to my second-floor office where Ed was doing his paperwork on the computer. He looked so handsome sitting there. For a moment I wished again to see the likeness of him in our child—a fleeting thought that fell gently into my mind like a leaf floating down from an elm tree. It wasn't so tinged with grief this time.

I needed something from the bookshelf and turned toward it, scanning the books there. When I turned back toward Ed minutes later, there were three faces superimposed upon each other right next to his face. There was Leroy, then Ed, then a little boy with features the father and son shared. "His name is Elijah." I heard it so clearly in my thoughts.

"What's wrong?" asked Ed, wondering why I was standing transfixed looking at him but not looking at him at the same time.

"We would have had a son, and God named him Elijah. Eli." I know I must have said this as if I were in a trance, but it mesmerized me. "I just saw our son." I didn't really know how to explain it to Ed—the vision. But I knew as surely as I lived that the God Who'd sovereignly kept me in hope for all my life, was giving me reason to hope in that moment.

"What?" Ed asked as he rose slowly from the computer and looked intently at me.

"I just saw our baby's face...and you, and your dad. One on top of the other. And God said, 'His name is Elijah.'"

"So, it *was* a boy," said Ed, his voice winsome. I heard grief around the edges of it.

Ed and I looked up the story of Elijah in the Bible. We knew he'd been a great prophet, but both of us were intrigued by why God had chosen to name our little guy Elijah. I think it's because of how Elijah left Earth. He didn't die, but was taken up straight into heaven. Like our baby. "That would be our kid, babe," I said as I smiled from ear to ear. "He'd be just that good! So good that God would take him straight to heaven."

The vision was healing. Over the years we've talked about Eli and how he would have changed our lives. I doubt we would be helping the trafficked young adults we are now with a ten-year-old running around. Our lives would be focused on raising him—school, soccer, football, church and birthday parties. But I do believe our son is waiting for us in heaven. That when I go home to Jesus and He says, "Well done, Andi" that I'll see a little kid running toward me and hear his voice cry out, "That's my Mom!" I only hope that what I do in life is something that makes my son proud of me. In some strange way, I can almost hear him saying, "It's okay, Mom. I miss you, too. But those other kids really need you and Dad. I'll see you soon."

My brush with motherhood made the memories of my mother even more incongruous with reality. I even loved the *idea* of my precious Eli. Couldn't imagine hurting him or crushing his spirit with words I could never take back. Like many of the girls God sends our way at Beulah's Place, our mothers have set us on the path toward rehab facilities and homelessness. It can take a lifetime to get over our moms. I don't even know where mine is today. But I can point to the scars. And memories of her unreasonable and premeditated abuse crop up at strange times. Like when I see a child alone in a car.

Leanne often left us in the car when she ran errands. She would crack the windows about an inch, step out of the front seat, and turn to us as we slumped down into the cushiony safety of the back row seat. With her body draped across the front seat and her face as close to mine as possible, the woman would yell, "You stay in this car and don't get out because when I get home I'm going to beat the crap out of you! You just think about that!" I was in that car for as long as two hours sometimes. Praying to God she wouldn't beat me later on. A request not always granted.

Even a mother carrying a large purse can trigger a knot in the pit of my stomach. It seems I was in charge of Leanne's, but only if she forgot it. I remember a particular afternoon when we were living in Buena Park, California. I was ten and Joe Jr. was fourteen. He had a major asthma attack at home. Leanne called his specialist in Los Angeles and prepared to rush her son to the hospital there. For some reason, there was a friend of Leanne's, a nun, visiting her that afternoon; so, she encouraged her to ride along with us to the emergency room. Los Angeles traffic was bumper to bumper even back then in mid-afternoon, so the drive was long and boring. By the time the doctor saw Joe Jr. and the staff stabilized his breathing, it was very late in the day. We plodded to the car after the hospital discharged him and sank heavily into our seats, groaning at the thought of the long drive home in rush hour. When Leanne was settled into the front with the nun, she said, "It's so late and you've been so nice to go all this way with us, why don't you stay for dinner."

"Oh, that would be so nice," replied the nun as she put her hand to her mouth, hiding her smile. It made me wonder what was wrong with her teeth.

"I think we'll pick up some chicken on the way home, then," said Leanne as she pulled out from the parking lot and headed toward the 91 freeway. My stomach rumbled and I tried not to fidget in the back seat, but I was very hungry by the time we pulled into the parking lot of the Colonel Sanders in Buena Park. The intoxicating aroma of greasy chicken and salty French fries floated in a heavenly cloud through the open windows of our sedan as Leanne pulled up to the drive-thru window and ordered dinner. It seemed an eternity before the kid at the window handed down an enormous lard-stained bag, heavy and promising, down into the driver's side window, and Leanne reached down into the floorboard of the back seat and pawed for her purse. That's where is usually was. Always under my feet. But I hadn't thought to notice its absence. Leanne had forgotten it that day, clearly. In the rush to get to the hospital, in the commotion of taking her friend with us, she'd left her purse at home. As she groped for it, she continued her conversation with the nun. When she finally realized the purse wasn't there, she turned around and peered into the empty space. "Where's my purse?" she asked. Then she looked directly at me, her eyes burrowing into mine with the ferocity of a police dog that's just cornered it perp.

I didn't answer her. Instead, I pulled my legs up into myself and put my head down on my bended knees, hiding from the implicit accusation that I was somehow responsible for the missing purse.

"Here, let me pay," the nun suggested, further infuriating Leanne, who was too embarrassed to say no. Besides, the bag of dinner, steaming and aromatic, sat hunched in the front seat between the two women like an annoying child that must be tended.

"I'm so embarrassed," said Leanne to the nun as she watched the woman retrieve our dinner money from the small coin purse she carried tucked away in her habit. While she was counting out the change, Leanne turned in saccharin annoyance back to me. "Why didn't you get my purse when we left the house?" she asked, too sweetly. But her eyes said: "What's wrong with you?"

I wanted to answer, but dared not to. I was thinking: *I thought Joe Jr. was going to die. My mind wasn't on your purse. And I am only ten. Why was I responsible to help an adult remember her belongings?* But I put my head back down on my knees and endured the rest of the ride home, dreading what would happen when Leanne's friend left us alone with her again.

I barely ate my chicken, excused myself and escaped to my room while Leanne talked with the nun in the kitchen. Joe Jr. took his meal to his bedroom and closed the door. I knew when I heard the kitchen fall silent that I was in trouble. Leanne barged into my room and let me have it. I was a stupid pig, too dumb to remember anything important. All the stress and embarrassment of her day was poured out like a muddy dam, rolling over me in torrents of filthy language and unconscionable accusations. She used her words as the strap that time, and my heart was bleeding when she was done. I escaped the bruising and crying, but not the damage her words inflicted.

I was, and am, the child Leanne never wanted. I was a burden in utero. A thing to be borne, not embraced. When I think of how I loved even the thought that the beautiful union of Ed and me was creating a living person with some of him and some of me that we could marvel at and enjoy, I can't fathom hating the child. But, because of the grace of the God Who committed Himself to me as I sat on a curb in front of an obscure neighborhood in Southern California, afraid enough of the woman who was supposed to mother me that I wanted to die, I didn't become the bitter, angry and emotionally destroyed woman Leanne was. I should have. But I held onto the fragile thread of hope the God of that great big blue sky handed me when I was five years old. I knew He saw what went on in the miniscule world of our family—watched intently the abuse I experienced—and arranged my rescue. I never dreamed the hell that went on behind the closed doors of our house could ever be used for good—that there could ever be redemption or any restoration from the ash heap of our upbringing. But every time the phone rings at Beulah's Place and I hear the familiar voice of desperation on the other end of the line, I know why I made it out.

Chapter Twenty-one

ANDI—FINALLY, A MOTHER

After the death of Joe Sr. and the permanent break in communication with Leanne, I was an orphan physically, not just emotionally. Though I was never anchored to life by a stable, loving family, I still missed what I didn't have. When Jeffrey left, there was no one. Joe Jr. led his clandestine life under the radar. The loss left me with a gypsy heart, wandering bereft of earthly family connections.

I'd found a church in Redmond in the late nineties—Forest Avenue Baptist. It was there I began to grow spiritually—to understand that God is not just a booming voice of my childhood, speaking from the blue, blue sky. I found a Father in Him, one whose character never failed me, whose love was a constant, and upon whose guidance I could depend. There were times in those years when He was all I had…and I learned He is all I really need. I became anchored in Him in a way that those with close knit, loving families might not need or understand. But still…

I met Janet at church in the fall of 1998. She and her husband, Stan, had five daughters and lived in a three-bedroom house with only one bathroom. He was a hardworking landscaper; she, a stay-at-home mom who could make an amazing meal using only two ingredients when that's all she had in the cupboard. Janet was a bright, bubbly package of abundant love with an artist's soul. We had an immediate connection, not only because we looked alike, but because we had the same energy and interests. To our mutual delight, people were always asking us if we were sisters. I'd never had one. I loved the idea of it.

Janet had five siblings and a mother, Betty Jo, who'd lost her husband, Janet's father, to cancer not too long before I met Janet. Betty Jo was a seventy-year-old woman with a southern drawl and an open heart that made me fall in love with her. She was often at the house when I had dinner with Janet's family, bustling around in the kitchen, laughing and talking, her Southern drawl stretching out the words like they were made of taffy. Her joy was contagious; her hugs, addicting.

I was still working at the Eagle Crest Resort at the time, and often at the end of an exhausting day, I'd find myself at Janet's, my arms full of leftover food from one of the many events I managed there. The family and I would relax over a meal we didn't have to prepare and talk about everything. I got to know them well. I admired Janet for the way she kept her family together and happy. There were still two of her five daughters living at home—one was a child born with Down Syndrome, which was one of the reasons Janet wanted to make sure she was always available to her. As my extended family, Stan and Janet always vetted any new man that happened to come around, and Janet always wanted to fix my hair for the occasional first date. It was my time for big hair! Janet knew how to tease it up so that I was a couple inches taller than usual. I also learned to appreciate Stan's qualities: he saw hard work as honorable, paid his bills, adored his wife and kids and loved his God. I'd so rarely been around a functional family that being in their home was always mesmerizing to me.

It was at one of these family dinners that I told Janet about a thought I'd had that day—or maybe more like a daydream. We were sitting around the table before we cleared the dishes and I said, "Janet, I have this recurring daydream, or vision, that…well, that your mom…um… adopted me."

Janet laughed out loud, her hand over her mouth. "Oh, my," she said through her giggling, "I bet my mom would love that!"

And she slapped her hand down onto the cotton tablecloth for emphasis.

"Wouldn't that be cool?" I asked. "You'd be my sister."

At the time, it was only a vague hope of my damaged heart. We didn't ever talk about it again.

Then into Betty Jo's life walked Paul Beard, a charming widower with a penchant for adventure and a lonely heart. He swept Betty Jo off her feet with his charisma and attentiveness.

"Hey, Andi," said Janet when she called me one afternoon late. "Mom's met somebody."

"What?" I asked, shocked.

"Not only that…they're going to get married." Janet didn't say this as though she was thrilled at the prospect.

"No way!" I said. "Man, that happened really fast."

"I know." Janet took a deep breath. Then she announced, "Well, I'm going to make the cake and take care of the flowers. I want her to be happy."

"Let me help, then," I said. "Who is this man, anyway?" I realized I was feeling a twinge of jealousy about this person Betty Jo was so enamored of.

"Paul Beard," she said. "A widower with no children. Mid-seventies, maybe. He seems absolutely crazy about Mom. They're like two teenagers!" Another sigh. "I don't know. Let's hope it turns out okay."

I loved Paul the moment I saw him, from his clear, sparkling eyes to his tall lanky form. He was a gentleman—old school—but he had an edge, like he'd be up for just about anything. His dad had been an itinerant preacher in Alaska, so he'd grown up working hard and loving God. Paul embraced me as part of the family, and I was at their wedding working the cake and the flowers right alongside Janet when he and Betty Jo married in March of 1999.

In July of that year, I picked up the phone to hear Betty Jo's voice, a smile ringing in it. "Hi, Andi," she began. "How are you?"

"I'm doing great, Betty Jo," I said, though it wasn't necessarily the whole truth. "How are you...and how's Paul?"

"Wonderful. Just great," she said. "I wanted to call because Janet was talking to me a day or so ago and mentioned that you'd had a vision of being adopted." Betty Joe paused. "Paul and I would love to adopt you."

I was flabbergasted. I'd not talked with Janet about this since the evening at the dinner table months ago. I responded with a nervous laugh. *Oh, wow, what a healing thought.* My mind tried to take it in.

Betty Joe went on. "We don't have the money to do it, but Paul and I would be thrilled to be your parents!" She giggled at the whole idea of it. I'd be her seventh child—Paul's first and only. And a daughter at that! I'd be a real daddy's girl.

"Oh, Betty Jo, that would be so wonderful. And I wouldn't want you to have to pay for it. I'd take care of everything." I could hear my heart pounding in my ears. This was unbelievable.

"Well, Paul also wants you to know there won't be an inheritance. We won't have anything to leave you." Betty Jo sounded a little disappointed. I didn't want them to have any doubt about why I wanted to be their child. That the two of them even cared about leaving me money was more than I'd ever received from Joe Sr. and Leanne.

"I will have all I need because you love me," I said, my mind and heart still trying to conceive the joy that left me breathless and elated.

"Well, we do, honey. We surely do."

And a warm blanket seemed to wrap its folds around me and draw me in.

The next week, I met with a lawyer who also was a member of our church. I wasn't sure whether he'd think I'd lost my mind or not, but when I pulled up a chair in his office, he said, "Adult adoptions aren't as unusual as people think. We probably do two or three a month. There are many people out there who are disillusioned, disenfranchised and abused these days." The attorney shook his head like he didn't quite understand the world.

"I fit into all those categories, so I guess I'm a good candidate," I said, hoping to sound flippant, wanting to dissipate my nervousness. "But I'm not surprised by it. Not at all, really." And for a moment I saw Joe Sr. looking at my reflection that night in the television and Leanne's face in mine, screaming her profanities. "A lot of us have a new life to write in a new way...adopted into love to even understand what it looks like. This is a fresh start for me... something I need to do." I took a deep breath and asked, "What do we do from here?"

"You'll need to contact the newspaper in the town where your parents last lived in order to give them an opportunity to object. We'll do the same in the Redmond newspaper."

"It's just my birth mother. My birth father died. I'm sure no one would care, anyway," I said, confident I'd not be any more missed than I had been for the past several years. "Then what?"

"When the time period lapses with no objections, we will draw up the paperwork. There's a three-hundred-dollar fee. I'll change your original birth certificate to indicate the new parents. And that's it!"

Finally, my birth certificate would reflect other names, other lives, a different family tree. To eradicate the evil of my childhood and trade it for the heritage of a man and woman who loved God and me...it was transformative. I would be reborn on paper. The past altered in such a way I didn't have to be ashamed of my parents. I would have a new mother and a father.

Almost as an afterthought, the lawyer warned me, "You won't get any inheritance from your birth family. I just want to make sure you know what you are doing."

"I don't think the woman has anything, anyway, and if she does, I don't want it," I replied. It would feel like blood money to me, anyway.

"All right, then," he said, as he leaned forward in his big leather chair, "let's get started."

I met Ed in September. By December of 1999, I had a legitimate family for him to meet. My dad, Paul, my mom, Betty Jo, and my sister, Janet. And I had a birth certificate to prove it. There was a place to go for Sunday lunch. There was laughter and joy. Ed and Paul spent hours talking about how they were going to go to Alaska one day and build a boat together. I'd found parents who loved me, respected me, were proud of me and who adored my man. And I was my father's only child. Adopted by him in much the same way my heavenly Father did—rescued from my desolation to be precious and protected.

When Ed and I married in June of 2000, Betty Jo and Paul Beard were there as my bona fide parents. Dressed in his tuxedo, looking dapper and debonair, my dad walked me down the aisle. It's hard to describe how complete I felt, walking on the arm of my new father to be married to my man. A whole new chapter written in the book of grace that has become my life.

"Who gives this woman to this man?" asked the pastor.

"My heavenly Father," I answered.

"And her mother and I do," said Paul, squeezing my left hand as it looped around his arm. I will never forget the smile on my father's face as his eyes brimmed with tears and danced with pride. Like the stroke of a wizard's wand spreading stardust over my pain, gone in that magical glance were all the years of struggling to somehow find approval from the ones who brought me into this world. Gone was the sense that somehow I'd been at fault—somehow caused them to be the monsters they were. When Paul looked at me, his daughter, I finally understood that I deserved to be loved and cared for. And God saw to it that I was.

Chapter Twenty-two

ANDI—THINGS TURNING SOUTH

When Ed took me on our first date for coffee, he described to me in detail, room by room, the home he wanted someday. It would be set in the middle of a large plot of land—no other homes for acres in every direction. The kitchen would be large and inviting. The master would have picture windows that looked out onto the grassy fields and tall pine trees. And in the den there would be a huge fireplace and a bear skin rug on the hard wood floors. That would be home. I was all about the bear skin rug, but I'm a people person, so the acres and acres of nothing but shrubs wasn't that appealing to me.

Ed's dream came true in March of 2001, when we purchased a bankrupt property in Sisters, Oregon, and set about remodeling it. I worked as the senior publicist for an international publishing company at the time. Ed still had his masonry work. We were excited about using the home as a place for church youth groups to gather. Ed created a gorgeous fireplace (*sans* bear skin rug) and designed an enviable master bathroom. There was Italian marble tile in the entryway. The home was really coming along in 2006 when we decided to sell it and move closer to Redmond. By then, the publishing company had been sold, and I was running my own public relations firm out of the house, so it didn't matter where we lived. It took just ten days to sell the house, and we sold it high for the market at the time.

Ed wanted acreage this time, but he wanted it to be irrigated, as he said, "before he was too old to work it." We discovered that people were swooping up acreage in Oregon like it was the last chance on Earth to own land, so our quest became somewhat desperate. On Easter Sunday, after church, we were searching online and found a property that seemed too good to be true. The next day we had our realtor take us to see a ten-acre ranch in Redmond. The family selling the property owned a forty-acre plot and needed to sell this section, including the house, in order to resolve some of their financial difficulties. Of the ten acres, eight were irrigated—Ed's dream. The neighborhood was a far cry from the beautifully manicured ranches of Sisters, but this ranch was lush and green. The afternoon sun glinted off the peaks of Broken Top, Mount Bachelor, The Three Sisters, Mount Jefferson, and Mount Hood, which displayed their grandeur in plain sight through the west windows of the home. They looked like a huge painting framed and hung in the den for all to admire.

While Ed and the owner walked the entire corner acreage, I sat in a rocking chair in front of the west windows and enjoyed the view. Light poured into the home's many windows, warming the rooms with serenity. I knew this would be ours.

We made an offer and sunk three hundred twenty-five thousand dollars cash into the purchase. Reconnecting with our Redmond life was refreshing. Our neighbors became great friends and were expert ranchers. The rancher's wife helped me learn the ropes of country living without making me feel ignorant and incompetent. But we reached a point where Ed and I thought I should rejoin the corporate world so we could sustain our lifestyle and have health insurance. His masonry and construction firm was doing well, and we both knew how to work hard. It seemed like the right thing to do.

I became a trainer for a well-known cellular call center. It was close to the house and I've always enjoyed instructing adult learners. I had no idea the job would almost cost me my life.

2008 was a pivotal year for us. The downturn of the economy negatively affected the construction business, and Ed had monumental financial problems as a result. General contractors who owed us money were declaring bankruptcy. Ed already had materials and labor out, so we needed to cover the costs. Despite our best efforts to collect, the first two contractors refused to do anything except yell expletives at Ed. We used our meager savings to keep crews working through the cold winter months though that decision would cause Ed tremendous heartache down the road.

One particular government job put us $30,000 in the negative in December 2008. The project was in a rural location that prohibited the moving of crews back to town or delaying deadlines. Ed and his crew literally camped out there in the bitter cold and returned to town on the weekends. It was the only way Ed could keep people working and compensated for those dismal months. We always paid employees on time, but towards the end, our funds were low and the government checks were slowing.

One Sunday afternoon, we received a threatening call from the wife of one of Ed's crew members. "It's pay day and you'd better pay my husband right now! If you don't, I will make a call to the employment board on Monday morning!" *Unbelievable.* Ed was a mess.

"I'm going to get him some cash," Ed said as he reached for his coat off the rack by the front door. "I'm sick of the guys complaining about the cold and the job site. I'll go get the woman her money." As he opened the front door, he turned back to me. "You know, I helped get that guy off drugs. Gave him a job when no one else would." He shook his head. "You'd think of all the guys on the crew, it wouldn't be him demanding pay on a Sunday afternoon."

Ed went to three ATM's to pull cash and cash advances from our credit cards to pay the man's wife. The crew finished the project, but we paid dearly for our choice to do the right thing.

The crunch Ed was feeling with his business made my position as a corporate trainer more important to our finances. In the first eighteen months I worked there, however, there were three different general managers and three different training directors, not to mention numerous middle management changes. The stress level was over the roof. I could feel the heaviness in the building the second I walked in each day. I didn't know how much of a toll it took on me until one Friday afternoon when I began to feel strangely ill. I'd had heart issues in the past—diagnosed as having Paroxysmal Supra Ventricular Tachycardia (PSVT). The symptoms of the condition are anxiety, shortness of breath, racing heart palpitations, rapid pulse and chest tightness. I was somewhat accustomed to a racing heart given the workload at the call center. Although that morning I had a headache that wouldn't go away, I pushed on through the morning to get my team ready to go "on the floor" by Monday. I was supposed to take beta blockers for my heart condition, but they made me groggy with even the smallest dosage. It was impractical for me to use them when I had so much pressure at work, so I'd discontinued taking them. I was usually able to live over the complications of my throbbing heart.

As that Friday rushed forward, I skipped lunch and downed antacids and peppermints that didn't seem to help my growing indigestion. Growing more intense, also, was the pain in my back between my shoulder blades. Though there was pain down my left arm, it wasn't like I'd experienced it on other occasions. I passed a Christian co-worker in the hall and stopped her, asking her to pray for me. If I'd been more aware in the moment, I'd have been concerned about the worried way in which she looked at me. Later, she would tell me that she'd never seen anyone's skin look so gray before. I wish she'd told me then because I rushed on to complete another three hours with my class.

With no letup of the pain and palpitations, I approached the training director. "I need to go to the emergency room for an EEG," I said, trying to catch my breath against the dizzying PSVT. "I'm having heart issues that I can't seem to get under control." I hated the vulnerability my health issues created.

He took one concerned look at me and said, "Go, Andi. I'll take over here."

Once I was in the car, I began to think maybe I was taking myself too seriously. After all, several previous cardiac visits had proved to be uneventful. That always made me feel like the doctors might think that I was a hypochondriac. And, I was uncomfortable with the physical contact that was always a part of these visits. But I never went to the emergency room except when I was very concerned about my condition. An emergency room doctor told me in 2001 that I shouldn't take chances when these episodes arose. I was to head straight to the hospital. I thought about calling Ed, but I didn't want to stress him out. If it was bad enough to keep me overnight, I was sure the hospital would call him. He'd picked me up off the floor when I had V-tach episodes in the past, helped me to stabilize. I couldn't help but think what a simple life he'd had before I arrived on the scene. If I had to stay, I'd be all right once Ed got to me.

I started the engine and prayed. "God, please help nothing horrible to happen to me on the way to the hospital. Please don't let me pass out before I get to the parkway. I need to make it there, Lord."

Thankfully, I reached the exit and could see the hospital looming in the moonlight, lit up with little glowing squares on level after level—someone in each room; someone needing care. I panicked then. All I wanted was to be home with my husband. I gunned the engine and flew past the exit, sprinting home like a race horse that can see the finish line. If I was about to breathe my last breath, it would be in the arms of the man I love. My fear had taken my reason captive.

"Are you okay?" Ed asked as I stumbled through the door and headed toward the couch, stripping my coat off and throwing my shoes to the floor. Ed caught me as I fell and helped me to land on the couch where I stayed for the rest of the night, completely crashed from exhaustion. He kept a watchful eye on me, but let me sleep.

For two days, I barely moved. I wasn't hungry. My body felt like a wilted flower, too weak to keep its head up—like I'd had a bad flu. There was what seemed to be an elephant sitting on my chest, making it hard to take deep breaths, compressing my ribs.

"How do you feel," Ed asked on Sunday night. "You don't seem much better."

"Tired." I sighed. "Tired to my bones, in my heart. Very, very tired."

"Are you going to be okay if I go to work tomorrow, Andi?" Ed asked, his concern evident in the somber pitch of his voice.

"Yes. I'm sure I will," I said. "I just need to rest some more."

Ed had ten acres to manage and his business to run. I didn't want him to feel like he needed to worry about me with all that was stressing him. When he left for work on Monday, I called in sick at the call center. I was up, but disoriented and my mind was foggy. I knew where I was, of course, but nothing seemed to make sense. I couldn't taste anything, so I didn't eat. I wound up back on the couch for the day, lying still and breathing, one breath at a time. The call center director wanted me to go to work on Tuesday. "There's just too much to do, and, Andi, you know how short staffed we are." My company needed my body whether it was breathing or not. It made me so depressed that I slept most of Monday.

Tuesday I was back at work, shrugging off whatever had happened to me on Friday, mustering up what I needed to teach these adult learners, who, it turns out aren't much better than high schoolers when they smell weakness. I couldn't let on that I was sick. By midday, the class was ready to go live on the floor, taking actual calls. The students were nervous. Tensions, as expected, were high. Their stress seemed to leach from me the last bit of energy I had. I swayed with light-headedness, woozy and tottering. *Oh, no! I can't have another episode! There's no way they'll let me out of here again!* I caught the wall of the nearest cubicle and leaned against it in case I fainted. Maybe I'd slide down it instead of falling face first onto the hard linoleum floor.

"Andi, what's the matter?" It was one of the supervisors.

"Andi, your face is flushed. You don't look good." The woman lightly touched my forearm. "Should you be working at all?"

"No, probably not," I managed. A bead of sweat was finding its way down from my forehead, rolling across my cheek. "But we are understaffed. You know that as well as I do," I said as I tried to focus on the woman's face. I didn't understand the sweat because I was shivering. My body seemed to be at war with itself.

"I'm going to talk to the training director, Andi," the supervisor said as she patted my arm then began walking away. "He needs to know how sick you are." Over her shoulder she called back to me, "I'll see if he'll let me take over your shift."

Reluctantly, the director allowed the supervisor to cover for me. She returned and helped me around the cubicle. I was wobbly and uncertain as I picked up my things and left. I went home and slept for the next forty-eight hours.

On Thursday, I called a friend of mine who is an emergency room nurse and who understood my cardiac situation. She went ballistic on me. "That was probably more than just a bad episode," she nearly screamed. "Women have heart attacks differently than men. You had the classic symptoms, Andi. Pain and pressure in your chest, pain in your shoulder and down your left arm, shortness of breath, cold sweat, lightheadedness and nausea. Five minutes! That's all the time you're supposed to wait before you head to the emergency room! Five minutes! If you ever forget this advice, I will personally see to it that you are admitted for…for a psychiatric examination!"

She was afraid for me. I hadn't listened to my body. *Thank you, God, for sparing my life.* I sat trembling after our conversation. I'd bartered my life for corporate benefits. I'd ignored my body so I could get my work hours in. What good would that have done Ed if I'd lost my life as a result?

My cardiologist ran tests but found nothing significant after the episode—no heart damage. Again there was the prescription for beta blockers. Again, they made me too groggy to work or drive. I took them for a week or so, then placed them on the medicine cabinet shelf to expire.

Back to work again within a week of my heart episode, I labored under extreme fatigue. It was all I could do to get up in the morning, get to work, start my class, teach then finish my shift only to get home and collapse. I used every ounce of my energy to keep my job. I withdrew from most of my other activities so I had what it took to continue at the call center.

I was still struggling with my health in May. I just never recovered my energy. Fatigue would often wash over me making the mounting pressure at work even more stressful. I wanted to be able to support Ed in his business, manage our household as frugally as possible, and still keep my friends close and stay involved in church activities. It took its toll.

"Why don't you quit, Andi?" Ed asked when he came home late one evening to find me, once again, stretched out on the couch, my hand over my eyes. "I'm not sure this is worth it."

"I can't," I said. "What would we do? Besides, I just got that raise." I sat up and headed toward the kitchen where Ed and I got ready to make dinner together. I put my arms around his waist. "We'll be fine," I said, with more confidence than I felt.

"You don't seem fine," he said as he kissed my forehead. "But it's your decision."

I was sharing my problems with lethargy with a friend who suggested I read up on adrenal fatigue. As I pored over the information, I became hopeful…even happy. The symptoms described me perfectly. I called my friend's doctor, who was a naturopath. Testing showed I did indeed have not only adrenal fatigue, but many symptoms of other health issues that caused the doctor to put me on limited disability from work. For twelve weeks, I was to rest and take the natural treatments prescribed for me.

Nothing had really changed for the better when I returned to work three months later. In fact, the same old tension seeped from the building when I opened the door to go inside. I felt it like a cloud, climbing up from my ankles to my chest then covering me fully. The same dread that shrouded me before—the pressure that had laid me low before, beckoning me to the battle once again. I was greeted by a new training director, a woman for whom I had little respect. Her sense of entitlement made it difficult for her to be a team player. I'd made such great progress with my health in the past few weeks, I decided I wasn't about to throw that away just to please her.

By the time I returned home that night, my body was tensed up and my heart just not in it anymore.

"Ed," I ventured, "what would you think if I quit?"

"I'd think you were finally taking my advice." He smiled that smile. "It was pretty bad today, huh?"

"Yes. That familiar tension in the building. There's a new training director I'm pretty sure I can't work with without imploding. Maybe it's time for me to move on."

"I agree." Ed actually looked relieved for me.

Though I loved many aspects of the job, I gave notice the next day. My last two weeks passed quickly, and I looked forward to leaving like a kid looks forward to Disneyland. On my last day of work, as I walked past the security check point and out through the big glass doors, I left a world of weight behind me.

Chapter Twenty-three

ANDI—BEULAH'S PLACE

On a Friday night not too long after I left my job, I was a guest speaker at a women's fall retreat. I'd had dreams when I was little of speaking to large audiences. The experiences were so real they often awakened me. Back then it might have seemed absurd to others that I might be captivating an audience because my lisp was so pronounced that sometimes I couldn't be understood. In fact, one kid in elementary school assumed I was mentally handicapped because of my speech. He spat on me. And over the years, it was a place of shame in me. Leanne, of course, belittled me because I didn't "talk right." But there was always something in my young heart that made me stronger than the difficulty my speech impediment created—knowing that I could be better than those who made fun of me. And there I was, standing before a rapt audience, speaking of the very God Who had made me a conqueror.

In the audience that night was a woman named Kaitlin. I didn't know her before that evening, but I felt during my talk that God wanted to speak to her specifically. So, I looked in her direction to say, "God wants you to know He loves you and knows what you are going through."

As all the ladies were filing out at the end of the evening, Kaitlin touched my shoulder. "May I speak with you for a minute?" she asked.

"Of course," I said as I turned to look into her eyes, obviously red from crying.

"I came to this retreat tonight convinced that God didn't give a darn about me," she began while she retrieved a tissue from her purse. "I work in a lockdown facility for juveniles. It's often hell on earth there. I see some unspeakable things." Kaitlin dabbed at her eyes with the tissue and cleared her throat. "I know that the demons I've dealt with there have created a space for themselves in my own heart." She swallowed hard. I could tell it was a difficult confession. "Made me bitter…you know."

I put my hand on her shoulder, wanting to comfort her.

"But tonight, when you spoke to me…personally…to let me know God loves me," she continued as fresh tears streaked her face, "something broke in me. It's like *He* was speaking to me through you."

"He *was*," I said. "I didn't know those things. But He does. He knows what you need."

I took her hands in mine and we prayed together. Kaitlin wanted a firmer faith. One that soared over the purgatory in which she worked every day. She wanted to know God sees her and these kids…and that He actually cares about them. Knowing you are loved and watched over is a powerful impetus for life. That's the knowledge Kaitlin went home with that night.

The next day, Saturday, was hectic, but I didn't feel overly tired. I was still exhilarated from the night before. But when I awoke on Sunday, I could feel the toll the weekend had taken on me. I was exhausted, but I really wanted to get to church to see how Kaitlin was doing. Ed was already up; I could smell the coffee. I knew he was downstairs in his office. I climbed out of bed, slid into my robe, stepped into my slippers and headed for the stairway. I always hold the hand rail. I remember reaching for it as I put my right foot forward to step down. Then there was tumbling through what felt like a black hole…down, down, down. *I'm going to break my neck and die*—the sound of my own thoughts in the blackness of the plummet to the bottom of the stairs where I lay still. Out cold. Until I heard Ed screaming, "What happened? Andi, what happened?"

Our office was to the right of the stairs, and Ed had come careening out of it when he heard the noise of my fall. Later he told me that my eyes were rolled back in my head, and he didn't know what to think. "Andi?"

I heard him then. Opened my eyes, but I was dazed and confused. It took me a moment to realize I was lying on the stairway, my body folded in an awkward clump.

"Are you okay? Are you hurt?" Ed asked, panicked.

"I think so." *I can feel my arms and legs. I must be okay.*

Ed gently lifted me to an upright sitting position, then eased me to my feet. I felt dizzy—weak in the knees. Once on my feet, Ed helped me to the bathroom where I threw up. "Are you going to be okay?" asked Ed from the other side of the bathroom door.

"I think so," I managed, as I swathed my face with a cool washcloth.

Still feeling disoriented and not quite right, I managed to get to the kitchen and pour myself a cup of coffee thinking that would clear my head. As I became steadier, I walked back upstairs to get dressed for church. But my back was very stiff and as the morning progressed, I was more and more unwell. Even the music at church, which I always enjoy, made my head hurt. Another lady who'd been to the retreat the night before asked me, "What's wrong? Are you okay?"

"Not really," I answered. "I fell down the stairs this morning, and I'm kinda stiff."

"I bet you were pushed by the devil because he was so mad about what happened to Kaitlin last night!" she responded, not without irony.

And I thought, *Yeah. Maybe that's true.* To this day I don't know how I happened to find myself splattered on the stairway. That I was pushed seemed as good a reason as any.

We had been planning all week to go to Crater Lake for the night—had made reservations weeks before and put down a two-hundred-dollar deposit. I didn't want to ruin our plans by saying I didn't feel like going, so we packed the car and drove off into such a nightmare of a snowstorm that it took us much longer than it should have to get to the lake.

The lodge was lovely. It's nestled in Crater Lake National Park and overlooks a crystal blue lake and is surrounded by cliffs almost two thousand feet high. Built in 1915 and renovated in the 1990's, the huge stone and wood building usually has a rustic and inviting feel. But this night it was covered in snow, so the enormous stone fireplace in the lobby was a comforting sight as we rushed through the front doors and into the lobby for check-in. Ed was hungry and I was stiff and tired, so we left our suitcases on the floor of our room and went to the dining hall for dinner and a nice bottle of wine that I was hoping would ease my stiffness and relax me. After making small talk with a nice couple we met, I decided to go to our room. I left Ed playing checkers in the lodge lobby and went up to bed. My head felt as big as a watermelon...like it was swollen twice its size...and my eyes were bulging open. It was a very long night.

The next day, the pain increased. I couldn't get my arm up over my head to shower or dress myself. A knowing crept up on me. The sense that I had injured myself more severely than I first thought. Nausea and dizziness continued as we packed to leave around eleven that morning. Ed needed to stop to check on a job on the way, and by the time he was done I knew I couldn't go on with the pain another night.

"I think we need to get me to urgent care in Redmond, Ed," I said as we neared home.

"It's gotten that bad, huh?" Ed asked as he reached across the seat and put his hand on my knee.

"I'm afraid so," I winced.

The doctor who saw me at Urgent Care knew nothing substantial about closed head injuries. The doctor I'd seen once or twice before wasn't there. It made me nervous and unsure.

"Did you hit your head?" asked the doctor as he tried to maneuver my arm, sending crashing pain through my entire body.

"I don't know," I barely breathed through the pain.

"I'm concerned about your arm," he said. "I think you need to see your physician."

We left. I couldn't get in touch with my doctor until Tuesday, by which time I'd been injured for over two days without diagnosis. When my doctor saw me that day, he was concerned about my injuries, but not overly. He sent me for an x-ray to check for a broken rib. There was no broken rib. He suggested I might have a concussion and sent me home after he told me to call him if I was still having problems in a few weeks.

In the meantime, I was doing some very strange things at home. For instance, there was a calendar on the wall in the garage next to a treadmill we'd set up for exercising at home. Ed came in one afternoon about a week and a half after the accident and asked me about the things I'd been writing on the calendar. "What are you talking about?" I asked, nonplussed by his question.

"There are notes all over the calendar, Andi," said Ed, unable to hide the concern written all over his face.

"I don't remember writing anything," I answered, embarrassed, my face suddenly hot and my heart pounding. *Am I losing my mind?*

On some days, I couldn't tell Ed what I'd done all day. Not because I hadn't done anything, but because I simply couldn't put the day back together in pieces that made sense. There was one day when I came home with groceries and couldn't remember why I bought them. Water hitting my head in the shower caused pain. If I tried to sleep on my right side, the pressure of the pillow case made my head hurt.

When I showed up during the second week after my fall for physical therapy at the urging of my doctor, the therapist told me she couldn't work on my back because it was still too swollen. "Did you hit your head?" he asked.

"I must have," I responded, though I still couldn't put together everything that happened as I tumbled down the stairs.

"I suspect you broke your vertebrae, maybe T-5 or T-6" he said. "It's too swollen to tell for sure which one."

Because I still had so much trouble reaching over my head, I eventually asked a hairdresser friend of mine if she'd mind washing my hair. It's very thick and curly, so no one had noticed what she did when she began hitting it with the spray of water, exposing my scalp. "You have a huge black bruise on your head, Andi!" she said, obviously alarmed. "How did you get it?"

"I don't know…maybe from the fall I took." No wonder it hurt.

"I thought you must have known, and that's why you wanted me to do your hair," she said as she gently massaged in the herbal shampoo.

"No. No," I responded, "I didn't. But it makes sense."

That was the impetus, seven weeks after the accident, for my calling the neurosurgeon who'd done Ed's back surgery. He declared my brain to be normal organically, but did say that brain swell can cause some loss of function. He ordered an evaluation with a speech therapist which eventually showed that twenty-five percent of my brain—mostly the executive functions—had been impacted.

Still not feeling right, I went back to my doctor. "I didn't know you'd blacked out," he said as he held my chart in his hand. "Not sure how I missed that the first time." Putting my paper-work against his chest and looking at me compassionately, he went on. "I think it could be your heart, Andi. We need to get this checked now!"

Again, there was nothing new wrong with my heart. Still there were the symptoms—dizziness, loss of balance, nausea. When I finally had an appointment with a brain specialist, he diagnosed non-positional benign vertigo. I was given therapy to control it, and that helped some; but, my back pain and memory issues persisted, as did some of my speech pattern challenges. The bills piled up for us as my insurance had been canceled, and I had to forego therapy because we couldn't afford to continue it.

Miraculously, with the help of Disability Group in Los Angeles, I was able to file for disability insurance. I was told it could take years to receive it, but within five months I had disability pay and insurance to help us through the continuing ordeal and to help pay for the medications I needed to deal with continuing pain and to somewhat reimburse us for all the out of pocket expenses my health issues had accrued.

In the most incredible way, because God is never doing just one thing in our lives, the disability became the opportunity to envision Beulah's Place. Because I couldn't manage the grueling corporate schedule of a new position with a Fortune 500 company that opened up during this time, Ed and I were open to God when the opportunity came to think outside the box. To keep moving forward no matter what!

On Thanksgiving of 2008, when Ed and I participated in feeding hundreds of homeless in our local community, birthing Beulah's Place seemed to be the answer to why other doors had closed—so this one could open wide.

It would take us the next few years to see our dream transformed into reality. The thread of hope which pulled me along from the sidewalks of my childhood drew me into the real possibility of rescuing teens from the same kind of abuse I suffered. We reached out to Childhelp, USA, the group founded by Sara O'Meara, whose sanctuary I visited with Jeffrey. Mothers Against Sexual Abuse also partnered with us. By the year 2011, we had our 501c3 non-profit status approved in just eleven days! By 2012 our organization was registered in twelve states.

2013 was a defining year for us. We took on our first Central Oregon teen and acquired our first corporate sponsors: Walmart (Redmond), Dutch Brothers coffee, McDonalds (Redmond) and Les Schwab Tires. Walmart, McDonalds and a wonderful fish restaurant in Bend (McGraths's) have been crucial in job placement for our teens. Donations of food, clothing, toiletries, and transportation began coming in from individuals, churches and businesses throughout central Oregon. As time passed, we received grants from Ronald McDonald House charities in Bend, Umpqua Bank in Redmond, the Redmond Chamber of Commerce, Walmart (Redmond) and Les Schwab Tires in Redmond and many other private foundations. Host families were located. The dream was finally changing lives...one at a time.

Shayley was one of the first teens to come to us for help. I'd met her at a school function where I was invited to speak about Beulah's Place. She was there with another girl, listening to our mission to rescue homeless teens. Although she'd escaped a difficult situation and was then on her own, Shayley was more interested in helping us with other girls at first. When I stepped down from the podium at which I'd been perched, Shayley strode up to me, confident and absorbed in the thought of helping other trapped and desperate young men and women. "I'd like to help," she said with the sincerity of it playing in her large dark eyes. "I know what they are going through...these kids," she continued.

"Well, that's certainly something to talk about," I replied as I looked up into her face. Shayley is tall and strong, with thick dark shoulder-length hair. She's articulate and passionate about her convictions. "Why don't you tell me a little something about yourself?" I asked, searching for two empty folding chairs where we could relax and get to know each other.

"Sure," Shayley agreed and followed me to the edge of the auditorium where she told me why she was in Redmond living with the friend of a relative.

Chapter Twenty-four

SHAYLEY—MARCHING TO A DIFFERENT BEAT

I know I should probably start from the beginning with my story, but I much prefer taking it up where I am today: I am twenty-two, have my own place and am enrolled in school. I owe my new life to people like Andi and Ed, who sacrificed and gave to me when there was no real reason I could think of that they should care about someone like me. I was one of the first to be helped by Beulah's Place; housed, fed and encouraged by perfect strangers when my life fell apart. But there is another thing. And I would have told you it would never, ever happen to me.

This girl named Belinda was a friend of my cousin's. I met her because I was staying at my cousin's house and babysitting her kids after I left home a couple of months before I graduated high school in the spring of 2012. Though Belinda's a couple of years older than I am, we began spending time together, having fun, talking. She is the reason I found myself at the high school auditorium one night listening to this little red-headed lady talking about rescuing teens from abuse. Having been in need of rescue myself, the talk made me want to help in any way I could. Beulah's Place was the name of the woman's organization. Andi was the woman's name. I volunteered right then and there.

Belinda is also the reason I went to church. Believe me when I say, church was the very last place I thought I'd ever find myself. I grew up with Bible verses flung across the room from mouths that used them like bullets to the heart. No kidding. When my family and extended family got together and fought, they'd use their favorite passages from the Bible to condemn and ruin each other. My final evening at home, when my heart disengaged from my family completely, my relatives were drunk, screeching Bible at each other like curse words. They'd been drinking shots of tequila when the disagreement started. Not "drunk on the Spirit" as their Bibles commanded, but, well, just plain drunk.

Belinda came over to my cousin's house one Sunday night and said she was going to church.

"Alone?" I asked.

"Yeah," she said. "I don't have anyone to go with me."

I was sad she'd have to go by herself, but I surprised myself when I said, "I'll go with you, then."

"Really?" Belinda seemed really happy I offered.

"Yeah, but don't expect me to get into it or anything. Church is definitely *not* my thing." I was only being nice. That was all.

"That's okay," replied Belinda. "It didn't used to be my thing, either."

With that understanding, I accompanied my friend to the local Baptist church in Redmond, Oregon. I was unfamiliar with Baptists. Didn't know what they believed. Didn't understand altar calls and such. What I knew was that the armor I'd built around myself to effectively protect my life from religion was impenetrable and deliberate. It had absolutely nothing to offer me. I would never use the Bible for anything…much less to hurt someone else.

Belinda and I took a seat about halfway down the aisle of the big Baptist church. The ceilings must have been twenty feet high, the walls sparkling white against the scarlet carpet that ran down the aisles and underneath the pews as if a can of paint had been turned upside down, coating the floor with blood-stained significance. I'd never been in such a sanctuary where the crimson robes of the fifty-person choir rustled everyone into silence while the organ began to play a hymn I didn't recognize and the preacher strode up to the platform dressed in a dark gray suit with a red-flecked tie pouring out onto his chest between his lapels. It was all very grand, but I settled into the pew determined to daydream…or maybe nod off. I was there for my friend. Nothing else. But…

From the first song the Baptists sang, there was a strange tugging at me. I was irritated by it at first because it made me so uncomfortable. It felt like no matter how much I wanted to disengage in the church service, I was riveted to something in the atmosphere I couldn't put my finger on. I honestly couldn't tell anyone today what the sermon was about except the preacher was talking right to me. Like his words came from up front and floated out toward me and wrapped me in a comforting and protective cocoon. Warmed me in a way I'd never experienced. I tried to shake it off. Tried to remember all the times the Bible had been a threat. But the feelings kept getting stronger. My heart listened before my ears did. "Jesus loves you."

Love wasn't something I associated with religion. Religion is hard. It makes *people* hard. Religion tells people they are always right, even when it's clear they are wrong. In my life, the religious experiences I knew of were calculated to make a person proud in a way that is cruel…maybe even evil. I couldn't even think what it might mean that Jesus loves me. Or even knew who I was, for that matter. Or that He was even real. He was the hammer that kept my family in line. The justification for abuse. The ultimate rule-giver and judge.

But what if He does love me? Wouldn't that change everything? My heart beat with that thought the same way it would beat inside my chest if someone had just kissed me. Someone I loved, I mean. It melted me, dissolving my objections and making my arguments against it diffuse in a mist of awe. The service was winding down and the preacher was asking us to stand with him while the piano played softly. I stood. But it felt like I was in a daze. Standing without thought given to the action. Following some strange inner command.

"Jesus is here. Right now." The pastor was speaking in a low voice. Softly wooing.

Normally I wouldn't be wooed by this stuff.

"I ask you to come forward if you'd like to ask Jesus into your heart right now." The music was still playing as the pastor came down from the pulpit and stood at the front of the auditorium. "I'd like to pray with you." He looked out over the many people there and waited.

And this is what I said I'd *never* do. I could feel my face flush, and my heart pulsing like a drum in my throat. I was sensing a battle going on between my mind and my heart, a furious conversation over what my feet wanted to do. Almost out of body, I walked…no…I pretty much ran…to the front of the church, fell into the arms of the preacher, and found myself with my head buried against his chest. It was like I was watching myself do this. Like I was compelled in a way that was more than my mind, more than my heart. Pushed into Jesus as I cried and cried. Sobbed into the pastor's red-flecked tie all the pain I'd kept inside for all my life— vulnerable in a way that should have embarrassed me to death, but it didn't. The pastor held me like I think Jesus would, gave me the cologne scented handkerchief he kept in his coat pocket, and when I'd calmed down, blown my nose and stepped back to look at him, he said, "Would you like to ask Jesus into your heart right now?"

"Yes," I managed, still crying softly at the immense relief of emptying years of abuse onto his lapels which were damp and stained with my tears. "Yes, please."

"You can repeat after me if you like," he almost whispered. "Jesus, I know you died for me…"

"Jesus, I know you died for me…" I repeated.

"I ask you to forgive me of my sins…"

"I ask you to forgive me of my sins…" By then I knew there were many.

"Please come into my heart as my Lord and Savior," he finished.

"Please come into my heart as my Lord and Savior."

When I was done praying, there was a shift in me. I can't explain it to someone who's never experienced it except to say I'm different now. I'm a new me. I didn't get religion that night. I got *rid* of it. Knowing Jesus is not a religious experience to me. It's finding the love of God. That's a whole other thing.

It's hard to talk about how I grew up because I think it could make *God* look bad instead of my family. Everyone at home is very religious. My grandfather was even a pastor of a local congregation in the California town where I grew up. My mom's father. Maybe that's why she was so messed up. Why she escaped her kids rather than deal with my father. Passive-aggressive behavior is what I think my counselor called it. The upshot of it is that I was the one my father confided in and depended upon to run the household and take care of my four younger brothers from the time I was six years old.

I'm just now learning that we all think the way we grow up is normal. That other families must be like ours. The world from the eyes of a six-year-old is small, just her house, her yard, her school, her church, her room or her mom and dad. It takes more experience to know that the girl down the street might not be expected to balance a check book, bathe her brothers, listen endlessly to her father's work and home problems, but, instead, her most arduous task might be trying to stay between the lines in her *Beauty and the Beast* coloring book. I had no idea, at the time, that *I* was expected to take on the responsibilities of a wife and mother. It was my normal.

Mother had five children in seven years. Dad wanted them. That's what she told me before I left home for good. Dad wanted them, and she didn't. It was too much for her. In order to relieve the pressure, my mom became the neighborhood do-gooder. Always out and about at church or at the neighbors helping out. That might be commendable to some, but it's really not. In the name of God, Mom left us home to fend for ourselves. I was making family dinners from the time I could reach the stove. And Dad would come in from working as a diesel mechanic all day and talk to me about all the stuff he should've been telling Mom. Or complaining to me about Mom. All this when I, like other little girls my age, should've been coloring in a Disney book.

I don't remember a specific day when the beatings began. I really don't like to talk about it. Dad was so angry about his life. I guess that was it. Or angry with his kids. Or God. Who really knows? And we never knew when it was coming. It wasn't always connected to some bad thing we did or said. Dad would just come home in a mood. If Mom was home, she'd go off into another room when it started. No protection. I'm sure she didn't want to get in the way of his fists. But we couldn't run away when we were little.

On Sundays, the extended family would get together. Always there was Bible spouting and arguing about what the text meant. Generally, if we met at our house, there was talk about how dirty it was. Judgement. *Always*. It was the truth about our house, but I did the best I could. I carried responsibility they couldn't even imagine. And when the condemnation came, I always took it personally.

Abusive parents, I have learned, have great difficulty communicating with their children as the children become adults. Adolescents aren't as easily controlled. Children have ideas, plans, thoughts, hopes, dreams, and ambitions as they mature. Dad interpreted our need to express ourselves as disrespect, a lack of humility, as rebellion or sass. My brothers and I suffered blow after blow in Dad's effort to beat our lives back into submission to him and his God. It was what the Lord would want him to do so we didn't grow up into rebellious sons of guns.

I learned to drive when I was fifteen. Dad bought a car he fixed up for me, and I finally had a way of escape. However, he learned quickly that he could control my coming and going by parking his truck at an angle so I couldn't leave when he didn't want me to. I found ways to work around that, but it was costly.

As I neared my sixteenth birthday, he had a new tactic. I came in from school one afternoon and set my books down on the kitchen counter. My brothers had walked home and were in the den having a snack and watching television when Dad banged into the house through the back door. That was never a good sign, so the boys quickly turned off the TV and stood at attention around the sofa, hands behind their backs as if they were soldiers ready for inspection. I'd just reached for a soda from the fridge and was closing the door when Dad stomped in and slammed it shut for me.

"Don't you kids ever do any work around here?" he screamed. "You lazy butts!" I could smell beer on his breath. "Where's your mother?" He headed to the den before I could answer. I didn't know, anyway.

"What the hell are you doing slouching around in here like a bunch of dummies?" Dad screamed at my brothers.

"Dad," I interrupted as I ran in from the kitchen. "They just got home from school!"

He turned on me so fiercely, his eyes bloodshot and angry, I felt like prey, not his daughter. "I don't need you to tell me about my own sons!" he screamed. "I can see they were sitting around watching television instead of doing chores! You think I don't know what you kids do when I'm not here?" Dad moved closer and put his face in mine. "What makes you think you can talk to me that way?" He breathed in my face, nostrils flaring, like a bull in a bullfight.

I turned and began to walk away when Dad jerked my youngest brother by the arm and swung his body between us. Willy. He was only nine years old and scared to death as he hung there lifted off his feet by the grip of Dad's hand under his little arm. "None of you can disrespect me, do you understand?" This he yelled at me. Then to Willy, who was crying and hiding his face with his free hand, Dad screamed, "Are you listening to me? Do you hear what I'm saying?"

"Yes, sir," whimpered Willy right before Dad's fist landed solidly in his stomach.

"Ah…" choked Willy as he doubled over, screaming in pain.

Oddly, Dad looked at *me* then. And I knew what he was going to do next before his fist slammed once again into Willy's quivering body. As my brother recoiled once again in screaming pain, Dad slapped him hard across the face and threw him onto the sofa, where Willy writhed in pain while my other brothers stood helpless, motionless, petrified looking only at our father, fearing for their own safety. But Dad was looking at me. "Don't smart mouth me again, Shayley," he warned, his finger in my face, his breath coming hard as if he'd just run a marathon, the spit from his words landing in droplets of spite on my face.

Dad shifted his feet, straightened his t-shirt and walked out of the room like an admiral who'd won a war. The rest of us folded onto the couch to comfort our brother, who was doubled over in pain and overcome with shame. Willy moved toward my lap and put his head onto it, the tears dampening my jeans and breaking my heart. We all cried. Together. I could hardly stand it—watching Dad beat my brother. I would, with all my heart, rather take the beating than see him hurt. Of course, Dad knew that.

I spent nights crying myself to sleep because I felt I was somehow at fault for the black eyes and bruises inflicted on my brothers. It still gives me nightmares.

By this time, I was in charge of the household finances, too. I've always been good at math. It comes naturally to me. Dad was without work for a couple of years and we almost lost our house. I spent time on the internet looking for ways to save us from foreclosure. I put Mom and Dad on a budget. We eked out salvation. But I had by then become the mother and father to my mother and father…and to my brothers. I felt completely trapped. *What would my brothers do if I left?*

My grandfather had an affair about this time, too. It wasn't very well hidden. Some woman in the church. Mr. Religious-Never-Do-Anything-Wrong was a big fat sinner. My grandmother was so submissive…or maybe subservient is a better word… she denied the affair and allowed this woman to be a part of our family gatherings! I know! Really? Well, my mother reasoned, we couldn't prove her daddy was having an affair. Meaning, we hadn't seen him do it. Still his prideful, righteous self was at the center of our family gatherings where I endured listening to him judge us for everything under the sun in the name of God with that woman sitting on the sofa beside him.

For me, it was over on Easter of 2012 when the family was gathered to celebrate the religious holiday. Grandad's house has a large game room with a pool table and big screen television dominating the space. It was the favorite gathering place for us when we all got together. As usual, the meal was a potluck: fried chicken, ribs, baked potatoes, a couple different kinds of salad and cherry pie, Grandad's favorite. Our family walked in around noon, each of us carrying a dish covered in plastic wrap in our hands. There was already a commotion, and I felt my stomach seize up. I was hopeful, though, as I took my dish toward the kitchen, that the person I'd see standing there cutting the pies she'd lovingly made for her husband would be my grandmother. Alone. No blonde intruder mocking her forty-year marriage to my grandfather. My hopes were dashed, however, before I turned the corner from the hallway into the kitchen. I could smell the other woman's perfume wafting from her in currents so strong I'd swear she'd fallen into a vat of the stuff. The house literally reeked with it. Grandma was standing at the sink. The other woman's body was draped lazily against the refrigerator as she watched my grandmother slice pies, the knife in her hand shaking with a tension I thought I understood. I felt my face flush. I wanted to cry and lash out at the same time—sad and angry that this pathetic scene was playing out in my grandparents' home on Easter Sunday.

The girlfriend wasn't all that young. I didn't understand the attraction, really. She was maybe a little taller than my grandmother, but she wasn't thin and curvy. I'd call her plump. Her stomach arched out like she was a few months pregnant and the inch or so of dark hair sprouting out from her scalp was in stark contrast to the frizzy blonde hair that lay straight against her shoulders, like the blonde was a brazen afterthought. The woman's lipstick was too red, her heels too high and her neckline definitely too low. If Christians are supposed to look a certain way, I doubt she'd captured it. I set my dish down on the countertop without saying a word and went into the recreation room with the others.

We ate our lunch on trays around the pool table. The men commandeered the conversation, as usual, with talk about cars and sports. Stuff that I wasn't interested in at all. On one side of Grandpa was the woman and on the other, Grandma. I didn't eat much.

While we women cleared the TV trays and loaded the dishwasher, the men racked up the pool balls, and we could hear the clack of them as they hit each other or glided into the edge of the table. I was bored and felt lazy when we wandered back to the rec room as the dishwasher hummed and the younger boys ran around in the yard chasing a Frisbee. I turned on the television and lay across the forest green sofa in front of it. I dozed off for a little bit, but was awakened by the shrill, overly-condescending voice of the blonde. "I brought some tequila!" she bellowed. "Who wants a shot?"

I didn't even know what that was. A shot, I mean.

"I'll take one over here," my grandfather said with a strange look in his eye and a creepy half-smile.

I didn't think he drank.

"Anyone else?" she asked as she bent low to hand Grandpa his shot, and the sweetness of her perfume seemed to pour out of her dress along with her breasts.

"Sure," said my dad. "I'll take one."

"Then I'll take one, too!" I said, angry that all these non-drinkers were now knocking back tequila like they were in a bar or something.

No one objected. We all drank. Too much. And that was the beginning of the end for me. Even if I could remember what started the argument, it's not important. What happened was the last straw. Someone picked a fight. Grandpa took the bait and opened his pocket Bible to slay those who didn't agree with him. Everyone was shouting. Everyone was right. Everyone knew their verses—the ones they used to slice each other to pieces, accusing and justifying. Though this behavior was normal for us, that day was the first time I was able to actually stand apart and look at it.

"What are you doing?" I screamed it. "What are you doing, you guys?" I felt hysterical—filled with a grave and horrendous understanding that our family was a complete dysfunctional mess and I couldn't be a part of it for another second. The tequila had warmed my blood—made me brave. I had years of pain ripened and ready to reap. "I can't take another second of this...this...this mess! Our *Christian* family is sitting around drinking shots that Grandpa's *girlfriend* gave us while Grandma sits there like nothing's wrong!" I hadn't noticed the tears streaming down my face until then. I'd lost all composure—all sense of the right things to say. "And you use the Bible like it's a deer rifle. Like you want to kill each other with it!" My hands were clenched at my sides, curled into fists, and I was shaking, raging. "I can't take it anymore! I won't take it anymore!" *There.* I'd declared it. Red-faced and sweating, energized by the power of the truth, I felt glued to the floor while the room spun round and no one moved. It was the single longest moment of my life. But something happened in the void. I was set free. From what they thought of me. From the bondage of abuse. From responsibilities too great for one single person to bear. I turned from their horrified faces and walked out of the room with them yelling after me, "You come back here, young lady!"

I didn't even cry as I ran to my car and started the engine while I heard the screen door slam and my father's angry voice shouting, "If you leave, don't bother to come back, Shayley!"

That was three years ago. I stayed with my cousin in Bend. She has two children and needed a nanny. I finished school online. But by midsummer, I was more of a burden to her than a help and she asked me to find another place to be. That's when my volunteer work for Andi and Beulah's Place turned into my needing a home.

It was over two years before I sneaked back to California to see my brothers. I know they were crushed that I left, and I thought they might hate me for it. I'd abandoned them to Dad. Some days that seemed very selfish and I felt ashamed. But their hope was my hope: leave as soon as possible and don't turn back. I wound down the bumpy dirt road to the house about three in the afternoon, a time when I thought I could catch my brothers alone. I slowed the car down so I could see the driveway before I turned toward the house. No cars. It was safe. I wasn't worried about Dad hitting me again. We were past that now. He couldn't control me that way anymore, but I was concerned that he might hurt my brothers because they'd let me in. It felt weird pulling the car up into my old space in the rock yard that served as a parking lot for our family. I felt the familiar knot in my stomach that was a part of my every day for so many years. Being home made me want to be sick. I would have left except I had to see if my brothers were okay…and if they still…well, loved me. They'd been my world for most of my life. I needed them to still know I loved them, too.

I turned off the engine, sighed my resignation as I breathed a prayer and quietly mounted the front steps of the house. I quietly tapped on the rotting edge of our green screen door and heard the sound of running feet as at least one of my brothers hurried to answer it. When the door opened just enough to see me standing there, Willy screeched with delight that it was me. He threw the door wide open and literally jumped into my arms. I felt like the wind had been knocked out of me in that moment. A quick breath seemed to stop my heart and a sob I wasn't expecting shook my whole body. Holding Willy mended some deep place in me. Feeling his little heart beat so fast against my own and feeling the warmth of his tears on my neck cracked open this hard place I'd been holding onto for years. When I ran away, *I* was all I had. Survival was what I cared about. However I could. And that makes people hard. I always have my guard up. I mean, I ran away because those who are supposed to love me didn't. So, what could I reasonably expect from strangers? I hadn't connected with anyone for two years…been held so tightly. I didn't know how much I'd yearned for that because I'd had to shut that part of me down. But whimpering against my shoulder was my Willy, and he still loved me.

"Where did you go, Shayley?" he asked, yelling it into my ear while his arms tightened around my neck, holding me in a death grip. "Why did you leave?"

"I'm sorry I left you, Willy," I cried, "but I couldn't stay any longer." Grief and joy can explode a person all at once. I'm proof of it. I cried an ocean.

Two of the other boys heard us and came running. I'd barely stepped into the house, the door still ajar and the screen door flapping against the stucco in the afternoon wind, sounding as if it were applauding my return. They stopped in their tracks to see me there, holding Willy aloft, and their eyes filled first with confusion and then with tears. I set Willy on his feet and looked at my brothers, afraid of the bruises I might see that would brand me the traitor I often felt I was. But they didn't give me time to fret about my shame. "Shayley!" they screamed and hugged my waist and danced around me like I was Mrs. Santa Claus.

"Group hug," yelled Willy, and we kissed and hugged there in the doorway as the screen kept on flapping. As family reunions go, it couldn't have been much better. Except…

"Where's Bobby?" I asked, as I blew my nose on a tissue I'd re-trieved from a half empty box on the kitchen counter. The brother just younger than I am wasn't there. It dawned on me later that I shouldn't have expected him to be since he was almost nineteen by then. But I knew he was the one most likely to have taken on the burden of abuse when I left.

"He works now," Willy said. "Down at Del Taco." His head was down, and he was shuffling his feet and sniffling.

"Are you back for good?" the boys asked in unison, their eyes trained on me so hopefully it made me heartsick.

"No," I said. "I live in Oregon now. I was just passing through and wanted to make sure I got to see you. I can't stay." I headed for the door again, not wanting to still be around when my parents returned. They'd not even tried to contact me since I left. My drop-ping in wouldn't be received well at all. I wish I could've packed my brothers up and taken them with me.

"Not even for dinner?" asked Willy as he pulled at my arm to stay.

"Not even for dinner," I said, but that didn't keep me from re-gretting it as soon as I started the engine and watched my brothers waving despondently while I backed down the driveway, hearing the familiar sound of gravel crackling my departure.

Chapter Twenty-five

ANDI—NO MORE RUNNING

In the face of every teen we take in I see the same desperation I felt in my years of abuse in the home in which I grew up—an abuse no one who knew us would have guessed was the bedrock of our dysfunction. Like Shayley's, our home was supposed to be a Christian one, but behind the closed doors of our ranch style stucco house, I never knew what I'd done to enrage the woman, Leanne, into her fits of anger. Never knew why sexual domination and abuse were a thing I had to endure. *Was it like this for everyone? Could no one be trusted to be safe?* As a child it seemed reasonable to me that everyone's home was like this. Neighborhoods filled with manicured lawns, front porch swings, smiling neighbors, biking kids and houses with front doors that, once closed, hid a haunted house with screams, witches and surprises that jumped out without warning. If every family lived in such treachery, no place was secure.

The year I turned sixteen my life had once again become unlivable. Beaten and coerced into me was the fact that I was unlovable, a fat pig, ugly, and stupid. I didn't have to guess whether that was what Leanne thought of me. She informed me of it daily. At times of greatest stress, my speech impediment was more pronounced, too, fueling the consensus that I was irreparably damaged—a reject. I remember one morning that year awakening and thinking: *I'm sad I woke up today.* I craved continual sleep—a respite from the chaotic carnival of my life. Death—a sweet reprieve from the prison guarded by Leanne.

It was all about a gift Joe Sr. had given to me. He'd recently gone on a jaunt to Asia to purchase inventory for a shop he briefly owned. Among the items he sold in the shop were unique pieces of costume jewelry. The evening before my desire to just not be alive anymore, Joe Sr. came into the living room where Leanne was sitting grading a stack of tests. Behind his back he held a gift which I guess he wanted to present in a grand manner. "I have something for you," he began, with a slight smile creeping across his face.

"What?" Leanne asked disinterestedly.

"You have to look up at me before I tell you," Joe Sr. said rakishly.

Leanne lifted her head from the pile of papers in her lap and adjusted her reading glasses further down on her nose so that she could peek at her husband over the edge without removing them entirely. "Okay…what, Joe?"

On cue, he brought one hand from behind his back and gave Leanne something hidden in a little velvet pouch. "Open it," Joe Sr. said like a kid who'd just given his mother a gift he'd made at school. He was almost panting for approval.

Leanne untied the delicate silk string that held the pouch closed and a necklace fell heavily into her lap, making a clinking noise. When she held it up, she gasped. "Oh, my, Joe," she breathed as she held the necklace up and put her glasses back up onto the bridge of her nose so she could look more closely at her gift—a gaudy diamond *L* dangling on a heavy gold chain. Her initial, bright and obvious. "It's beautiful!" Leanne exclaimed as she undid the clasp and placed the bauble around her neck. It slapped back against her dress, too heavy. Maybe a little ridiculous.

"I have one more surprise," Joe Sr. announced. "Where's Andrea?" Then he called for me. "Andrea, come in here a minute."

I'd been in the kitchen and heard the gifting from there. Joe Sr. was always trying to get on Leanne's good side, and this pretty much always worked for the short term. I had no idea what he wanted with me when she seemed so happy. Why mess with a good moment?

"Okay," I said and sauntered into the living room.

"Look what I just gave your mother," he said proudly, looking over at Leanne.

"It's nice," I replied. *Was this why he called me into the living room? To see her flaunt her big diamond initial? Sheesh.*

He reached into his pocket and pulled out another velvet pouch. "I bought another one for my favorite daughter!" he announced as he grabbed my hand and put the pouch into it.

I could see the look on Leanne's face and was afraid to even empty the pouch into my free hand. It was always amazing how quickly she could turn. "What did you get *her*?" accused Leanne as she set the papers aside and moved forward on the couch to see clearly what I was about to unveil.

"The same thing I got for you," Joe Sr. replied, unaware of the explosion about to erupt all over his happiness. He was turned toward me, waiting with a cocky smile for me to unwrap my diamond *A*. "Come on, Andrea, let's see it," Joe Sr. said.

When I dropped it from the pouch into my hand, Leanne shrieked a little. Like someone had just pinched her.

"Thank you," I said, but I wanted to run. I could see what Joe Sr. couldn't yet—her face. Leanne had removed her glasses and her eyes filled with a murderous glow. There was only her, all the time, and I was in the way. I didn't even want to put the thing on. I didn't want a gift that was the same as hers any more than she wanted me to have one. I just wanted to fade into our hideous wallpaper and be done with it.

"You gave *Andrea* the same thing you got me?" Leanne was standing by then. Her hands were balled up into fists, and her face was scarlet with anger and hubris. From the neck of such a creature hung a flashing, glimmering *L*, out of place and banging lightly against her heaving bosom. "Your daughter gets the same gift as you give me, Joe? What the hell were you thinking?" She puffed up her chest and her breathing was an erratic wheezing, like a faulty engine ready to blow. As she seethed, spit flew from her mouth, the words escaping from between clenched teeth. "She's not your *wife*!"

Before I knew it, Leanne was bolting from the couch and heading toward me with such vengeance that I ran into my bedroom and slammed the door before she could get to me. My heart was beating so hard my body shook and my temples pulsed. She didn't follow, but my blood curdled as I heard Leanne screeching her vitriol at Joe Sr. for thinking to bring me a gift equal to any that he would bring her. "She doesn't deserve it, the little piece of crap!"

He probably answered something. It went back and forth for a while. It always did. The sexual lines were always blurred in our hyper-dysfunctional family, and this fight was more about that than the gift. I was the collateral damage—intended and unintended. Leanne finally fell quiet, and I knew she would give me the cold eye and him the silent treatment for days. When she got like that she stomped around the house, snorting like a bull trapped in its corral, and she'd beat down my door to call me to breakfast or dinner with such rancor the house shook. The whole thing made me feel like my soul had been sucked out of me. I was caved in like a punctured inner tube with all its air oozed out. A piece of junk. A throwaway. Nothing.

Between classes at Marywood High School the next afternoon, I slipped into an empty room and slumped down into a desk. My lips quivered; my eyes overflowed with the tears of my desolation. I was worthless and constantly reminded of it. And if "nothing" goes away, there is no one to notice. I didn't really understand prayer that well. My experience with God was that He was watching over me, but He was not personal to me. I couldn't *feel* Him. So many years before, I'd made a promise to the God of a magnificent blue sky. That promise was all that kept me together many days. But this particular afternoon without the expanse of blue, I felt closed in by my own unfolding history, one that repeated itself as it arced in the concentric circles of my never-ending heartbreak. With no way out, what I knew I could expect was what I'd already come to grips with day in and day out. I was a hamster on a wheel, observed and manipulated by a wicked witch I couldn't melt, Dorothy-like, into oblivion. I was the despised unwanted child of the mother I was given. I sank into the depths of the little wooden desk in that muggy dark classroom and despaired of having taken my first breath. I squeezed my eyes shut, forcing the tears to streak down my face in rivulets that spilled onto the white blouse of my school uniform. I knew I couldn't cry enough to fix all of this. I'd tried. It didn't solve anything—it only watered the pain. In my heart of hearts, I simply didn't want to be in this world anymore. Shrinking into nothing, evaporating without a trace, flying toward the blue sky…no real specific plan for my demise was forming. Just the peace of not existing—a peace that was ephemeral and exciting. I had the power over my last breath. Leanne couldn't take that away from me even if she wanted to. It would be the final word, and I would have it! Just the thought of my life careening toward death exhilarated me…stopped the tears. I could never slap her when she slapped me. I had no real means of retaliation for the excesses and the abuse. It seemed the older I became the more aggressive her behavior was. I was too grown up for her to control in the old ways. I could run. I could hide. I could scream. And her perceived lack of power made her more iron fisted than ever. My sixteen-year-old self didn't think I could endure it for one more day.

I flicked back my tears with my fingers and sat upright in the desk. With my elbows sitting on the desktop, I put my bowed head in my hands and talked to the God of my childhood. The One Who promised to take care of me until I got big. *I know you hate suicide, but I just can't do this life anymore, God. I am trapped…humiliated, violated, abused…and I'm sick of it.* I wasn't crying then; just stating the facts. The classroom became very quiet, like all the air had been sapped out of it, and I existed in the black hole of a very small universe. God didn't speak to me like before, but I knew He was there all the same because my thoughts seemed poured into my head from some canister of wisdom I'd missed in the uproar that was my life. *I'd managed to stay alive this long.* That was the gist of it. I'd survived the high waves of an ocean in which I should have drowned long ago—held my breath and ridden out the maelstrom. *Why would I take my own life now when I'm almost out of her clutches?* Dawning on me was the realization that my suicide would be a win for her. My best option was to survive. *Okay, God. I'm going to stay here. You'll have to make this work for me. But I promise I'll never kill myself. I've come this far. It would be a waste of all I've been through to quit.* And my mind was made up. I chose life.

That's not to say that anything got easier. It didn't. I was allowed to get my driver's license when I turned seventeen, but I was only allowed to drive our old blue Datsun station wagon to and from school or work. Leanne's hyper-vigilance about my whereabouts was stifling, but once I was in the noisy jalopy, I felt a freedom I'd never known before. By then I was a senior in high school and was not only working hard toward graduation, but also working three part-time jobs, one at Bullock's department store, a part time job with Joe Sr.'s business partner and the other as a helper in the school cafeteria at Marywood. By this time, Joe, Jr. was in college, so I was the only child at home. As much as was humanly possible, I stayed away, too. On a rare afternoon when I was home early from work and school, I found myself in the middle of a heated argument between Leanne and Joe Sr. about going out to dinner.

"Put on some decent clothes, Joe!" Leanne was yelling from their bedroom when I walked through the door around six o'clock in the evening.

Joe Sr. was sitting in his tattered old leather recliner in the living room with his shoeless feet dangling. In his hand was a glass of iced tea that dripped its sweat onto the old Notre Dame t-shirt that fit tight across his belly. On his head was a baseball cap, crinkled from its many trips into the washer and dryer, and his legs were bare from the knees down, sprouting from his Bermuda shorts like two hairy tree trunks. I could tell the last thing Joe Sr. wanted to do was get dressed to go out with Leanne. "Where'd you say we're going?" he yelled back, still stuck to the recliner as if he'd been glued into it.

"The Millers!" she called from the open door of their bedroom. "You've known about this for a week, so come get dressed!"

In an effort to avoid the argument and the dinner date, I crept toward my bedroom and safety. "Andrea!" *Caught!* "I didn't hear you come in," Leanne said as she stepped into the hallway, blocking my path. "Get dressed. We are going out to dinner."

"I have so much homework. Can't I stay here?" I pleaded. It wasn't a lie. I had piles of homework to do and my work schedule always left me with little time to accomplish it.

"No." Leanne slipped into the bathroom to smear on her lipstick. "We're all going." She peeked around the door. "Now get dressed."

There was no use arguing with her. I'd have to find time to catch up later. As I turned to open my bedroom door, I heard the pit-pat of Joe Sr.'s bare feet slapping the brown path of worn hardwood floor that led to his room. "Why didn't you remind me about this? I don't have time to shower, even."

"I did, but you never listen to me!" Leanne yelled, still from her place in front of the bathroom mirror. "You've got ten minutes!"

It was a teacher friend of Leanne's who'd invited us to dinner…well, invited *her* to dinner. Seems Leanne couldn't trust her husband or her daughter to behave without her. I didn't even know her friend. We were rounded up like the sheep we'd become and forced into the car exactly ten minutes later, cranky, sweaty and out of sorts. Joe Sr. turned the car air conditioner on full blast as he barreled out of the driveway like he was Mario Andretti after a pit stop, giving Leanne and me whiplash because he was so irritated to be dressed up and going out. "You're driving like a maniac!" screamed Leanne, as she yanked her seatbelt from its place near the window and threw it across her chest, buckling it loudly to make her point.

"You wanna take the wheel, Leanne?" offered Joe Sr. with such gruffness that it quieted his wife. I could see the set of his jaw in the rearview mirror, his teeth grinding out his anger, keeping him from saying all he really wanted to in order to keep some peace. And the air conditioner wasn't working. The icing on his cake.

We turned south on Beach Boulevard out of our Buena Park neighborhood and merged into the busy traffic that was always crawling through the main thoroughfares near Knott's Berry Farm. We were going to be late. Each traffic light seemed to be colluding with fate to turn red right as we approached it. The tension in the car was palpable. Leanne was a ticking time bomb, her foot tapping on the floorboard restlessly. Joe Sr. sighed with resignation each time we missed an opportunity to fly through an intersection.

"We're going to be late," fumed Leanne. "We're going to be late because you didn't get your butt off the couch and get dressed in time. I can never count on you for anything."

"We're going to be late because we are trying to get you to dinner at some friend's house in rush hour traffic." Joe Sr.'s words came in a loud steady monotone.

I was feeling more and more exasperated when Joe Sr. pointed out that this was Leanne's friend we were squashed into a hot car at rush hour to go visit, triggering the unfairness of it all in me. "I don't know why I couldn't just stay home," I said, mostly to myself, but Leanne heard me. I'd signed my own death warrant.

"Pull over, Joe, right now!" Leanne screamed at the top of her lungs, the volcano that had been building in her erupting into furor. She looked back at me from the front seat, her anger scalding her face a bright purple.

Joe Sr. kept driving. A small grace. All I could think was, *Crap, here we go again.*

"Turn this car around!" Leanne demanded. "Turn it around right now!"

I was sitting in the back seat behind Joe Sr., and Leanne's short stubby arms couldn't quite reach me as she turned in the front passenger seat and lunged at me with her right fist balled up, ready to land solidly onto my face. I cringed into the corner of my seat and covered my face with my hands—protecting myself like a lightweight boxer up against the heavyweight champion of the world. It was always my go-to position in every fray with Leanne, though she didn't hit my face too often for fear of leaving bruises the outside world could see. She was a teacher, after all, and knew the rules.

Perspiration beaded on Leanne's face with a slick sheen, like it was covered in egg white, and the sun bounced off it, making her look like an alien. She was fuming as she turned back around in her seat and heaved like a bridled horse ready to return to its stable. We couldn't get home fast enough for her. The wringing of her hands intensified the closer we got to our front door and my inevitable punishment. I'd already begun to take the Datsun key from the key ring I kept in my purse. It clanged together with my house key and a work key as I unwound it until it dropped off into my lap. "Give me the car key, young lady!" Leanne ordered, her left hand reaching toward me in the back seat though she didn't turn to look at me.

"It's already off," I said in a near whisper as I dropped the key into her open palm. Lately, giving up the freedom of driving was the ramification of my having crossed her. It didn't usually last too long, though, because neither she nor Joe Sr. wanted to be my chauffeur. I had no idea this time crossing her would almost cost me my life.

As soon as the car pulled up in the driveway, I threw open the door and ran inside. I was too big to get under my bed like I did when I was little. I'd slide under it and move to the farthest most corner and shrink as small as I could into a miserable ball, shivering as I waited for her to storm down the hallway, her feet stomping and shaking the earth like the dinosaur in *Jurassic Park,* the treachery making my heart dance a dirge against my tiny ribs. All I could do now that I was grown was stand petrified in my bedroom and hope she didn't open the door. But the floor did shake and the monster did enter my bedroom, fists raised and body energized like someone had switched on a button in her that put her anger into hyper-drive. I thought she might actually implode.

"You little bitch!" Leanne yelled with all her might. It erupted out of her, venomous and horrifying. "You're just a whore! An ungrateful son of a bitch!" And the hateful edge of her screeching hysteria landed on me in a choking grasp around my neck as I tried to move slowly back toward my bed, defenseless and terrified. Her hands were wet with perspiration and hot around my neck. So transformed was her face, too close to mine, that I shut my eyes to keep from looking at her. Her humid breath smelled rancid as if came in a putrid stream out of the mouth of a fuming dragon. Possessed with the power of her own rage, Leanne began to shake me back and forth as she spewed her expletives at me, her hands tightening their grip around my neck, choking me, cutting off my breath. In an effort to gasp enough air to keep from passing out, I pushed at her and squealed. This only made her more furious as she rocked me violently back and forth, shaking me until I thought: *Oh, my God! She's going to break my neck! I'm going to suffocate! I'm going to die tonight!* Panicked, I kicked at Leanne's shins and writhed to get free of her. I locked my knees to keep from falling onto my bed as she spread her legs wider for balance and clutched my throat with her elbows outstretched like a raptor killing its prey. Just when I thought I would pass out, Joe Sr. slammed open the bedroom door and screamed, "What the hell are you doing?"

He ran over to us, squatted his six-foot frame down to Leanne's level and threw his arms around his wife's waist and pulled with all his might, forcing for a blessed moment her hands from around my neck. As she jerked away from his grasp, Leanne grabbed my throat with her flailing right hand and began strangling me again. "I'm going to kill her, anyway!" She spit the words into my face, her eyes glowing red-hot like a horror story demon's. "I should've done it a long time ago!"

"Damn it, Leanne! Stop it!" Joe Sr. demanded as he grabbed her wriggling body and wrapped his arms tightly around her flailing arms. The more Leanne squirmed to get away, the stronger were her husband's efforts to constrain her. I somehow managed to stay upright as Joe Sr. dragged his wife away from me.

"I hate that little bitch!" she shrieked, as she turned her head toward me and tried to fight free of her husband so she could get back to her assault.

As Joe Sr. held his wife in a death grip to keep her from killing their only daughter, I slipped from the bed, coughing, exhausted and inconsolable. *My mother still wants me dead.* Washing over me for the millionth time was the certainty that I was worthless... at least to Leanne. I ran from the bedroom and into my adjoining bathroom, slamming and locking the door behind me; then I propped myself against it while my heart beat furiously against my chest and its throbbing filled my ears with the rhythmic swooshing sound of blood finally able to flow from my constricted jugular vein. I was exhausted. Like I was a really old person who'd seen so much of life that I'd despaired of living it. I took a hobbling step toward the sink, nearly falling forward over it, then grasped its sides with my shaking hands. When I glanced up into the mirror, the face looking back at me was tear-stained, red-eyed and oddly *young.* My neck was ringed with the scarlet residue of the attack, the edges where Leanne's fingers pushed into my trachea already turning an eggplant purple. It would leave bruises which I'd learned to cover up. What I couldn't fix was the quiet desperation that had come to a head. As I splashed cool water onto my face, I heard the door to my bedroom open and peeked out of my bathroom door as Joe Sr. led Leanne out into the hallway. He had her hands held together in front of her like she was a shackled prisoner about to be led to her death on a guillotine, and he walked backward leading them toward their bedroom where they entered and closed the door. The beast was still once more.

I turned back to my bathroom, washed my face and buried it into the towel I'd used to dry away the moisture. It felt safe—my face in the darkness of the terry cloth, the smell of soap, the buffering of my sobs. I just could not do this again. Anything would be better than the random visits to hell that was my normal.

I stepped back into my room and closed the door Joe Sr. had left slightly ajar. It was dark outside by then, but I didn't turn on the lights. I lay across my bed and stared up at the acoustic ceiling that was staring back at me like so much popcorn scattered overhead as though it had spilled from its box at the movies. I lay there as the moonlight began to stream in through the flimsy curtains dangling from the windows in my bedroom. The headlights of passing cars lit up the darkness, spilling random patterns onto the pale gray walls that closed me into the prison my room had always been. I had homework to complete…lots of it. I was a California Scholar winner, a very diligent student, but on that night, I couldn't concentrate on school work. It seemed petty to worry about writing essays and studying for tests in light of the almost deadly events of the evening. I just didn't get it. I actually was all my parents wished I could be, I thought. I was obedient to Leanne's hyper-vigilance, not breaking her rules. Though others at my all-girls school were having sex, getting drunk and even doing drugs, I was engaged in studying and work. Leanne and Joe Sr. should have been proud of me. But I was never good enough. It seemed Leanne was constantly trying to purge from me some sin I hadn't committed.

I rolled over onto my side, gazed out the open window and waited for the house to get quiet. For the beast to sleep. All I could think about was escaping the dungeon that was home—to run away. The urge seemed primal—necessary. I didn't think about *where* I was going—*going* was the important thing. Not being in this house. Being anywhere else. Like a prisoner who escapes the penitentiary through an underground tunnel it took years to dig, I would escape only with my life, if I was lucky. Freedom was the prize. Never looking into Leanne's bulging red eyes. Never hearing the screech of her voice. Never smelling her dragon breath. Never feeling her inappropriate touch. Never, ever, ever again. That thought alone gave me peace, settled my stomach and became the catalyst for my flight.

The back door always stuck. I knew as I tiptoed down the hall toward the kitchen and freedom that it would be my only obstacle—getting it opened without arousing my parents. I'd thrown a sweatshirt on over my jeans to keep warm. The heat of the day had given over to the usual cool California night. I hadn't thought to pack a backpack or even take my purse. Running was my only thought—running like a gazelle chased by a tiger. Panicked that I'd be devoured before I made it out of the clearing and into the trees. It felt like life or death.

The kitchen was dark and quiet, perfectly clean, the counters polished and glistening in the dappled glow from the street light that stood like a tall rigid sentinel at the edge of the sidewalk that wound its way past the front of our house. I reached for the back door and tugged it gingerly at first, hoping beyond hope that it would give me some grace. It was, however, unrelenting in its effort to keep me from passing without its usual grinding and lurching. Finally, with a great effort, much pushing and pulling, the door gave way with a bang against the wall beside it. "Where are you going?" Joe Sr. asked.

I turned too quickly to see him, and stumbled into him standing in his bathrobe right behind me. "Leave me alone!" I said in as loud a whisper as I dared, pushing my body away from his. "I'm leaving! You don't love me any more than she does!"

He didn't say a word to me as I stomped out the door and headed down the sidewalk into the misty darkness. I hugged myself and looked at the watch still on my wrist. Eleven at night. I hadn't even thought about where I'd go. No getaway car for this prisoner. I was on my own.

This guy named Billy ran the ice cream counter at the Thrifty drugstore a few blocks away from our house, so I thought I'd go there and talk with him. Though he was older than I, he was always nice to me and struck up a conversation every time I stopped by. That always made me feel special. I headed that direction past dew covered cars that slept along the curbs of our street and houses whose eyes were shuttered against the night. Our neighborhood was heavily barricaded with large trees originally planted there to block the noise from busy Beach Boulevard. That night they became shadowy figures with hairy arms reaching out to grab me. The only sound I heard was the echoing clap-clap of my flip-flops against the slippery sidewalk. I tried not to be afraid. What I was leaving was surely as bad as what might greet me in the neighborhood and beyond. It was almost a mile downhill from my house to Beach Boulevard where the cars were still randomly cruising by and the only thing lit up was a bus stop where prostitutes often sat waiting for a ride. My fear was momentarily conquered by my need to escape, so, slightly out of breath and wary, I turned down Beach toward the big drug store four blocks away and picked up my pace to get there. I thought I might tell Billy I'd run away, that life at home was hellish, that I couldn't take it anymore. I don't know why it occurred to me that he'd be interested, but my heart beat faster and faster at the idea of confessing my plight to another human being. Once there, I crossed the empty parking lot where a small mortuary sat dark and emptied of mourners grieving their dead, who lay cold and lifeless in permanent satin- lined beds. It felt creepy and desolate. Made my skin crawl as I headed to the two large entry doors of the drug store, but Thrifty was closed. I tried the doors a couple of times, but they didn't give against my pushing. I was locked out of my confessional.

I didn't have any money and suddenly felt ill prepared for my journey. I couldn't even take the bus somewhere. The local police station was at least two or three miles away, but I started walking in that direction. Maybe I could tell them about Leanne—show them the bruises on my neck. Maybe they'd believe me. But then, maybe not. There would be more hell to pay at home in that case. We didn't have family close by. They certainly wouldn't buy that Leanne was an abuser. And I couldn't think how to tell them to make them believe even if they lived close enough for me to walk to their homes. I'd been so isolated that I didn't have any true friends, either. The dense curtain of descending fog shrouded me while I walked dejectedly along the sidewalks of my neighborhood, mirroring my own inability to see clearly what I was supposed to do. My grand dramatic gesture of leaving home for good had no unobscured path forward. I was stuck outside wandering aimlessly with not a soul who cared and with no one to rescue me. I was going to be pathetic whether I went home or wandered away.

The back door jerked and choked as I opened it only a couple of hours after I left. The house itself looked like a dark sleeping hulk when I approached it. *No one is awake.* I'd slip back into my bed—my life. I sighed, suddenly exhausted and aware that my neck really hurt and my head was pounding. I'd retreated. *I'm a deserter in the battle. A loser…again.* Covered in the shame of surrender, I walked into the kitchen, closing the door behind me. "It's not safe for you out there, Andrea," my father said as he scratched through a kitchen drawer looking for matches. He was always giving up smoking because Leanne told him to. Like an alcoholic hides booze, though, Joe Sr. always hid some matches so he could light up a stashed Pall Mall Gold when his wife wasn't looking. He found a crumpled matchbook and pulled a shriveled paper match from it. "She'll cool off in the morning," he said as he wandered outside to smoke.

"I don't really care," I said to his back. "I'm going to bed."

He didn't even hear me. The match lit the darkness and illuminated Joe Sr.'s face in an ethereal glow as he stood in the yard in his pajamas, almost ghost-like in the enveloping fog. I watched him there for a minute—wished for a conversation that would never come. Some recognition from him…or someone…that my life was a living hell that I didn't cause. That Leanne was crazy. That her abuse wasn't normal. But, then again, the man was just as messed up as his wife.

The hall seemed longer than usual, making it feel like a death march, as I headed to my bedroom. As I closed the door and pulled the sweatshirt off over my head, I could smell the Pall Mall Gold burning in Joe Sr.'s mouth, the smoke blending with the night, heavy on the air that circulated slowly toward my windows. I was suddenly nauseous. But it wasn't physical so much as it was a reaction in my soul. Wanting to throw up the past and redo it. To have a different life if only I could purge myself of the one that existed. Maybe that would bring some peace, like right after vomiting there is often relief that the awful thing that caused such fits in my body was now gone.

I pulled back the bedspread on my bed and nestled under the covers. Joe Sr. wasn't any more capable of knowing me than was his wife. They were trapped with each other, abusing and being abused, a never-ending cycle of proffered pain. Had I known as a teenager what I now know, I would have fled that night to anywhere. Told someone—anyone. Tried to find just one person who would believe that my mother sexually molested me; that she verbally abused me; that she beat me. And that she wasn't the only one who used me for gratification. I would have understood the woman's multiple personalities and her husband's philandering. I would've known my normal wasn't normal at all. But I was a child damaged by their dysfunction, lost in their world and needing a savior.

I lived through another year. One day at a time. Some days, one hour at a time. I wasn't sure about what praying really meant, but I began writing poetry—talking to God through it. Much of it was a torrid yearning for a judge to hear my case. I desperately needed to be understood and believed. Some of it was what I imagined a love relationship with God would look like. I knew God was not unaware of my plight, but nothing really changed in the landscape around my life. Talking to Him…writing my hopes and fear…kept me going until I went to college at Loyola Marymount the next year. Healing, though…healing is an ongoing process even now. My journey has been formed by my abuse much of my life, but the very real presence of God in the months and weeks that preceded my brief hospital stay in Cerritos, and after my breakthrough there, have given me the courage to look homeless teenagers in the eye and with great conviction know they will not *have* to go back to the crucibles of their pain. Evelyn, Shayley, Allison and Nevaeh… all the others…I *get* them. Whether physically thrown out onto the streets by parents or guardians who abused them or deciding to run because they felt they had no other choice, life had become unbearable. In their attempts to be courageous or to be heard or to be loved, they found themselves in the ironic situation of once again being used and discarded. I can say to them with conviction and truth, "I know what you are feeling." Their normal isn't strange to me. It's sadly familiar, and the fact I know their pain and have broken through into a healthy purposeful life assures me that if anyone can reach their hearts, rescue their bodies and inspire their souls, surely I am more than qualified. In the binding up of their wounds there is a quiet kind of victory, a peace within myself. Le-anne's legacy will not be replicated, at least not on my watch. The midnight of their souls will no longer be ignored. Each one is precious to me—a treasure. No longer will one of them be left to bleed on the side of the road without hope of rescue.

Chapter Twenty-six

THE MISSION

Eighteen miles of steep rocky road separated Jericho from Jerusalem. The rugged terrain and uninhabited hillside often harbored robbers who would hide in the brush and wait for lone travelers, often on foot, to pass their way. It wasn't uncommon to hear tales in the local taverns about how a group of thieves held up a patron on his way to or from the Holy City. It was a story the crowd could relate to when Jesus told them of the man who lay beaten and unconscious on that very road.

The man was perhaps a Jewish merchant hauling goods from Jerusalem to Jericho. The day started as pleasantly as most, clear skies, the air still cool from the night desert air. His wife likely packed him a lunch, and he carried a wineskin full of aromatic Chardonnay from his neighbor's vineyard. The man's clothes were clean, his feet washed, his hair tucked back neatly with a cloth tie his wife had fashioned for him and his beard was freshly trimmed. He kissed her cheek as he set out with his donkey, which was laden with loose bags filled with the goods from his silver shop. He'd ride the animal home later in the week when his purse was full and his bags were empty, but this day he would walk alongside, staff in hand.

"Be careful," his wife hollered after him. "Yakim's brother was robbed on that road two weeks ago!"

"I've made this trip many times, my bride," the man hollered back. "All will be well. You'll see." And she watched him until his gleaming red tunic was only a small dot on the horizon.

The sun was high when the merchant stopped to rest. Took a sip from his wineskin. Tore a corner from the soft leavened bread his wife had packed. He was sitting on a large rock. The same one he'd rested on many, many times before. As the donkey swayed beside him in the heat of the day, flicking flies away with its bushy tail, the man laid his head back and thanked God for such a day.

In the hills above, three men had watched as the merchant strode down the slope. At first he was only a tiny burst of crimson on the landscape, now they saw him, now they didn't, as he wound up the road. There was nothing that made their hearts beat in anticipation. People came this way daily. Not everyone had anything these men wanted. And, not everyone was alone. As they watched haphazardly at first, lying high up on a smooth ledge, they didn't have any expectations about the person moving ever closer to them.

One of the men was a criminal, recently escaped from a Jericho jail where he was being held for attempted murder. One was a loner the other two knew very little about except that he'd joined them recently. The third was a thief by trade. Never been caught. He had a large home in Jericho built and paid for by his pillaging of decent folks just trying to get from one place to another. His neighbors would never have believed it had they known how he made his living. He seemed to be a good husband and father. A decent enough man.

The traveling merchant wiped the dripping sweetness of the wine from his mouth and the salty perspiration from his brow and packed up his lunch. "We have a ways to go, my man," he said to the donkey as he patted the animal's back, the signal that lunch was over and it was time to move on. The donkey stomped backward and forward, his body swaying with the heavy load he must adjust for balance. "Come on, you beast!" the man said as he laughed. "You are like a stubborn child!" And he took the reins in his hands and pulled his traveling silver shop back onto the road.

It was the sound of the jangling metal in the bags that jostled back and forth on the donkey's back as it wafted up from the road below that roused the three men on the hill to action. Crawling on their hands and knees to the edge where brush hid them from view, they watched as the merchant approached the crest of a hill, singing to his donkey as he pulled it along behind him. Without speaking a word to each other, the men ran and slid as fast as they could down through the rocks and brush to the road. "Stop right there!" screamed the career criminal, whose face was concealed behind a wrap on his head. The other two men grabbed the merchant who was so completely caught off guard that he didn't fight back at first.

"What are you doing?" the merchant screamed as the criminal grabbed the reins to the donkey and began to run with the animal up the hillside. "Where are you going with my goods?" he cried as he struggled against the men who then threw him viciously against the boulders that lined the roadway.

"Shut up!" the men hollered.

But the merchant rose to his feet and made a futile attempt to chase after his donkey and its load. His feet slipped on the gravelly road. One of the men grabbed his arm and twisted it, laying the man on his back. The other, the loner, was the first to strike a blow to the merchant's face, breaking the man's nose and bloodying the rock against which he fell. Unsteady, the merchant tried to regain some form of balance, but before he could stand up fully, he was attacked again. Hit hard in the stomach, then in the ribs then kicked mercilessly as he lay on the ground until at last he lost consciousness. The men ran away after also stealing his crimson robe and expensive leather belt, leaving the merchant bleeding and alone, half dead and in need of emergency care.

The flies that had only moments before swarmed the beast at the merchant's side now buzzed and fussed around the wounds that oozed his blood. Coming from Jericho, a priest was making his way up the long stretch of road back to Jerusalem and the temple there. His heart was beating with the effort of the ascent, and sweat was pouring from beneath the turban set somewhat askew on his balding head. It was a surprise to see the merchant lying in his blood on the side of the road—nearly naked; nearly dead. *What could have happened to the man?* Only a passing thought to the busy priest. Not a call to action. Not a reason to attend to the man's needs. After all, he was a priest and couldn't touch anything as unclean as the man lying still by the side of the road. There would be seven days of cleansing in the temple if he touched a corpse. Too much trouble. Not enough time. And the blood on the body offended the sensibilities of the priest. He walked by on the other side of the road and soon forgot about what he'd seen.

As the afternoon wore on, and the merchant's condition worsened with the heat and the swelling of his face and the darkening bruises that covered his body, a Levite stumbled upon the scene on his way from the temple. His job there was to assist the priests with the offerings. A respectable and holy job assigned to his tribe by God. Favored above other Jews because of his lineage, the man was proud and smelled of rich cologne as his robes swished by the merchant now groaning as his consciousness returned. The Levite heard a faint, "Please help me." But the man on the ground covered in dirt and blood was not someone he knew from the temple in Jerusalem. The Levite disdained his filth. Knew nothing of why he was lying there in such bad shape. And, of course, he had work he must get to in Jerusalem. With disgust, the Levite walked past the carnage as far as was physically possible on the other side of the road.

Daylight was fading as a Samaritan man rode toward the merchant still lying semi-conscious in the road. He was Jewish, but not from the lineage of Judah. Long ago, the tribe of Judah split from the other tribes of Israel which didn't worship in Jerusalem at the temple as did those descended from Judah. The other tribes had also intermarried with non-Jewish people, making them essentially unclean and unfit to worship God with the pure strains of Judah. The separation was deep. Jews didn't associate with Samaritans. Nor help them. Nor care what happened to them. That is why, when the Samaritan man stopped his donkey and stepped to the ground beside the wounded merchant, an unusual thing had happened. An unclean Jewish pariah reached out to a Judean worshipper of God and said, "Sir, sir, how did you come to be here?"

Only moans came from the merchant, whose teeth were missing and whose eyes were swollen shut. At last someone had compassion on him. At last his pain was acknowledged.

Without hesitating, the Samaritan man pulled the wineskin from his donkey and tore the hem of his own garment into thin strips in order to treat the festering wounds of the victim on the road. There was no talk of who was unclean. In his need, the Jewish merchant didn't despise the kindness of the Samaritan, though on another day they might not have noticed each other. In his compassion, all the Samaritan saw was the wounded, hurting man lying desperate on the side of the road.

"Here," said the Samaritan, "take a drink." He cradled the merchant's head in one hand as he poured wine into his parched and blood-caked mouth.

It stung on the merchant's tongue and filled up his swollen throat. He coughed as his head lolled back onto the Samaritan's arm. Gently he was laid back onto the ground so the rescuer could cleanse the wounds with wine and oil. After gently bandaging the man with the strips of cloth, the Samaritan lifted him up onto the donkey. The man was on his way to Jericho. Had reserved a room at an inn not far off the roadway. The stars were already appearing in the sky as the two men approached the ancient city. The innkeeper was surprised to see the load the Samaritan bore—a wounded Jew from the Holy City. "He'll probably be offended when he finds out he was riding a Samaritan's dirty donkey!" laughed the aging innkeeper. "What happened to him?"

"I don't know," answered the Samaritan. "He isn't able to tell me anything."

After making the arrangements for the room, the Samaritan carried the wounded merchant to it and laid him on the bed. He stripped the dirty undergarments from the merchant and washed his bloodied body in vinegar and water. From his baggage, the Samaritan took clean clothes and dressed the man. Poured warm soup down his throat and sat through the night by his bedside in case the merchant needed anything.

In the morning, the Samaritan had to leave, continuing his journey. But the merchant was in no shape to be moved. "Here," he said to the innkeeper. "Here is enough money to take care of the man until I return in two days. Make sure he is comfortable, please."

"What is he to you?" the innkeeper asked, still amazed that this Samaritan man, a man like himself, would take care of a person who would never think to do the same in a similar situation. "He is a Jerusalem Jew who wouldn't give you the time of day if you were left for dead beside the road!"

"And you would expect me to pass him by? Really, Jacobi? You would expect me to deny this man help because you think he wouldn't help me?" The Samaritan was in the innkeeper's face, his tone not harsh, but challenging. "That would be no way to treat my neighbor, sir."

"Suit yourself," said Jacobi. "I will take care of the man until you come back. But what if it costs more than what you gave me? You can waste your time and money on him, but I don't have to."

"If you spend more, I will repay you," said the Samaritan with an exasperated sigh. "You know I'm good for it." And with that, the Samaritan mounted his donkey and went on his way.

Jesus told the crowd, who'd assembled to hear him, this story because a lawyer in their midst had asked Him: "What must I do to have eternal life?"

"What does the law of God say? How do you interpret it?" asked Jesus.

"You shall love the Lord, your God, with all your heart, soul, strength and mind, and your neighbor as yourself." The rote and memorized answer of every knowledgeable Jewish man brought up in the synagogue.

"That's right," said Jesus. "Do this and you will live."

It wasn't enough for the lawyer. He really wanted to know who he *had* to love—not everyone is his neighbor, of course. "Just who *is* my neighbor?" asked the lawmaker with a self-satisfied expression on his face.

The answer was the story of the Samaritan, and when it was finished, Jesus turned to the lawyer. "Which one of these men proved to be a neighbor to the man who fell among the robbers?"

Of course, it was clear to the lawyer and everyone in the crowd where Jesus was going with the question, but the man felt there are just some people too disgusting to care about. There were some even the Jewish law said were unclean and untouchable. The lawyer felt flustered because there was only one answer to this question Jesus posed. It stuck in the lawyer's throat and embarrassed him. The obvious point was that the righteous Jewish men from the Holy City were unmerciful. Unloving. Self-absorbed. There was only one hero in the story, and he was himself unclean. It was a trick. The question. The *story*. "The one who showed mercy to the man." The lawyer choked it out.

"That's what you should go and do then," said Jesus. "Show mercy to the unlikely, unlovely—the wounded and abused. Those are your neighbors who need mercy.

***

There was a time for Ed and me that we were working so hard at working hard that we barely noticed the young people who walked around Redmond and Central Oregon with backpacks strapped over tattooed arms, cigarettes hanging from their mouths and the smell of the streets wafting from their minimal clothing. But all that changed on Thanksgiving of 2008 when we realized that, while we had restricted resources from the economic crash of 2008, the one thing that mattered most wasn't money, but our compassion. We decided that day to make every lost and homeless teen our neighbor just as surely as we would those who come with casseroles in hand, live in neat homes and wear clean clothes. Homeless teens need mercy and rescue. Like I needed mercy and rescue. A safe place to lay their heads and the salve of love to heal their wounds. If we love like Jesus does, Ed and I know it is up to us to go find the least likely neighbors and bring them back into community. Each time we rescue a teen, I am reminded of the prayer I prayed when I was five years old: "If you keep me alive, God, I'll do whatever you tell me to do. I'll love who You love. I'll serve who You serve. I will follow You."

To the degree Ed and I have shown mercy and love to the least of these—the homeless, aimless, depressed and forsaken—we have done it to Jesus Himself. We can no longer see the teens hitchhiking by the side of the road, sitting under trees in the park or hovering together on city sidewalks as we once did. It is our precious mission to throw them a life rope—to extend to them a thread of hope that there exists for them a place that is safe and merciful. A room at the inn that is Beulah's Place.

EPILOGUE

Evelyn: Evelyn moved back to Alaska for a few months in order to donate one of her kidneys to her mother. Though their relationship was rocky and her mother's drug problems were still an issue, it was Evelyn's desire to do for her mother what she could. "How could I deny her a kidney when mine was a match?" was her reply when I asked her why she would do that. When she recovered, she moved to the East Coast and enrolled in college there. During this time, Evelyn became a surrogate mother for a young childless couple. When I asked her why, she responded: "While I don't want children of my own, I didn't think it was fair to have a gift that would help someone else and not use it." The couple now has a precious baby boy. Evelyn graduated this year with degrees in criminology, psychology and sociology. She has a great job and her own two-year-old son, Malachai.

Allison: At twenty-three years old, Allison has found great success in the beverage industry. She earned her Class A Commercial driver's license and a huge pay raise. Allison is in a healthy, long-term relationship and is constantly giving back to the community by volunteering to speak for Beulah's Place and offering to help other at-risk teens navigate the process of becoming successfully independent as she has done.

Nevaeh: Nevaeh earned Dean's List accolades for her work during three semesters of the community college from which she recently graduated. Because of her outstanding performance, Nevaeh has been accepted to every college to which she applied and will be deciding which to attend this year. Pre-law is her interest because she wants to provide assistance to others and a solid life for herself. Nevaeh raises awareness and funds for Beulah's Place and receives great satisfaction in helping others who are in need, especially the desperate.

Shayley: Shayley is living independently in Oregon and has worked for the same company for two years, receiving several promotions and working on the number one team in the company. Starting winter term this next year, she will be going to college to study clinical psychology. She tried to live with one of her parents briefly, and that triggered memories of childhood sexual abuse she'd buried. Shayley is now bravely walking through counseling and looking forward to the day when she has the honor of turning around and helping other young women through their journeys. She looks forward to purchasing her own home in the next few months.

Acknowledgments

FOOTPRINTS

While there are so many who have left their footprints along our path to rescuing at-risk homeless teens, and the success of Beulah's Place, it is here that those *early and continuing* footprints are celebrated:

Steve Gardner / Pixelworks
The ARIA Foundation
The Crevier Family Foundation
Leadership Bend Impact Summit
100 Women Who Care Central Oregon
Dr. Claire Reeves, MA, C.C.D.C., PhD.
Dr. Mike Bechtle, Ph.D.
Diane Bechtle
Kedo Olson
Joan Lauren
Cheri Frey
Liz Farruggia
The Torgrimson Family (Aaron, Cassandra, Amber, and Paige)
Frank & Judy Waterer
Pam Forester
Cornerstone Christian Fellowship
Westside Church / Community Assistance
Diane Bishop / Clothing Across America
Rys Fairbrother / What If We Could

Farm2Friends

Desert Song Hygiene Bank

Ann Arends & Sally Kuhl

John & Sherry Elbek

Tate and Tate Catering

Super Walmart (Redmond, OR)

Cinder Butte Meat Co.

The 1017 Project / Shiloh Ranch Church

Dr. Philip Wallace, MD / Central Oregon Spine & Sports

Dr. Patricia Buehler, MD / In Focus Eye Care

Dr. Abrianne Goss, ND

Dr. Linda Hillebrand, D.O.

Dr. Richard Gilmore, DMD / Gilmore Dental

James Toffolo, PT ND

Step and Spine Physical Therapy

Pastor David & Debbie Brown

Pastor Craig & Kim Smart

Julie Myers

Craft3/Jeff Baker

Bruce Barrett, Realtor

Michael Badami / Eight East Productions

Highland Baptist Church

Redmond Community Church

Mountain View Fellowship

Zion Lutheran, ELCA (Central Oregon)

Todd & Lori Coulter / Les Schwab

Penni St. Pierre

Marcus & Hollis Lopez

Cameo Chambers, LOVE Inc.

St. Vincent de Paul (Redmond)

Scott Christiansen (Christiansen's Contracting Co.)

Ronald McDonald House Central Oregon

Mayor George Endicott (Redmond)

Chief of Police Dave Tarbet (Redmond)
Janice Debo
Aaron Mitchel
Bill Farish
Dale & Hazel Jenson
Keri & Sean Satterlee
Kit & Kaye Bowlby
Sean Neary, Attorney at Law
Lisa & Andy Spencer / Les Schwab (Redmond)
Kathy & Paul Rodby /McDonald's Store Owners
Melanee Rossa
Shane Mayfield
Alayna Weimer
Robin Boivie and Family
Thom & Lauri Deason
Katie Flock
Lowe's Heroes Program
Umpqua Bank (Redmond)
Deschutes County Commissioners
Redmond Chamber of Commerce
A&E Masonry and Construction
Martin & Rosa Brooks (Michigan)
Jill Cummings
Amber Wilson
The McCoy Family (Brett, Lynai, Sarah, Trystan, Zane)
Shawn Baker
Amanda Albrich
Linden Gross
Kayde Johnson
Mike & Kylie Bisutti
Congressman Chris Smith (NJ)
Congresswoman Ann Wagner (MO)
Chicks Connect Central Oregon

Stonecroft Ministries - Pat Abernathy
Deschutes Children's Foundation
Bill Hocker / Kelly Imaging
Redmond Athletic Club (RAC)
Redmond Service League
Kiwanis Club (Redmond)
Crooked River Ranch Lions Club
Rotary Club (Redmond)
Lindsay Kacalek
Nicole Bowers Wallace / NBW Films
Blanquita Cullum
Andrejs Auskaps
Jim Bohannon
Congressman Greg Walden (OR)
Congressman Pete Olson (TX)
Congressman Chip Roy (TX)
Congresswoman Debbie Lesko (AZ)
Congressman Jim Costa (CA)
Elaine Chao, U.S. Secretary of Transportation
Heather Fischer, Special Advisor for Human Trafficking / The White House
Greg Provenzano, Co-Founder and President, ACN*
Tony Cupisz, Co-Founder, ACN*
Mike Cupisz, Co-Founder, ACN*
Robert Stevanovski, Co-Founder, ACN*

Every volunteer and donor who has helped Beulah's Place has saved at-risk, homeless teens. By doing so, we, as a united community, give back the basic human right for these young adults to live safe, free lives.

Special Thanks to the Charter Members of Voices Against Trafficking LLC. VoicesAgainstTrafficking.com/Join

INFORMATION

For information about Beulah's Place
or to donate, visit beulahsplace.org.

You may also follow us on Facebook.com/Beulahsplace
or Twitter@Beulahsplace

To schedule Andi Buerger for personal appearances
or speaking events, please contact:

Blanquita Cullum
Cullum Communications
703-307-9510
Bqview@mac.com